The GUINNESS Book of
Tank
Facts and Feats

Russia's most successful tanks—the outstanding T 34/76.

Hail and farewell—British Chieftain of the 1960s and Mark V of 1918.

The GUINNESS Book of
Tank
Facts and Feats

A record of Armoured Fighting Vehicle Achievement

edited and compiled by

Kenneth Macksey

with contributions by
COLONEL P.H.HORDERN DSO OBE · COLONEL E.F.OFFORD DSO MBE
MAJOR J.K.W.BINGHAM RTR · MAJOR W.F.WOODHOUSE RTR
artwork by MIKE ROFFE

GUINNESS SUPERLATIVES LIMITED
2 CECIL COURT, LONDON ROAD, ENFIELD, MIDDLESEX

Published in Great Britain by
Guinness Superlatives Limited, 2 Cecil Court,
London Road, Enfield, Middlesex

SBN 900424 09 5

Set in Monophoto Baskerville Series 169,
printed and bound in Great Britain by
Jarrold and Sons Limited, Norwich

Contents

Acknowledgements

The editors and compilers wish to extend their thanks to the many organisations and individuals who gave generous assistance during the preparation of this book, and particularly those listed below:

Aberdeen Museum, U.S.A.
Armor, Washington, D.C.
A. B. Bofors
British Museum
Bundeswehr Tank Museum, West Germany
Canadian Public Archives
Department of the Army, Washington, D.C.
Lieutenant-Colonel R. Everard, R.T.R.
Fosters Ltd.
Imperial War Museum, London
Lady Liddell Hart
Ministry of Defence (Army), London

National Archives and Records Service,
    Washington, D.C.
National Army Museum, London
Major M. C. Norman, R.T.R.
Royal Armoured Corps Centre, Bovington Camp
Royal Military College of Science, Shrivenham
R.A.C. Tank Museum, Bovington Camp
R.H.Q., Royal Tank Regiment
4th Royal Tank Regiment
J. P. Scrivenor
Vickers Ltd.
Major S. J. Williams, R.T.R.

Introduction

S ince the dawn of time, when man crept from his cave in his daily hunt for food, women and the
expansion of his domains, a deep urge has driven him to enhance proficiency at arms by the improvement of his weapons. While first it was thought sufficient to fight on foot, armed merely with
a stone axe—or simply with bare hands—it soon became recognised that the acquisition of expanding
power depended also as much upon protection against hostile weapons—a protection to be provided
either by wearing personal armour or by the ability to move more nimbly and swiftly as well as further
than an opponent. Thus was created man's demand for armoured fighting vehicles to transport him to
battle, to sustain him in the fight and, perhaps, enhance his ability to exploit victory or to reach safety in
defeat.

An interest in armoured fighting vehicles—of which today's tank is the supreme example—is first
recorded from the third millennium on the celebrated Standard at Ur—a relic which displays the
earliest known example of vehicles drawn by beasts, manned by armed men and protected by what
appear to be hides. From that moment onward the evolution of fighting vehicles kept pace with
advances in society, economy, technology and industrial capacity, each step forward the product of
man's ambition to widen his power and influence. Tales of war more than ever become the story of
battles won by new weapon systems overcoming those which were outmoded, either by some advance in
technology or an improvement in fighting technique. The pages of history are adorned by accounts of
sieges and battles dominated by the changing balance between the penetration of attack and deflection
by the defence. Analysis shows that the greatest politico-military achievements fall to the credit of those
generals who were able not only to strike hard but, at the same time, inflict decisive losses upon the
enemy by outmanœuvring and cutting him off from his sources of supply—eventually paralysing his
will to continue at war. The opposite—stalemate—almost invariably led to catastrophic losses that
were the negation of the primary purpose of war, for stalemate can undermine the aggressor's determina-
tion as surely as it exhausts the defender. Such a course was close to realisation at one point during the
American Civil War and was actually reached in 1914. For at the very outset of the First World War, it
was discovered that man had achieved such an enormous facility for destruction that to advance towards any decisive objective had become well-nigh impossible, in the face of a prepared opponent,
without suffering unacceptable losses. Yet the evidence of man's subservience to weapons and machines
had long been apparent. If they had not been recognisable at the time of the Napoleonic Wars, at the
turn of the nineteenth century when steam power was revolutionising industry, they were fully on
display during the Crimean War in 1853–56 (when a steam tractor was employed to tow stores and guns)
and wholly existent during the American Civil War when armoured trains came into action, machine-
guns and breech-loading artillery were in use and the cable-telegraph was already speeding the passage
of orders that compelled armies to react more accurately and swiftly at the behest of commanders who
were installed at remote centres of control.

But if, today, machines tend more than ever to dominate war they remain the servant of man, their
achievements the servant of his will—that vital urge which provides the essential motivation for the
feats which are the subject of this book. Here are recorded achievements and facts that are to the credit—
and sometimes, all too often, the shame—of man and armoured fighting vehicles. It is not a subject in
isolation for it lies at the heart of conflict and encompasses almost every activity that energises society.
In the third millennium man's existence was dependent upon beasts of burden and upon the use of wood,
hides, bronze and stone: these were the prime elements of the earliest fighting machines. Today man is
dependent upon, some would say dominated by, the automotive vehicle while his future is engrossed
with the harnessing of vast resources linked to new materials and a host of complex techniques in the
field of communication, transport, metallurgy and physical power. The present-day tank—the high-
powered, armoured weapon platform that is controlled by an increasing conglomeration of electronic
devices—draws upon a broad field of modern technological expertise for its creation and employment.

Thus the data which appears in this book, though it concentrates on armoured fighting vehicles and is the result of a close search for the latest available information, is by no means exhaustive. Apart from the fact that research is constantly revealing fresh information about the past, evolution is keeping armoured fighting vehicle technology on the move in the never-ending competition between nations and inventors. Moreover, the subject encroaches into fresh areas as naval and air power exert their influence, and as costs compel a rationalisation in outlay of wealth. As time passes this book will have to be updated to keep pace with the continuing accretion of armoured fighting vehicle feats and facts.

K. Macksey, 1972

Glossary of Tank Terms

Appliqué armour: Extra armour attached to the basic plates.

Assembly area: Pre-battle position, usually located out of enemy sight.

Bazooka plates: Armour plate suspended at a distance from the sides of a tank hull or its turret.

Bins: External boxes for carrying tools and loose equipment.

Bogie: A wheel forming part of a tank's suspension. Usually one of several within an assembly.

Brinell: An index of metal hardness.

Buffer: See Recuperator below.

Calibre: Internal dimensions of a gun-barrel.

Differential: An arrangement of gears enabling driving wheel or tracks to revolve at different speeds when the vehicle is turning a corner.

Driving sprocket: Wheel (usually toothed) which transfers power from the gearbox output or tank final drive to the tank's tracks.

Fascine: A roll of wooden palings (usually a large one) designed to be dropped by the tank into a trench enabling it to cross.

Fighting compartment: Space inside the tank which encloses those of the crew who man the armament.

Final drive: Mechanism which transfers power from the gearbox to the driving sprocket.

Forming-up place: Immediate pre-battle position.

Glacis plate: Frontal hull armour.

Ground pressure: The main parameter determining a tank's performance on soft ground. Usually expressed in pounds per square inch (lb/in²) of the area of track laid by the tank on level ground.

Gun trunnions: Supporting projections which act as a pivot for the gun in elevation.

Harbour: Area behind the lines where tanks retire after battle for rest and maintenance.

Hull down: A tactical position in which the tank exposes only its gun to the target thereby shielding its hull from view *relative to the target*. This is the best type of fire position, but see also Turret down.

Idler wheel: Unpowered wheel which carries the track and often is adjustable so that it can act as a track tensioner.

Laager: Close defensive formation adopted by tanks at night. Usually unarmoured vehicles are parked within this formation.

Louvre: Ventilation inlet usually shielded by armour protection.

Mantlet: The turret's frontal plate—sometimes rigid, sometimes movable and occasionally resilient.

Master switch: Overrides all electrical systems in an A.F.V.

Muzzle brake: A fixture at the end of the gun-barrel to help reduce recoil by deflecting propellent gases to the rear.

Recuperator: In conjunction with the Buffer absorbs the gun's recoil, reduces strain on the mounting and returns the gun to its run-out (firing) position.

Rollers: Unsprung wheels that are part of the suspension.

Schnorkel: Tube provided to enable a tank and (sometimes) its crew to breathe when engaged in deep underwater fording.

Sponson: Gun mount attached to a tank's side giving only limited traverse to the weapon.

Suspension: The linkage or connection between a tank's track and hull which provides a means of support for the track.

Torsion bar: A flexible rod anchored to the vehicle's hull, the opposite end carrying a sprung crank, at the end of which is a suspension bogie or wheel. Movement of the wheel and crank twists the rod.

Track link: The basic element of a tank track, usually linked to its neighbours by pins.

Turret: A rotating armoured structure resting on ball-bearings, running on a traverse ring with rack. Power for the traverse is usually provided either by hand cranking, electric or hydraulic motors.

Turret down: A tactical position in which the tank commander alone can see the target thereby shielding the entire tank from view *relative to the target*. Unlike the Hull-down position (see above) only *indirect* fire can sometimes be aimed against the enemy from the Turret-down position.

SECTION I

From Chariot to Armoured Car

—the increasing pace of advancing technology

It is a fact of the art of war on land that fighting men take slowly to new ideas and techniques. Though man's desires to conquer the elements of sea and air were always among his most cherished dreams, his endeavours to raise pace and efficiency in his natural environment remained chained to harsh reality—a reality enforced by economic necessity and the limitations of technical knowledge. Thus when soldiers were given insight into the possibilities of some new weapon they often as not had to postpone its purchase because current industrial capability made it too expensive, while stocks of existing weapons could not be scrapped in order to make way for the new. Whatever the age, weapons of war represented a heavy charge on any exchequer and, as often as not, an unproductive one too.

There was also the difficulty of discussing and disseminating information. Not until the first millennium can it be said that existing communication systems permitted a reasonably free interchange of ideas between neighbouring communities and a modest proliferation of the latest discoveries. For instance, it took from the third to the second millennium for chariot technology to advance beyond the four-wheeled to the two-wheeled model and for the solid wheel to be replaced by the stronger and lighter spoked wheel. Nearly 1,000 years elapsed between the first use of bronze as armour and its replacement by iron—and another 1,000 before steel came into more general use. The chariot epoch was itself prolonged for at least 3,000 years until armoured horsemen replaced these horse-drawn vehicles as the vital, battlefield arm of mobility: indeed, even though chariots ceased to reign supreme in the Middle East after 700 BC, they were still to be found in action against the Romans in the hands of the Celtic tribes in the British Isles as late as AD 83.

It is a remarkable yet significant fact that horsemen were to reign supreme on the battlefield for over 1,000 years. They did so because their superior mobility gave them the advantage of concentrating their arms against foot opponents whose weapons and armour were weaker and whose powers of combination could not be made to match the individual. Yet once the cross-bowmen, long-bowmen, artillerymen and musketeers began to acquire the weapons and skills that could hold the horsemen at bay, the day of the chariot in modern guise returned. Success for John Zizka's battlewagons in the Hussite Wars of the early fifteenth century came about because the wagons acted both as mobile fortress and weapon-carrier for the new instruments of destruction. By giving dynamic protection to the fighting man they neutralised the forces of mobility. It was from the fifteenth century onward that the pace of mechanisation of war noticeably quickened. Inventors turned their minds to creating armoured fighting vehicles that were great improvements on Zizka's farm carts. Innovations abounded and gave impetus to fresh concepts as the dissemination of thought became easier. Better roads encouraged travel while the invention of printing multiplied understanding. When Guido da Vigevano designed a windmill-driven combat machine in 1335 he was delving in dreamland and Robert Valturio was hardly more practical with a comparable idea in 1472—for these fighting vehicles depended upon the elements that left too much to chance in combat. On the other hand Leonardo da Vinci's celebrated underpowered "tank" of 1482 was a more practical proposition since it relied upon men to propel it. The fact was that the only fighting vehicles worthy of consideration had to be those which depended upon internal means of traction. Therefore there could be little improvement in their practicability until a stronger and more compact power plant could be invented.

That this had to wait until the early nineteenth century was perhaps just a trick of fate, for in the meantime weapon power had increased so enormously that it threatened to preclude battle as a viable politico-economic proposition. Artillery and firearms had advanced fast and far in their power of devastation and in their reliability as the techniques of working in iron became better known. The matchlock hand-gun came into use in the fifteenth century and would make do into the seventeenth century, when the flintlock appeared. In 1718 James Puckle was successfully demonstrating the first manually operated machine-gun, though it would be 1862 before a machine-gun was first used at war, during the American Civil War. By then the breech-loading cannon would be appearing, along with its much greater rate of fire over that of the old muzzle-loaders. Soon, in 1862, would come the first Gatling machine-gun and then, in 1885, partly as the by-product of smokeless powder, the fully automatic Maxim machine-gun. Each advance in weapon technology happened as the result of some basic scientific discovery, one thing leading to another and all multiplying in number as mass-production methods supplanted the arts of individual craftsmanship. The introduction in 1856 of mass-produced steel by the Bessemer process was typical of this trend—and quite fundamental, too, since it meant that in due course high-quality, armoured steel plate could be produced in quantity and at low cost compared with the extremely expensive material which, until then, had represented the small output of a few experts.

One important ingredient which was to turn the tank into a practical proposition had first seen light in 1770 when Richard Edgeworth had taken out a patent for "a portable railway or artificial road to move along with any carriage to which it is applied". This was forerunner of a score of ideas for chain or caterpillar tracks which were to be conceived in the following century. And if they originated mainly from a desire to improve transport over the then appalling roads, it would not be beyond the armament manufacturers' enterprise to convert them to military purposes. Everything waited, however, for the power plant—the gradual yet accelerating inventive progress towards a practical steam engine, growing out of J. Savery's machine of 1698, through James Watts's important improvements of 1763 and 1769 and, in that same year, the first journey by Cugnot's steam tricycle in France. By 1855 Boydell's steam tractor with its "footed wheels" would be dragging heavy loads in the Crimea, leading inexorably to the demonstration by Daimler of a petrol-fuelled, internal combustion engine in 1885 and later that year, Benz's motor car.

Inevitably the merging of ideas gave birth to the first genuine internal-combustion-powered armoured fighting vehicle—that of F. R. Simms in 1902. There were projects, too, to employ "footed wheels" or "chain tracks" to warlike purposes—making use of the first commercially built "track" of the American Holt Company that were then beginning to give agricultural machines access to land which was hitherto impassable by vehicles.

As background to this intensified industrial development there stood the threat of the huge armies brought into being by the adoption of conscription by the European powers. Great steam-driven, armoured naval fleets were expanding in size alongside monstrous land forces which were intended to go to war in a procession of railway trains, to be flung as masses into battle behind intensive artillery fire which, it was visualised, would open a magic door to the winning of battles. Few foresaw that this mass would be powerless in the face of new weapons. Man went to war on land in 1914 protected only by a woollen tunic even though armour was of the essence in maritime vessels. Armoured vehicles on land were almost wholly rejected. Thus the year 1914 marks a watershed in land warfare. The massed armies of infantry, backed by artillery and cavalry cancelled each other out. The vital element of a protected, mobile, weapon platform was missing—but not for long.

The first recorded armoured fighting vehicles. Chariots of Ur—3000 BC.

The first recorded examples of armoured fighting vehicles are those shown on the Standard which was unearthed at Ur of the Chaldees. It dates from about the year 3500 BC and depicts a number of four-wheeled vehicles each of which was drawn by four onagers. Wheels are constructed from two solid, wooden segments and the frames seem to be armoured by hides. Some of the vehicles are carrying stores but others are crewed by two armed men.

The earliest example of a campaign dominated by chariots is that fought by the Egyptians in 1680 BC in defence of their country against the invading armies of Hyksos—the "Shepherd Kings" who are sometimes believed to be of Arab origin and, at others, Israelite. The chariots in use were a great improvement on those of Ur since they were made of light wood, were drawn by horses and were more highly manœuvrable because their running gear comprised a pair of spoked wheels. The Egyptians were to copy this type of chariot and use them for many centuries—until, in fact, they were superseded by the next generation of chariots incorporating iron components.

The first identified example of metal armour, bronze, seems to date from about 1400 BC in China, though this metal made an almost simultaneous appearance throughout the Middle East, and then Europe.

The first examples of iron came from Egypt in about 3000 BC, but it was to be at least another 1,000 years before it entered into general use, and not until 800 BC, or thereabouts, that it was extensively employed by the Assyrians in the construction of their chariots and the armouring of their soldiers.

The most advanced military nation, as well as the most civilised, in the Middle East between 1100 BC and 670 BC was Assyria—no mean distinction when it is remembered that this nation was implanted in the heart of a region seething with perpetual conflict. The Assyrians developed their own style of mobile war based on chariots that were often of the three-horse variety. They used chariots backed up by excellent foot armies, companies of archers and well-conceived siege-trains that could assail cities either by mobile battering-ram or wheeled fighting-towers pushed close to the walls. Personal armour was usually made of iron while that of the chariots and fighting-towers could be of wicker-work. Provision was also made to float chariots across rivers by means of inflated goatskins attached to the vehicles' sides.

The best-documented battle in which chariots were used was that of Cunaxa fought in 401 BC on the banks of the Euphrates near Babylon between the rebel Lydian Army of Cyrus the Younger and the Persian Army under Artaxerxes II. This was a chance encounter when the two armies stumbled upon one another in improvised charge and counter-charge, foot and horse mixed up with the chariots, the latter equipped with scythes attached to their wheels. Artaxerxes was the victor.

The decline of the chariot set in with the eclipse of the Assyrian nation yet we know that the Persians went on using them until they were wiped out by the Macedonian Alexander the Great, and that their last major use in the Middle East was at the Battle of Orchomenus in 86 BC when the Romans defeated the King of Pontus and Crimea. But the Britons were to use them against Julius Caesar in 55 and 54 BC and again against Agricola in AD 83—just about their last ever appearance in any numbers. The reason for decline lay in the ability of the disciplined infantry and cavalry of Greece and Rome to combine effectively against chariot crews who merely advanced in open order to the fray and then dismounted to fight as individuals rather than as a team. Those chariots whose crews remained mounted for fighting, as did the Britons, could do little more than make a nuisance of themselves by hit-and-run tactics. In the future such tactics were better carried out by the armoured horsemen who now took precedence as the mobile arm. It is therefore significant that such use of vehicles as now took place in battle was in a defensive role to fend off horsemen.

Gunpowder may have been first discovered in China (though this is perhaps a legend). It was found in Europe about the middle of the fourteenth century, its discovery credited either to Berchthold Schwarz, a German monk, or the Englishman Roger Bacon.

The first battlefield use of artillery may have been at Metz in 1342 or Algeciras in 1342, but there is no doubt that Edward I used cannon against the French at the Battle of Crécy in 1346. The early cannon neither had long range, high lethal power nor much reliability, but they made a loud and frightening noise (to friend and foe) and appeared ever more frequently in action as methods of iron foundry were refined. Yet it was well into the fifteenth century before they in any way seriously challenged the dominance of cross-bows and long-bows and they only did so in the end when it became apparent that it was easier to train a man to shoot straight with the new matchlock hand-guns than it was with a bow or the earliest firearms.

The first use of artillery from armoured vehicles came in 1419 when the one-eyed Hussite leader, John Zizka, successfully resisted a force of Bohemian knights by forming his heavy, wooden farm carts into a defensive circle and holding the enemy at bay from what we know today as a wagon-leaguer. Rapidly Zizka organised his entire people into wagon armies, in peacetime using the wagons for their original agricultural purpose and in war either as infantry or artillery carriers. Mostly the wagons sought static refuge on important ground, joined to one another and using the leaguer merely as a temporary base for an offensive defensive battle. But at the Battle of Kutna Hora, when they were caught by the enemy in open ground, they actually fought on the move in close formation. Possibly the Hussites also have the distinction of being the first to fire guns from the shoulder—as indication of their insight into the advantages of flexible firepower.

The first suggestion for a fighting vehicle that moved independently of muscular power came in 1335 from an Italian physician, called Guido da Vigevano, who proposed a windmill-driven machine with power transmitted from the sails to the wheels via pinions. The trouble was that such a vehicle could sail only before the wind and so, since there was no guarantee that the enemy would remain downwind, the idea lacked practical application.

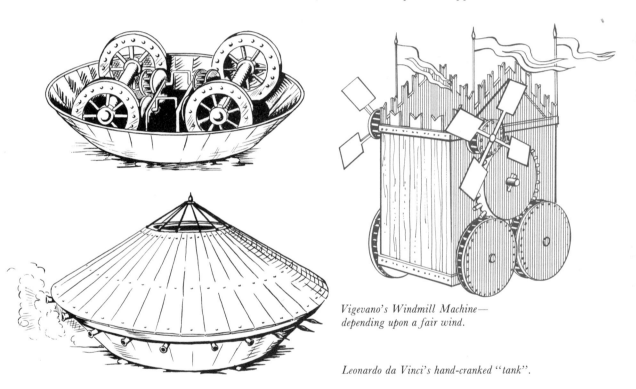

Vigevano's Windmill Machine— depending upon a fair wind.

Leonardo da Vinci's hand-cranked "tank".

Thus Leonardo da Vinci qualifies as the first man to invent a fighting vehicle which could operate independently under manpower, the men concerned travelling within an armoured shell turning cranks that drove the road wheels. This machine, devised in 1482, was a genuine armoured fighting vehicle with a preconceived tactical application. Da Vinci wanted men to move to their objective under covered protection, yet be able to fight through slits cut in the vehicle's sides. But of course its pace would have been slow because the power-to-weight ratio would have been terribly low—a limitation which applied to every other similarly conceived machine in the following years. Those of Holzschüher, Ramelli, Napier and many another merely represented variations on da Vinci's theme.

The breakthrough towards a practical steam engine came in 1698 when J. Savery produced such a source of power for commercial purposes. It is perhaps worth recording, too, that it was **Savery who coined the term** "horsepower" as a measure of performance. In 1763 and 1769 James Watt took important steps forward by inventing methods that made the steam engine infinitely more efficient. He multiplied its commercial attraction by vital improvements in economy and reliability.

The first steam-driven road vehicle also appeared in 1769—a tricycle invented by the Frenchman, Cugnot, that ran for twenty minutes at a speed of 2·25 mile/h with a load of four passengers. This machine can be seen to this day in the Conservatoire des Arts et Métiers in Paris.

The first working machine-gun had already been produced in 1718 by James Puckle who intended it as a naval anti-boarding weapon. Ignition of the cartridges was by flintlock—a limiting factor of efficiency—ammunition feed to the barrel by a manually operated rotating magazine. This weapon is to be seen today in the Tower of London. Although its development was stifled it was, in fact, proved feasible—the father of all the rotating-chamber machine-guns to come.

The first matchlock firearms began to appear in the mid-fifteenth century and were the crucial invention that turned firearms into a decisive weapon on the battlefield. For whereas the primitive method of igniting the charge had been by slow-burning powder chains, the matchlock transferred the flame more quickly from a burning "match", attached to the trigger, direct to the charge, enabling the firer to hold a gun to his shoulder and obtain positive aim along the barrel with almost instantaneous ignition. This new method was slow to become universal, but was in general use by the early seventeenth century.

The first flintlock gun was invented by the Frenchman Le Bourgeoys in 1615. His method gave "spark" ignition and thus eliminated the problems of maintaining a match in flame. It was just one more important advance in the search for reliability and accuracy for firearms that had to find their way past military conservatism into practical use. It has to be recorded, however, that throughout the seventeenth century, the weight of personal firearms was reduced from 25 to 11 lb each and that the Swedish military genius, Gustavus Adolphus, was instrumental in introducing the first cartridge by which the charge and bullet were incorporated in a single bag, or round, the charge carefully measured to assist in obtaining uniform performance from each. This was a much more scientific method than expecting each soldier to measure the right amount during the heat of battle.

The next major advance in ballistics came in 1805 when the percussion cap was invented by the Rev. Alexander Forsyth—an advance that was promptly turned down by the British Army and failed to enter service until 1842, even though manufacture of copper cartridge-cases had begun much earlier and its first practical application had been demonstrated in 1816 by an American sea captain, J. E. Shaw. This invention increased the rate at which firearms could be loaded and discharged besides adding greatly to their reliability and accuracy. From now on, too, the chance of powder getting wet was significantly reduced.

The first steel was probably made by accident in the course of iron manufacture in the fourteenth century but,

The first large-scale production of steel of a fairly uniform quality had to wait until 1856 when Henry Bessemer's process came into use throughout industry, making steel a more common, cheaper and more useful metal than iron, and allowing enormous changes to become possible throughout the entire engineering world. From now on guns and vehicles could be given greater inherent strength along with lighter construction. At the same time came the gradual introduction of tougher steels—alloy armour plate—that gave superior protection against the new weapons. The research involved was a never-ending occupation for metallurgists.

Perhaps the greatest, and certainly the most misunderstood philosopher of war had his *magnum opus, On War,* posthumously published in 1832. It was Karl von Clausewitz whose book reflected the military experience of a lifetime that had witnessed the better part of the Napoleonic Wars. Clausewitz stimulated the imagination of statesmen and soldiers alike and led them to evolve national policies that harnessed entire populations for the purposes of war, along with economic schemes shaped to the cause of universal combat. His was a work which, in the wrong hands, made inevitable the allocation of those unlimited industrial resources which, alone, made machine warfare possible.

The first important example of machine warfare occurred in the Crimean War of 1853–56 when the Russians fought the Anglo-French armies. In this war there appeared *for the first time*:

> **A Minie bullet** whose expanding cartridge-case would extend the power and range of small arms when fired through a "rifled" barrel and make the "rifle" so much superior to the old, smooth-bore flintlock musket.
>
> **Russian artillery** firing "bursting" shells that greatly increased the lethal effect of each discharge.
>
> **Steam tractors** carried cross country on large "footed" wheels—the creation of an Englishman, James Boydell—and used as prime mover for guns and wagons behind the lines. But Boydell's tractor, designed for agricultural work, was to lead to a much more important proposal.

Cowan's combat vehicle 1855—first with a steam engine and footed wheels.

The first proposal for an armoured fighting vehicle powered by something stronger than muscle power was put forward in 1855 by James Cowan—a suggestion that a Boydell tractor should be enclosed by a metal cover, fitted with scythes and armed with cannon for use as a genuine fighting machine in the forefront of the battle. This idea was rejected by Lord Palmerston on

the grounds that it was "uncivilised". Its rejection underlined the tendency
for machines to be harnessed in war purely for their capacity to take life
rather than save it, for while the Crimean War, and those that followed,
showed quite positively how modern arms caused prohibitive loss of life, a
suggestion to mitigate the slaughter by protecting men against fire was
liable to instant rejection.

That first predominantly machine war, the American Civil War, was fought to a finish between
1861 and 1865, and confirmed the promise of the Crimean War. Indeed it
caused such heavy casualties that the prospect of men advancing in close
order in the old fashioned way against modern weapons became increasingly uncertain. Soldiers face the possibility of death if there is a recognisable chance of survival linked to positive gain. Such hopes had entered the
realms of a ridiculous gamble by 1865. Because of this the American Civil
War managed to score a number of dubious firsts throughout its course.

For the first time armoured warships came to grips in the celebrated duel of 1862 between
Monitor and *Merrimac*. In this contest the guns of two armoured ships
inconclusively slogged it out, firing immense volumes of metal at very
little cost in life and without sinking each other. Armour protection was
the saving factor.

For the first time breech-loading rifled gun-barrels, notably those produced by the Englishmen,
Sir William Armstrong and Sir Joseph Whitworth, were used to increase
the range and killing power of the artillery. But **the first breech-loading
cannon**—a 6-pounder—had actually been produced by the German firm
of Krupp in 1851.

For the first time railways were used to transport and maintain immense armies at the front.
This not only offered far more soldiers to the slaughter but raised strategic
mobility to new levels—incidentally making the possession and destruction of railway material a major objective of the war. It also brought about
the first, though rare, examples of fighting between rival armoured trains
armed with a variety of cannon and filled with infantry.

For the first time a machine-gun was used in battle when a manually operated gun, modelled on
the original Puckle principle by Williams, was engaged in the Battle of
Fair Oaks on 31st May, 1862.

For the first time cable telegraph, discovered in 1838 by K. A. von Steinkeil, was used to carry
messages throughout the battle zones, providing statesmen and com-
manders with rapid person-to-person communication, easing the passing
of messages yet multiplying the complexities of operations as it became
possible for leaders to conduct war by remote control in place of direct
surveillance. The pinnacle of command thus began to shift from the forefront of a battle to the rear.

For the first time, above all, when organisation and methods were making possible the greatest
ever concentrations of men and material on the battlefield, weapon
power was making combat excessively costly, if not prohibitive. In four
years nearly 620,000 men were killed, as well as numerous civilians—the
majority towards the end when the armies became fully developed. Immense damage had been caused as well, yet rising above the ashes was the
surging industrial power of America, capable of providing even more
efficient weapons to satisfy a world in search of arms.

The first smokeless powder appeared in 1885, a substance that burned far more efficiently than gunpowder. It gave renewed impulse to improvements in artillery and small arms. It was of vital assistance to an American called Hiram Maxim in his experiments to produce a fully automatic machine-gun—one that had its ammunition fed to the breech in a belt and was recocked and re-loaded by power generated from the firing of the previous shot.

Maxim's first fully automatic gun was first shown in 1884 and proven with the new powder a year later in 1885—a year made memorable by another highly significant advance in technology.

The first economic mobile propulsion unit, fuelled by petrol, was demonstrated by Gottlieb Daimler—a primitive machine which nevertheless bore a remarkable resemblance to present-day internal combustion engines except that ignition of the petrol vapour in the cylinder's combustion chamber was caused by a hot tube instead of a sparking-plug.

The first petrol-driven vehicle followed in the same year—a 3·5 hp model designed by Karl Benz, the engine and transmission the only truly remarkable features since this vehicle, like nearly all the early motor cars, relied upon the concepts of horsed carriage designers.

The first fully armoured fighting vehicle was that demonstrated in 1902 by the Englishman F. R. Simms who, in 1899, had made a four-wheeled motor cycle armed with a single Maxim machine-gun. Simms's wheeled machine of 1902 was the joint product of the armament manufacturers, Vickers and Maxim, offered for sale, though unsuccessfully, at a time when the European armaments race was only just getting into its stride. It had Vickers armour 6 mm thick, a 16 hp Daimler engine that gave a top speed of 9 mile/h and was armed with two Maxim machine-guns and a 1-pdr pom-pom. It has to be added that there had been many proposals for similar vehicles in the preceding years—one in 1896 by an American E. J. Pennington, and others in Russia, first by a man called Dvinitsky and another by Lutski: but none of these was turned into an actual running model and so full credit is due to Simms even though he may have cribbed a bit from Pennington.

First production armoured car by Charron 1904—Notice the detachable sand channels to raise mobility.

The first armoured fighting vehicle to be sold seems to go to the credit of the French firm of Charron Girardot et Voigt which was commissioned in 1904, by the

Russian Government, to build three armoured cars. Only one was delivered and may have reached the Manchurian front in 1905 where, at that time, the Russians were losing the war against Japan. This, in fact, was the war which showed, quite conclusively, that men without armour were doomed. The Charron car carried only one machine-gun behind armour only 4·5 mm thick, but it is said to have had a speed of 30 mile/h—though this is probably an exaggeration. What was important was the attempt made by Charron to increase the vehicle's cross-country mobility by attaching portable metal channels for use in bridging narrow gaps. Attention was turning, albeit slowly, to the demands for the capability for moving off the roads. Soon a successor to Edgeworth's "portable railway" would be in everyday use.

The first commercial tracked vehicle was built in 1906 by the American Holt Manufacturing Company—a converted steam agricultural tractor. It was for use in Louisiana delta lands by the Golden Meadow Development Company and marketed for $5,500—all part of the expanding work that was converting wild territory to everyday service.

The first commercial tracked vehicle. Made in the U.S.A. in 1906 by the Holt Manufacturing Company.

The first important British attempt to experiment with a tracked vehicle, however, was military. Somebody in the War Office may have read H. G. Wells's description of a steam, cross-country fighting vehicle carried on "footed wheels" of the sort produced by a Mr. Bramah Diplock. At all events they offered £1,000 for a cross-country vehicle that could haul a howitzer 40 miles without the need to refuel. The prize was won in 1907 by a

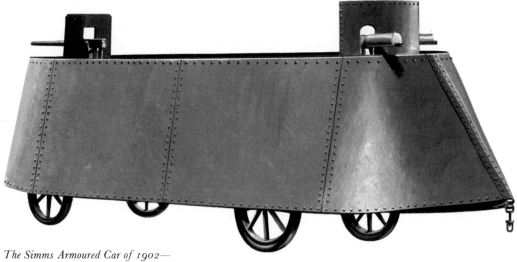

*The Simms Armoured Car of 1902—
first of a breed.*

The first French tank—Schneider CA 1

*British Mark V. Not all crewmen
wore this complete outfit.*

Roberts tractor—the first practical, if fragile, linked track on trial.

petrol-driven tractor designed by David Roberts and built by R. Hornsby and Son. The most striking feature was the original and rather complex track with its wooden-footed treads linked by lubricated pins—an arrangement that had a tendency to break all too easily. But as the Hornsby tractor passed its test it gave the idea for . . .

The first armoured assault gun, the suggestion of a Major Donoghue to mount a gun upon the Hornsby tractor and surround it with an armoured shield. This proposal was instantly rejected by those in earshot, yet in other places the idea for a tracked fighting vehicle was slowly beginning to catch on.

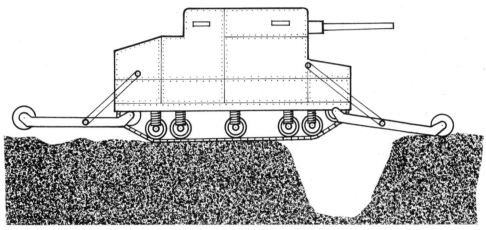

An Austrian proposal—Burstyn's "tank" of 1911.

The first of several "paper" projects, with a practical look about it, was that drawn up in 1911 by an Austrian engineer called Burstyn—a machine he termed "a land torpedo-boat". But Burstyn, though he envisaged a future need to cross wide trenches and armed his lozenge-shaped vehicle with a cannon, never solved the problem of building a track that would carry such a vehicle at 5 mile/h cross country. But he was aware of the need to give the crew a fairly stable fighting platform and so, unlike many machines that later came into service, made provision for a sprung suspension.

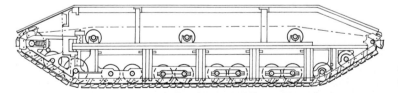

*An Australian design—
de Mole's "tank" of 1912.*

The second "paper project" of importance was that of the Australian engineer, L. de Mole, who proposed a tracked machine (without specifying armament) in 1912. De Mole suggested a linked track with sprung suspension, but seems to have concentrated hardest on achieving an efficient steering system. Until then it was the practice to stop one track and let the other revolve, thus driving the vehicle either left or right. De Mole thought it would be less wasteful of power if the tracks were "bowed", thus guiding rather than compelling the machine into a turn. His model was never put to the test and he, with like-minded inventors elsewhere, either saw his activities submerged by the coming war or simply consigned to the oblivion of the wastepaper basket. Yet mechanical fighting vehicles were already obtaining active service experience.

The first strong proposal to substitute motor cars for horses came from General Miles of the United States Army when, in 1905, he suggested that no less than five cavalry regiments should be converted from horses to armed motor cars of the sort that a Major R. P. Davidson had been demonstrating at the turn of the century. The proposal got nowhere, as was to be expected of so remarkable an idea bearing in mind the climate of military opinion which, for the next decade or more, was to resist every attempt at serious mechanisation.

First armoured car at war—Italy's Bianchi during 1912 in Libya.

The first battlefield appearance of an armoured car took place in Libya in 1912 during the Italo-Turkish War. This machine—a Bianchi made at Turin with a Fiat chassis—was used again that same year in the Balkans. Not that they made any fundamental impact, though some felt it better to have machines such as these on their side rather than against them, since, in those days, though **the first armour-piercing bullets** had been devised, there were not a great many ways for infantry to penetrate a 4-ton vehicle protected by 6 mm of steel. In other words an armoured vehicle carried with it a certain aura of invincibility no matter how light it happened to be.

The declaration of war by Austria-Hungary against Serbia on 28th July, started a chain of declarations which brought Russia, France and Britain into war with Germany and Austria-Hungary—a collision which was to exemplify the dying struggles of unarmoured armies. For the men of 1914 went to war almost totally unprotected, without a single armoured vehicle in their formal order of battle. Yet the speed at which events had moved out of political control had to be ascribed to a further new factor that affected international relationships. Messages could now be passed more swiftly from place to place throughout the entire world with unheard-of speed. Thus reactions moved faster than decisions, since, in addition to cable telegraphy which had helped revolutionise the American Civil War, there were now "wireless" transmissions.

The first successful wireless transmission was performed by Sir William Preece in 1892 over a range of a quarter of a mile. But by 1895 Guglielmo Marconi sent a message 1 mile—in 1897 9 miles. By 1901 messages were being sent over 3,000 miles, wireless sets were becoming smaller, more reliable and were being turned to military uses. Thus the armies went to war in 1914 with wireless communications installed, in some cases down to divisional level. But these clumsy and fragile devices could not be taken into the front line, although some were sufficiently light to be carried in the flimsy aeroplanes of the day.

The greatest war that history had known was initially fought by men and armies who were unaware of the false out-dated precepts in use. But the ingredients of change were ready—vehicles driven by internal combustion engines, armour plate, light and compact guns, track-laying vehicles, armoured cars and embryonic radios with the potential of imposing close command over troops in the forefront of the fighting. Combine all these elements in a single machine and a tank became reality.

SECTION II
The Return of Armoured Warfare
1914–1918

Nobody knows when the first automobile fight broke out as the armies of the Central Powers moved outwards to attack their neighbours, but it must have happened soon after the outbreak of war since, even though the principal armies had rejected armoured vehicles, they were none of them blind to the advantage of moving men and stores in lorries and motor cars. To supplement the railways and existing military horse-drawn transport a host of civilian vehicles were impressed and brought close to the battle-fronts, to help carry supplies, reinforcements (the celebrated reinforcement of the French Army with a division carried to the front in a fleet of Parisian taxi cabs in September 1914 is the first of its kind on a large scale) and to act as fast chargers for commanders and staff officers. Soon these vehicles came under fire, particularly where the battle-front was loose knit, in a war of ambush between mobile patrols. Thus wheeled fighting motor vehicles were nearly always a viable proposition and particularly in Russia where the front remained relatively free from trench lines and barricades. But in the West they became hamstrung since, by the end of October 1914, a continuous line of wire-encumbered trenches had been dug from the North Sea to the Swiss frontier. Yet before that phenomenon appeared there had been skirmishing between motor cars belonging to the British, Belgian and French armies against German cavalry patrols and infantry outposts—a sort of motorised guerilla warfare waged on the flanks of the main German armies as they surged forward to the gates of Paris and then went into full retreat during the Battle of the Marne.

Trenches totally prevented fighting by wheeled vehicles. Yet from then on only those nations with a pressing and unavoidable need to overcome continuous trench lines put any effort into seeking a way to improving the mobility of fighting machines. The armies of the Central Powers and of the Russians in the East had no such need because they possessed space in which to manœuvre to strike at the enemy's flank and rear. The Germans in the West had no immediate strategic desire to break through after 1914. Thus the Central Powers lacked the incentive to create a new type of assault vehicle. But the French and British not only believed the Western Front was the decisive one but also had strong political reasons for wishing to throw the Germans out of France. Gradually, however, it dawned upon them that the trench barrier was practically unconquerable by existing weapons and methods. Hence they were compelled to begin experiments in search of ways to break through with the assistance of automotive vehicles as a vital supplement to the traditional assault by men and artillery.

The evolution of the machines which were to take the name of "tank" is enshrined in the dogged-ness of a few enthusiasts who committed themselves to re-educating soldiers while pursuing research into a new technology that, eventually, would gather a host of separate components into an assault vehicle. The central thread in a tangled story is to be found in **the primary idea of a Lieutenant-Colonel Swinton** wending its way through a maze of inter-departmental minutes and committees until **the first trials of existing cross-country machines** showed that tracked vehicles were the best type to cross trenches and flatten barbed-wire entanglements.

The story introduces us to the many inventors in several nations who struggled against doubters (and among themselves) to devise something complex and brand new in a race against time to save the lives of men in a battle. Though everything that was needed existed in embryo, nothing was properly developed for instant use in the construction of a practical tank. Nearly every step forward was a "first step" and each improvement a superlative in discovery. Thus while tank technology advanced close to the frontiers of knowledge its crews went to war guided only by speculative operational instructions—instructions which could but stem from Swinton's imagination in the total absence of experience.

There came the first British and French experiments and trials in 1915 and the first British adventure into battle with thirty-six tanks on 15th September 1916, followed by an ordeal in combat that gradually acquired sufficient experience (as well as giving time to build more machines) to project tanks more skilfully against the enemy. This was a period when special tank forces were being formed and when the French were thinking bigger than the British on the side of production and usage. At last, on 20th November 1917, the first truly massed tank attack was made by the British at Cambrai, the turning-point in the tank's fortunes. For up to then the remaining nations at war had only tinkered with tanks. Like the Germans, neither the Austrians, Russians, Americans nor Italians had seen much future for the new weapon, though all were making or buying just a few in case they happened to be wrong. After Cambrai, however, there was no end to the number of nations who were convinced of the need for tanks—even if only as a temporary expedient. **For it is one of the most remarkable facts** about tanks that throughout their existence they have never won unreserved acceptance as an indispensable weapon system: always there have been strong bodies of so-called informed opinion to foretell their imminent oblivion.

The year 1918 was to witness **the truly great tank battles** in the West after the Russians had withdrawn from the war, thus allowing the Germans to concentrate their main effort upon defeating the British and French before the power of the U.S.A. could be fully applied. Yet the German offensive of March 1918 was supported by barely a score of tanks, and there were to be but two small tank-versus-tank fights before the war ended in November. **The last battles**, in fact, were completely dominated by hundreds of Allied tanks of new design, striking surprise hammer blows at a German Army which found itself outclassed in a new kind of technical warfare. And, as tactical usage progressed in company with technical improvements that made tanks faster, stronger and more reliable, the prophets of the future, the Briton, Colonel Fuller and the Frenchman, Estienne, began to publish their belief in armies that would be dominated in future by tanks taking the leading role. Thus from Cinderellas of the battlefield in 1914, armoured, fighting vehicles had become princesses in 1918 with a valid claim to supplant the infantry as "Queen of the Battlefield".

Link for British Heavy Mark V.
Width 20·5 in. Pitch 7·5 in. Weight per linkage 82·15 lb. Weight per foot 131·3 lb.

Belgium's Minerva armoured car in action in August 1914.

PART ONE—FEATS & ACHIEVEMENTS

The first indication in the First World War of the superiority of weapons over infantry came as the Germans met a sharp initial repulse against the Belgian fortifications of Liège. Here massed men were stopped by artillery and machine-guns which sheltered behind concrete and steel. The only way these forts could be broken was by a super-heavy artillery bombardment from siege-guns laboriously dragged into position, along with their ammunition, in a time-consuming process costing fourteen days. But for a while longer, with space in which to manœuvre, the great German cavalry and infantry force rolled through Belgium and France towards Paris.

The earliest fighting vehicle actions were fought by the Belgians in August 1914 using un-armoured Minerva touring cars sporting a single Hotchkiss machine-gun —a weapon system which caused German cavalry patrols a lot of trouble in the approaches to the besieged city of Antwerp. Later the Belgians employed armoured cars like cavalry patrols for reconnaissance and ambush, a method rapidly adopted by the French who began mixing armoured cars with their horsed cavalry.

The first attempt to organise an armoured car force to undertake an independent mission came in August from inspiration on the part of Winston Churchill, the British First Lord of the Admiralty. Churchill had made the Royal Navy responsible for operations along the Belgian coast to prevent Zeppelins becoming based there to make raids against England. He ordered Commander Samson to organise companies of armed—later, by local improvisation, armoured—motor cars to operate as a guerilla force to protect the airfields from which naval aircraft were flying on bombing missions against the Zeppelin bases. The armoured cars continued to be effective until the Germans dug trenches across the roads, but in their short spell of freedom to manœuvre they were able to prove the value of armoured fighting power—the effect of a single armoured car sometimes being equal to that of a whole infantry company.

The first proposals for trench-crossing machines to overcome these barriers, as they appeared throughout September, came from Churchill, who demanded planks to enable the armoured cars to cross small cuts in the road, and from Lieutenant-Colonel Ernest Swinton. Swinton's real task was that of official reporter—"Eyewitness" for the British Army in France—that Army being rather allergic to the presence of pressmen. He was an experienced Royal Engineer who, as Official British Historian of the Russo-Japanese War, had been compelled to study and understand the advent of trench warfare in that conflict. At the end of October he proposed that armoured caterpillar tractors, carried on Holt tracks, should be built as the means to break through the newly evolving trench barrier. His ideas were swiftly vetoed by G.H.Q.—the first of many rebuffs to come— but given an airing in London, through the Committee of Imperial Defence, reached the ears of Churchill who was, by then, dabbling with trench-crossing tractors as prime movers for dragging heavy siege-guns to the front.

Swinton

The first French proposal for a vehicle as a trench-assault weapon was primarily aimed against the barbed-wire entanglement which screened the front line. A design was submitted in November 1914, by J. L. Breton for a mechanical wire-cutter, and the idea was expanded under the guidance of a Schneider Company engineer, called Brillié, to fit the cutting device to an armoured "Baby Holt" tractor. The system was abandoned in February 1916 when it was realised that the tractor alone could crush the wire, and as it became apparent that a gun might be a good substitute for the cutter.

The original arguments that gradually led to the evolution of armoured fighting vehicles in 1915 revolved around trench-crossing ability—a competition between the merits of tracked and wheeled suspensions. Both in Britain and Russia there were proposals for gigantic machines weighing, in one case, 300 tons and powered by diesel engines of up to 800 hp. The Russian "Tsar" tank— of which a pilot model was built—had wheels that were about 29 ft in diameter; its British equivalent (never built) first conceived wheels of 40 ft. Neither came to anything worth while because they were obviously too vulnerable a target and so the final solution, after intensive experimentation, settled on tracked vehicles.

The most advanced nation in development work was Great Britain where, throughout 1915, the driving force of Churchill, Swinton, Royal Naval officers and a banker-cum-sailor called Albert Stern, acquired Government approval and sufficient Treasury funds to experiment with a plethora of cross-country machines until a practical solution to the problem of making a working armoured and armed tracked vehicle was overcome. They worked as a team even if, at times, their disagreements threatened to destroy the whole project.

Stern

A Mark I being loaded at Fosters Ltd. With sponsors removed the Daimler engine is exposed to view. Note the exhaust smoke and the Russian letters which read (for security purposes) "With care to Petrograd".

The first definitive paper specifying the technical and tactical requirements for a tank was written by Swinton on 15th June 1915. He demanded it should climb a 5 ft bank and cross a 5 ft gap, that it should carry a light quick-firing gun plus two machine-guns, be proof against armour-piercing bullets, have a speed of about 4 mile/h and employ a crew of ten. These conditions would be varied as experiments progressed, but they were enough for **the first tank designers** William Tritton and Walter Wilson, to work towards a recognisable objective and for **the first tank builders**, Foster's of Lincoln, to tackle the problems of construction.

The first actual use of the word "tank" was brought about by the need for secrecy to disguise the existence of so potent a special assault weapon. In December 1915 it was decided that a deceptive name must also match the shape of the vehicle's shell, which looked like some sort of water-container. "Tank" was adopted because it was short and less ambiguous than "container" or "cistern". As such it remains to this day even if the modern family of vehicles bears little resemblance to the original.

On 12th January 1916 the first fighting tank ran on its own tracks, and in successive trials that month and the next convinced all doubters that here was a practical device deserving full scale-production. On 12th February the first order for 100 tanks was signed by the British Army Council and put into operation by Stern on instructions from the Minister of Munitions, David Lloyd George.

The initial move on the part of the French towards making a true fighting vehicle was delayed throughout 1915 because their generals believed heavy artillery fire sustained for hours or days on end could act as an effective battering-ram. By September it was plain that they were wrong and so, at last in December, a Colonel Estienne, at the third attempt, persuaded his C.-in-C., Marshal Joffre, that there was a place for a tracked, armoured gun in the forefront of battle. In fact he visualised it merely as an extension of artillery philosophy, but it led to the first orders, in mid-February 1916, for a mass of tanks—400 Schneiders followed by 400 St. Chamonds called, at first, "artillerie d'assaut" and controlled by the Artillery Section in the War Department. But the British were by now well ahead in the tank race since they had carried out thorough experiments before entering production, whereas the French merely put an armoured box on a tracked chassis and hoped for the best.

Estienne

Rolls-Royce Armoured Car of 1914—a type which, in modified form, survived three decades of war.

The dominant armoured fighting vehicles throughout 1915, however, were armoured cars which were to be found lurking behind every front awaiting the opportunity to dash through any gap which might present itself. On the Western Front this was impossible and in the East there were too few machines to be of any importance, while at Gallipoli they were unemployable in their intended role. But it was in the desert that the scope of long-range armoured warfare of the future was suggested. In North Africa at an oasis called Bir Hakeim, the crew of the torpedoed British ship *Tara* were held prisoner by Senussi tribesmen fighting on behalf of the Turks. A force of forty-five vehicles consisting of Rolls-Royce armoured cars, under the Duke of Westminster, and some supporting light vehicles and ambulances, made a 120-mile dash across desert, moving by night and day, and in less than fourteen hours had effected the crew's rescue.

The first recruitment of a special tank force was begun by Swinton in March 1916, the original officers and men coming from the Navy, the motor trade and a cross-section drawn from the rest of the British Army. Gunnery training started soon after, but everything else had to await the **first production tanks** which began delivery in June.

The earliest tactical training was based upon a long and detailed paper "Notes on the Employment of Tanks", issued by Swinton in February 1916. In full it can be read in Swinton's book *Eyewitness*. Not only was it to perform duty in preparing the first crews, and thus lay the foundation of **the tanks' first introduction into battle**, but it was to establish a basic doctrine which for many years dominated the thoughts of tank men the world over. Swinton stressed the tank's vulnerability to artillery fire and the need for his machines to co-operate closely with friendly artillery and infantry. He laid down the stages by which an attack should be prepared, the time it should start—at dawn for preference—the density of formations and the timing of the tanks' movements to coincide with the arrival of infantry on their joint objective—the enemy front-line trenches. But he also envisaged the tanks breaking through to the enemy gun line in the first day's fighting, visualised them advancing under cover of smoke clouds and working in co-operation with bombing aircraft. He also asked for external communications by wireless and telephones, though these could not be provided in 1916.

The first action by tanks was, on rare occasions, to justify Swinton's vision. It began at first light on 15th September 1916 with the advance of a solitary tank, D 1, under the command of Captain H. W. Mortimore, along the eastern outskirts of Delville Wood—the prelude to the Battle of Flers Courcellette that opened the final stages of the Somme offensive which had been raging, to little avail except loss of life, since 1st July. Mortimore's advance was, in a way, prophetic of the tank's progress in future battles—the balance of his success just outweighing failure. His tank reached its objective and took prisoner a number of terrified German infantry, but it might have done more had not a shell hit the starboard sponson, killed two of the crew (**the first tank casualties**) and broken the track, making D 1 **first out of, as well as first into, action**.

The greatest initial tank successes were achieved where they operated most highly concentrated in number. Of the thirty-six machines out of forty-nine available, the largest concentration occurred in the vicinity of the village of Flers. Here the village was taken with tanks in the lead and this gave rise to **the first outbreak of tank terror** on the German part—"the Devil is coming", they cried—and **the first example of tank euphoria**, when enthusiastic reports told of cheering British infantry advancing behind a tank.

Tank fought gun for the first time a few hundred yards beyond Flers when D 5 under Lieutenant Blowers, reached a German battery position and dominated it by fire until shortage of petrol and the non-arrival of friendly infantry made him turn for home. Whereupon the German gunners, returning to their guns, hit and set D 5 on fire—one of the earliest incidents of what a later generation of tankmen was to call "a brew-up".

Deeds of heroism by the crews began when the first clutch was let in as the leading tanks advanced, for these were highly vulnerable vehicles and the crews were inadequately trained, knowing little of conditions at the front. Private A. Smith received the Military Medal for his work at Delville Wood on the 15th— **the first tank decoration**. But **the first award for gallantry** to an officer had to wait until 26th September when Second Lieutenant Charles Storey took his tank, D 14, in splendid isolation against the Gird Trench near Gueudecourt, driving along the parapets, firing at the occupants below and co-operating with an aeroplane which also added its fire to that of the tank—**the first example of tank/air team-work**. Under heavy fire which penetrated the thin armour or splashed round its joints, all but two of the crew were wounded before the tank had to give up from petrol shortage. Over 300 prisoners were taken and Storey received the D.S.O. — an unusual award for so junior an officer. **The first awards to the greater part of a crew** went to five members under Corporal A. Taffs who, after their officer had been killed on 13th November when penetrating as far as the enemy second-line trench in mist, continued to advance. Unfortunately the tank got stuck when it overran a German dug-out and two hours' digging by the crew failed to extricate it. So this crew then joined the infantry and fought on foot—a perfect example of the doctrine that tank crews are but mounted fighting men just as cavalry were meant to be.

Horses, men, trenches and barbed wire in 1917.

Credit for the creation of the first Tank Corps goes to the British Army which on 8th October, brought an organisation into being that was not so much to assert tactical control (for that remained an infantry prerogative) as to train, control and maintain a new weapon totally different to any then in existence. The first man appointed to command the new Corps as such (which, for the time being, retained its original title of Heavy Section of the Machine-gun Corps) was Lieutenant-Colonel Hugh Elles, a Royal Engineer officer who earlier had been deputed by the Commander-in-Chief, General Sir Douglas Haig, to advise him on tank matters. Of those who were to join the staff within the next few weeks three are historically pre-eminent:

Martel

Captain G. Le Q. Martel, the Brigade Major, who was to set up the first establishment and, in November, wrote **the first futuristic paper** on tank armies—a paper which stated: "In any case the tanks will be of such great importance that future great wars are almost sure to start with a duel between the tank armies of the respective sides."

Captain F. E. Hotblack the Intelligence Officer of incredible bravery who won the D.S.O. on 18th October by walking in front of a tank through heavy fire in order to ensure its arrival on the objective. He was to set up the first systematic tank reconnaissance arrangements in preparation for action.

Major J. F. C. Fuller who joined in December as G.S.O. 2, becoming G.S.O. 1 in April 1917 as the Corps expanded. As Elles's chief staff officer this brilliant individualist, who had already written an accurate prewar forecast of the state of war to come, was to shape the new Tank Corps by relating a shrewd analysis of battles past to a projection of the future. Constantly evolving battle-drills would emerge from his genius; action would thrive upon the driving energy that he imposed upon those around him.

Yet nothing of great importance would be achieved by tanks in the earlier battles of 1917. The British offensive at Arras in 1917 included only sixty tanks—the entire available force since production of new machines was still limited. Though the village of Monchy-le-Preux was captured by three tanks, working on their own (the first such achievement of its kind which ended with the loss of all three machines) most tank attacks ended in anti-climax.

The French launched their first tanks, against the Chemin-des-Dames on 16th April 1917, putting in no less than 128 Schneiders. Like the British their crews were composed of naval men and soldiers from all parts of the Army. And like the British in battle they suffered a high rate of mechanical failure plus heavy losses from enemy counter-measures. Neither Schneiders nor the St. Chamonds did well over broken ground.

French St. Chamond moving out of cover in 1917.

The initiation of tanks into the arid desert war took place on 17th April 1917, when eight British vehicles went into the abortive Second Gaza offensive in Palestine—on ground that had once been dominated by ancient chariots. As on the Somme they shared local success with failure and losses. Six months later another eight tanks took part in the Third Battle of Gaza and were given the record number of twenty-nine objectives between them—a task redoubled in difficulty by the demand they should start in the dark. Yet five of the eight took their full share in the attack and did much to break Turkish confidence.

Royalty visits—Queen Mary and a Mark IV Male.

Tank drowning took place under British auspices when they committed a great many of the new Mark IVs to the Passchendaele offensive in July, inviting them to wallow in bottomless mud under a welter of shell-fire. It was not perhaps unreasonable for some officers to wonder whether or not the morale of the crews had been irreparably damaged before they had been given the opportunity to strike a sizable blow on ground of their own choosing, working to the methods evolved by Elles and his staff.

The longest action fought by a British tank was of sixty-eight hours' duration. A Mark IV of F Battalion, Tank Corps, became ditched 400 yd in front of the infantry near Gallipoli Farm, between the lines, in the Ypres Salient on 22nd August 1917. The crew remained in action, dispersing several German counter-attacks and killing a great number, until on the night of 25th August, having run out of ammunition, the crew, all wounded, withdrew to British lines, leaving behind one man who had been killed.

An indication of what could be done by tanks was provided by the French attack at Malmaison on 23rd October 1917 using ninety-two tanks on a narrow frontage for limited gains. Many became bogged and six were destroyed, but several went along with the infantry into the German lines and some attacked the artillery position.

Failure at Passchendaele proved, however, the tank's salvation, and the innovator of the plan of salvation was Fuller with his proposal that a massed tank raid should be launched on the firm chalk downs near Cambrai where the Germans' heavily entrenched Hindenburg Line fortified ground that had hardly been touched by shelling. From the idea of a raid grew the concept of a renewed offensive in the hope of something good to offset the bad of Passchendaele.

This, the first tank offensive, began at dawn near Cambrai on 20th November 1917. The full strength of the British Tank Corps, no less than 476 machines, was committed (though only 378 were fighting tanks in the front row) to move behind an artillery barrage fired by 1,003 guns. Surprise was the keynote— the secret concentration of tanks, guns, infantry and cavalry in the attack position at the last possible moment before the attack began; the firing of the barrage only as the tanks started to advance, and the use of aircraft in large numbers to attack the German guns and communications. On the first day this attack led to an advance of up to 4 miles and the breaching of the line on a 12-mile frontage—remarkable enough under any conditions in 1917 and quite shattering to German morale. British infantry losses were about 4,000 that day and tank casualties 179, of which 65 were by direct hits from artillery and the remainder by ditching and mechanical failure. The German losses that first day were over 10,000 men, 123 guns and 79 trench mortars along with 281 machine-guns. Some of the tanks had been continuously in action for sixteen hours before the day was out. If their victory could not be made absolute by the pursuit of the Germans in depth, the fortunes of the tank had been assured. **During this battle the first "tank" Victoria Cross** was won by Captain R. Wain—for a dismounted action.

Captured British Female Mark IV in German use, 1918.

The after effects of the Battle of Cambrai amounted to this:

> **For the Allies.** A revitalisation of plans to expand their tank forces and to introduce new types of machine. By 1919 a force of 10,000 tanks was to be assembled, shared by the British, French and Americans.

> **The American Army**, which had written off tanks as a failure at the end of 1916, changed its mind and formed its own Tank Corps on 26th January 1918. Its commander was to be Brigadier-General S. D. Rockenbach, but it was to be several months before it could go into action since the men had yet to be trained and the tanks could come only from British and French sources.

> **The German Army** also formed its first section of tanks in January using five A7V tanks and, later, five British tanks to form a second section. Up to now, like the Americans, they had hung back in the tank race. Too late they set plans in motion for a vast expansion.

> **The Russian Army**, which had tardily awoken to the possibilities of tanks in early 1917, asked the British and French to supply some since their projects had broken down amidst the general chaos of their own industry. Some tanks were shipped and were in time to take part in the struggle of the Revolution.

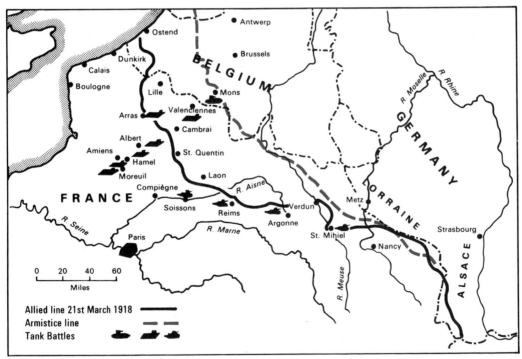

As the First World War progressed, tanks were increasingly used on the Western Front, sometimes in dribs and drabs but later in great concentrations. This map shows where the major appearances took place.

Tank fighting throughout 1918, to start with, was on only a minute scale at the beginning of the greatest offensive of the war when the German Army attacked in the West on 21st March. Dwarfed by the immensity of the bombardment that went on across an immense frontage, a mere five German A7Vs, plus the five captured British machines, crept through fog against the British at St. Quentin. Of these ten only three completed their mission in a local attack—the others either broke down or were knocked out. In the March days of the German offensive that followed, it was only the British and French who used tanks to any extent and then mostly in small groups to counter German penetrations of their line. As such they had a limited impact while their losses from being overrun in position were altogether too high.

The rising momentum of the tank struggle first appeared at Villers-Bretonneux on 24th April when thirteen German tanks were launched against British and Australian troops. The remarkable feature of this battle was not simply the overall success of the German tanks which prevailed wherever they went, but the tank-versus-tank fighting which broke out when three A7Vs came into conflict with three British Mark IVs—a fight in which honours were about even, though the Germans pulled back. Later seven British "Whippets", called up by an aeroplane to charge the German infantry, were driven off with the loss of one to a single A7V. The Whippet commander, in fact, was quite unaware that it was a tank which had fired upon him.

Throughout the summer of 1918 the Germans persisted in repetitive offensives on different parts of the front. Though rarely using tanks themselves they were often attacked by Allied tanks—frequently by the French:

At Adelpare Farm on 5th April six Schneiders attacked but only one reached its objective.

At Grivesnes Park on the 7th another six Schneiders went into action, reached their objectives but had to return, riddled with holes, because the infantry did not follow up. This was the first time the Germans employed their *Tankgewehr 18*, a clumsy anti-tank rifle firing a 13 mm armour-piercing bullet.

On 8th April three platoons of Schneiders were in action at different places and for the loss of three knocked out a number of German machine-guns in thick woodland. They helped infantry advance 900 yd.

At Cantigny on 28th May Schneiders were the first tanks to support the U.S. Army in battle, leading a classic attack by the 28th Infantry, behind a surprise bombardment, in the capture of the town.

In the Forest of Retz from 31st May to 18th June the new Renault FT tanks, occasionally mixed with other French tanks, came into action in a succession of skirmishes in which the number of tanks employed never rose above fifteen. But the effect on the Germans of these pinpricks was as disheartening as it was encouraging to the French who always made progress at a reduced cost in lives.

The Germans used ten tanks again at Soissons on 1st June and another five at Reims the same day, but nearly all ran into heavy artillery fire and were lost—the most distinguished work by the crews being in the nature of dismounted rather than mounted action.

The next massed French tank attack was reserved for 28th June and was by sixty Renault FTs at Cutry-St.-Pierre-Aigle. Competition between infantry and tanks was noticeable here—"an infantry unit would be dishonoured who would subordinate its advance to that of tanks". Generally speaking, in this successful action which was well planned in great detail, both tanks and infantry reached their objectives, despite heavy fire and shared casualties. Indeed it was often the tanks which beat the infantry to the objective and made the latter's subsequent advance possible.

A night attack at Bucquoy by five British Mark IVs on 22nd June was conceived simply as a raid —and was one of the few successful tank night actions, undertaken without damage, even though one commander was reduced to defending his tank by firing his revolver at point blank range.

The attack by sixty of the new British Mark Vs at Hamel on 4th July in which they, with ten Australian battalions and four American infantry companies inflicted heavy losses on the Germans in a hotly contested action, followed the trend of larger more deliberate counter-offensives in lieu of local skirmishes. Here the casualty figures were of great interest. The Germans lost 1,500 prisoners and 171 machine-guns, the attackers just under a thousand infantry. But of the tanks only five were destroyed, with but thirteen crewmen wounded.

The next major stroke by the French came at Soissons between 18th and 26th July when 211 St. Chamonds and Schneiders in company with 135 Renaults co-operated with French and American infantry to drive a wedge deep into the German flank where it rested in exhaustion at the end of another abortive offensive towards Paris. An additional 125 Renaults were used on an adjacent sector. For eight days the tanks struggled forward, though never so fast as on the first day and with dwindling numbers as enemy shell fire, soft ground and mechanical failures took their toll. Tank casualties, in fact, were high. In one case 48 out of 69 engaged were knocked out, in another there was 22 per cent of personnel made casualty. Some companies were continuously in action for forty-eight hours. But it was the infantry who were first among the exhausted, while it was claimed that the tanks might have done even better had the artillery concentrated on their support, by shelling German guns, instead of aiming as of old at wire and machine-guns that were the infantry's main threat. These latter the tanks could crush.

July 1918 brought an end to a plethora of smaller tank battles of which Moreuil, on the 23rd, was the most important since, here, thirty-five British tanks supported French infantry of their 3rd Division. One English speaking Frenchman travelled in each tank to improve liaison, eleven tanks were knocked out for a loss of fifty-four crewmen, but the objectives were taken. So pleased were the French that they awarded the tank unit (9th Battalion of the Tank Corps) the Croix de Guerre—**the first decoration given to a tank unit**.

This was the eve of the greatest tank offensive of the war when 604 Allied tanks were to strike a titanic blow east of Amiens on 8th August. But it has to be emphasised that, so effective had the tanks now proved themselves, nobody seriously contemplated an important action without having them present. Though the Allies were acquiring great numbers of machines from increasing production, even the latest arrivals were unreliable and vulnerable. Hence battle casualties were bound to be in excess of replacements and therefore became an important limiting factor in plans for a continuous offensive such as the Allied Generalissimo, Foch, envisaged.

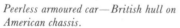

Peerless armoured car—British hull on American chassis.

The first light tank—the French Renault FT.

Dawn at Cambrai, 20th November 1917—tanks and infantry advance towards the smoke screen which blinds the enemy artillery.

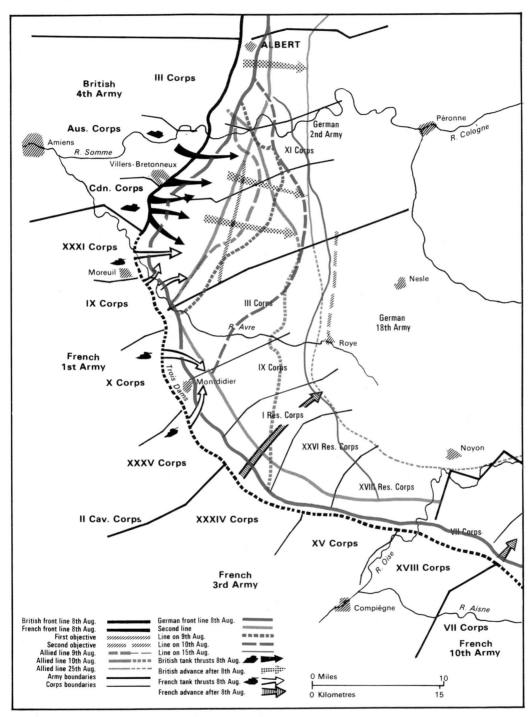

Battle of Amiens. August 1918. The artillery neutralised the Germans, the heavy tanks punched through, the infantry mopped up and medium tanks with horsemen exploited in the gap created.

A Whippet advances with Canadian troops near Amiens, August 1918.

Yet the tank as the principal and decisive weapon of the future was now being hotly recommended by Fuller. In a paper of 24th May entitled "The Tactics of the Attack as affected by the Speed and Circuit of the Medium D Tank" (later better known as "Plan 1919") he had pleaded the case for a tank force that could not only disrupt the enemy front line but also could plunge deep into his rearward area, striking at the artillery positions and paralysing his entire apparatus of control by hitting at headquarters. He wanted a "breaking force" of 2,592 heavies and a "pursuing force" of 2,400 mediums that would expand the British Tank Corps to 37,000 all ranks—and even then would merely be part of an Allied tank force of 10,000 machines. Here was the policy that was adopted by Foch for implementation in 1919—even if, by then, the Medium D tank could not be ready and its work had to be done by the less efficient Medium C and others.

The true indication of the practicability of Fuller's concept was demonstrated on 8th August during the Battle of Amiens when about 600 British and French tanks attacked on a 20-mile front. They used the basic methods of Cambrai to achieve a breach in the German line, but added the intervention of Whippets and armoured cars to deepen the area of penetration. After the heavy Mark Vs had opened a hole, the pursuit force entered the gap and by nightfall had advanced a distance of 6 miles, capturing immense quantities of men and material and so shattering German morale that their will to resist was temporarily undermined while their High Command, in the person of General Ludendorff, lost his nerve and concluded that peace terms must be sought.

The main innovations at Amiens that were to shape tank thinking most profoundly in the future were:

> **The use of heavy tanks** to carry machine-gun teams deep into the enemy rear and there dismount them for guerilla action.

> **The deep penetration of the enemy lines by armoured cars**, towed through barricades by the tanks, that led to attacks on German headquarters some 8 miles in the rear.

> **The attempt to combine Whippet tanks with horsed cavalry** in the pursuit—an attempt that failed because the two elements were incompatible: horsemen could not move where armoured vehicles stood up to enemy fire, horsemen went too fast for Whippets when opposition had ceased.

The most remarkable feat by a single tank was that of the Whippet, "Musical Box" which, under Lieutenant C. B. Arnold, cut loose in the German lines and, over a period of ten hours, fought a solo war against the Germans. "Musical Box" destroyed a gun battery and immense quantities of motor and horsed transport, killed great numbers of German reinforcements and successfully engaged a railway train before herself being hit and set on fire. The driver was killed but the rest of the crew survived as prisoners of war, after being beaten up by a very angry enemy.

Mark Vs in battle alongside New Zealand infantry in France, 25th August 1918. Captured German guns in background.

Tanks were constantly in action throughout the remainder of the war for, as the attack at Amiens died away, the Allied offensive was widened to the flanks, the French putting in a series of assaults to the south, the British making renewed hammer blows of the Amiens type at Albert. The limiting factor now became the availability of machines that were in short supply. For example, the British from having 1,184 machines fit for action on 8th August had only 266 on the 31st and had returned 819 machines to salvage by 11th October. Between 8th August and 11th October British tank crew casualties amounted to 550 out of 1,500 officers, and 2,537 other ranks out of 8,000—which some would have reckoned cheap for the enormous successes that had been achieved. The French were also taking heavy losses. At Nouvron-Vingre on 20th August an entire force of 16 Schneiders was knocked out while 14 Renaults either broke down or were destroyed with the loss of 30 per cent of their crews. Yet the tanks dominated every appearance and almost invariably ensured the success of each attack.

There was the Whippet tank which came home on its own at dusk after a fight near Croisilles on 24th August. Phosphorus bombs hit the tank, setting fire to parts of its superstructure and forcing the crew to abandon ship because of the fumes. The crew, after putting out the fire, restarted the engine and headed for home, but again the fumes became too bad, so while the tank moved slowly forward in bottom gear, the crew walked ahead, using the tracks as shelter from enemy fire, until they had reached safety and it was possible, once more, to occupy the fighting compartment.

The first battlefield appearance of the new American Tank Corps took place at the Battle of the St. Mihiel Salient, on 12th September when the 304th Tank Brigade with 174 Renault tanks worked in conjunction with French tanks of all kinds. It was not a happy début for the Germans were already withdrawing from this salient and largely evaded the net. On the 13th the tanks were held up for shortage of fuel because resupply had broken down in a traffic jam.

Among the first decorations won by American tankmen was the Distinguished Service Cross awarded to Major Sereno Brett for leading 326th Battalion into action on foot under fire on 12th September. But a truly dramatic D.S.C. went two days later to Second-Lieutenant Edwin McCluer when his three Renaults accompanied by five dismounted men penetrated 2 km into the enemy rear and there played havoc with a German infantry battalion, shot up artillery and destroyed eight machine-guns—his adventure ending in successful efforts to tow home the other two tanks after they had broken down. A fortnight later a Lieutenant-Colonel George Patton was wounded while leading tanks towards action—thus both he and Brett, who were later to play their parts in post-war tank development, earned fame because they were forced to control tanks, without the protection of armour, due to the total absence of intercommunication between tanks.

The greatest American tank appearance was a bloody affair during the Battle of Meuse Argonne between 26th September and 5th October. Into this action went 141 Renaults, plus a great many more French-manned machines, and soon they were heavily engaged, accounting for large numbers of Germans with their machine-guns. Yet because the American tanks were split up all over the front, to meet random infantry requests for assistance, it can hardly be said that they acted as a tank force proper in the British style. By the 29th only 55 Renaults remained to the Americans and by 5th October they were down to 30 with losses over 50 per cent in officers and 30 per cent in men. That day they were withdrawn, temporarily, from the front due to the almost total unserviceability of the force. Though the American

C.-in-C., General Pershing, might offer "anything in the A.E.F. for 500 additional tanks" they were simply unavailable because, while Anglo-French production was unequal to their own needs, American industry had utterly failed to deliver a single battleworthy machine of its own.

The first U.S. Congressional Medal of Honour won by a tank man went to Corporal Donald Call of the 344th Battalion on 26th September near Varennes. He was a driver whose tank was hit by a shell, half its turret knocked off and his officer wounded. Under intense shell and machine-gun fire he dragged the officer out and carried him over a mile to safety.

The first Ford tank—only fifteen built. Never saw action.

The war came to an end as the German Army withdrew towards its own frontiers, first in an endeavour to shorten its line and then to escape engulfment while an armistice was arranged. Their own tanks made but two more sallies—one at Fermicourt where two were inadvertently destroyed by their own infantry and the other at Nieregnies on 11th October. Meantime, as the Allied tank waves got smaller as they ran out of numbers, tank pressure on the Germans was commensurately reduced.

In the final stages it was Allied armoured cars which took up the running in the most mobile form of warfare that had been known in the West for four years. They crossed the Rhine on 6th December at the head of the British Army of Occupation.

Armoured cars, in fact, accomplished some of the most dramatic feats of the war and not the least of these took place in the wastes of the Middle East. Rolls-Royce types, supported by Ford armoured trucks, were frequently employed in Mesopotamia and Palestine, pursuing the beaten Turk forces whenever they were forced out of a strongly defended position. The main problem was usually one of fuel supply. For example, when the senior British Royal Flying Corps officer, in Mesopotamia, Lieutenant-Colonel J. E. Tennant, was captured after a forced landing behind the Turk lines on 25th March, shortly before the Battle of Khan Baghdadi, it was an armoured car patrol which was sent to rescue him and his companion. With instructions to operate out to 100 miles range, with fuel dropped by aircraft if necessary, the task was accomplished in the nick of time—just as the Tartar escort seemed on the point of murdering their charges. It was perhaps significant that Tennant's companion was a Major P. C. S. Hobart who, in later years, was to take the lead in advocating long-range operations by British armoured forces.

Rolls-Royce armoured cars tow a crashed aeroplane in Mesopotamia, 1918.

The development of the armoured car as an element in guerilla warfare (as envisaged by Churchill back in 1914) was taken up by Lawrence of Arabia in his conduct of raiding the Turkish lines in Arabia and Palestine. The cars supplied extra pace and fire support to the camel-borne Arab auxiliaries and were Lawrence's principal means of personal transport as well as a symbol of prestige.

Lawrence

The first elements of the British forces to enter Aleppo and bring the war against Turkey to an end were armoured cars whose staying power in a long pursuit after the victory at Megiddo far outdid that of horsed cavalry.

Modified German A7V in action against rioters in Berlin, 1919.

As the mobile element of an anti-guerilla force armoured cars were also discovered to have many uses since they could be switched quickly from one threatened place to another. In Russia, as the Revolution took hold, armoured cars of many varieties made increasingly effective public appearances either in open combat or for crowd control in the cities. The British introduced them into India where they soon found themselves clambering the mountain tracks of the North-West Frontier, escorting convoys to isolated garrisons and combating the large-scale tribal warfare which had escalated into a full-scale war against Afghanistan.

As the last shots of the First World War were being fired in November 1918, the first shots in the post-war campaigns were already ringing out. And foremost among the combatants were armoured fighting vehicles which practical soldiers deemed essential wherever danger threatened.

Production of tanks had been immense and the vast majority remained, either for use or scrapping. The total of operational fighting tanks made amounted, by nations, as follows:

	Heavy	Medium	Light
Great Britain	2,617	281	nil
France	nil	800	3,500
Germany	20	nil	nil

and in addition there were several thousand armoured cars.

The economics of mechanised warfare were emphasised by Fuller, British battle casualties per square mile of gain being:

Between July and November 1916	5,300
Between July and November 1917	8,200
Between July and November 1918	83

and in the American Army it was calculated that, although it was much more expensive initially to equip an infantry regiment with motor vehicles than with animals, the economic balance fell heavily in favour of the former after three years' operation and maintenance.

PART TWO—VEHICLES & TECHNOLOGY

First to make extensive use of the motor car in 1914 were the Belgians. The cars were unarmoured private touring cars pressed into service for use against marauding German cavalry and reconnaissance screens on the right flank of the invading Germans. Finding that protection against rifle- and machine-gun fire was essential, the Minerva and S.A.V.A. works in Antwerp began armouring the cars; soon standard body designs were in production, with improvised mild steel or armour plate protection for other makes such as Imperia, Mercedes and Excelsior. The "commandeered" cars began to be superseded by fully enclosed armoured versions of Minerva and S.A.V.A. about the middle of September 1914. The air-cooled Hotchkiss machine-gun was standard armament, although a 37 mm gun came to be mounted in some cases later. Both makes of car had similar engines, using the American "Silent Knight" single sleeve-valve arrangement.

Early French armoured cars, including a few vehicles engaged with the Belgian and British cars against the Germans in 1914, were mainly Panhard and Mors and used much more frequently in overseas territories.

Early German armoured cars were based on limited experience with pre-war lorry-borne balloon and anti-aircraft guns, both armoured and soft-skinned. The Germans built some seventeen armoured cars during the First World War.

They were high, ponderous and cumbersome, of Daimler, Ehrhardt, Büssing and Mannesmann makes, four-wheel drive and steerable from either end. They were chiefly employed for internal security, only taking part in military operations in the Balkans.

Armoured cars were not part of the U.S. Army's standard equipment, so that those which were built remained private ventures. Of the firms such as Davidson, Pierce-Arrow, Garford, Mack, White, Packard, King, Seabrook, Peerless and Jeffery, only the last-named manufactured significant quantities of complete machines. These, with numerous chassis, were exported to the U.K. and Russia, where armoured bodies were mounted.

The largest armoured car fleet of any country during the First World War was pre-Revolution Russia's, with some 1,500 vehicles.

The first British R.N.A.S. armoured cars were Rolls-Royce and Mercedes touring cars protected from rifle-fire by 6 mm mild steel plate bought locally from Forges et Chantiers de France in Dunkirk. By mid-September the cars were better protected when 8 mm armour plate was supplied from Beardmore's in England; but the plates were flat, as the technique of bending thin armour had not then been learnt.

The earliest that overhead protection became available was in December 1914 when the first Admiralty turreted Rolls-Royce, Lanchester, Delaunay-Belleville and Wolseley cars were delivered. These were followed in February 1915 by Seabrook 5-ton chassis armoured by Portholme Aerodrome Co and mounting a 3-pdr gun or a Vickers 1-pdr pom-pom, and four Maxims.

The War Office first began to build armoured cars based on the heavy A.E.C. "B" type London General Omnibus Company chassis in January 1915 at Woolwich Arsenal. Similar Thornycroft chassis were adapted later.

When the R.N.A.S. Armoured Car Division was disbanded in August 1915, with the exception of the Locker-Lampson Squadron in Russia and Rumania, the War Office took over all their equipment, and formed motor batteries to man the cars as part of the Machine-gun Corps. They kept the Rolls-Royces and the Seabrook armoured lorries, using the former for protection in the battle zone, and for towing 3-pdr guns in conjunction with the Seabrooks and a few A.E.C.s for surprise raids of short duration. Leyland armoured cars, bought by private subscription, were employed in German South-West Africa; and for some months, the R.N.A.S. squadrons overseas in German East Africa, the Dardanelles, German South-West Africa, and the Western Desert of Egypt and Libya operated as usual without changing their capbadges.

The first Tank Corps armoured cars were the sixteen Austin twin-turreted Hotchkiss machine-gun-armed 50 bhp cars of 17th Tank (Armoured Car) Battalion. **Their first action** was in support of the French 10th Army at Belloy, after a 60-mile night drive, on 11th June 1918. Thereafter the cars were con-

Austin Armoured Cars in Iraq, 1919.

stantly employed until the Armistice, sometimes being towed across shell-devastated ground by tanks until they reached roads on the German side of the line. **They were the first British troops to enter Cologne** on 6th December 1918, and the first to cross the Rhine, using the Hohenzollern Bridge, and carrying the Tank Corps colours. In six months, 17th Battalion had supported British, Australian, Canadian, New Zealand, South African, French and American troops, and had been mentioned three times in German dispatches. Every car had been hit at least once, and seven were destroyed at a total cost of five men killed.

These Austin cars were also used with the light armoured motor batteries in Mesopotamia.

The first German aircraft shot down by a British armoured car was a Taube, on 14th October 1914, hit by Maxim and rifle-fire.

The first British use of vehicle-borne machine-guns, other than in armoured cars, was in the Motor Machine-gun Service in October 1914, thirteen months before the Machine-gun Corps was formed. The battery was the fighting unit, consisting of three sections each of four guns. Mounted in the sidecar of a motor-cycle combination, the Maxim had a crew of two, each gun backed up by another combination carrying reserve ammunition. In action the gun had all-round traverse and an anti-aircraft capability, initially with no armoured protection. Armoured shields were issued later. At least one combination was also given complete armoured protection experimentally later, in 1916.

The combinations were Scott—578 cc parallel twin, watercooled rotary-port two-stroke, shaft drive—and Clyno—55-degree V-twin air-cooled four-stroke 744 cc J.A.P., belt drive—and, later, Royal Enfield, Douglas, A.J.S., or New Imperial. Wheels were interchangeable, with integral ball-bearing hubs, dog engagement and wing nuts. With spare wheel, 1,250 rounds of ammunition, a 1 gal can of water for the gun, the

Maxim and its tools, spares for the machine, and two men, the all-up weight of a Clyno was 10·5 cwt.

Each section had three Douglas solos for their "scouts", and two Daimler 1-ton box cars. With a box-car carrying two spare Maxims, and a two-seater Vauxhall staff car for the battery commander, the unit strength was four officers and fifty-eight N.C.O.s and men.

The heaviest idea for a wheeled landship was devised by Major T. G. Hetherington of the 18th Hussars, seconded to the R.N.A.S., in December 1914. Originally to mount a 12 in gun, its weight of 800 tons was to be propelled by submarine diesel engines and electric drive. But, as put forward, it was a 300-tonner mounting three twin 100 mm guns behind 76 mm armour. It was to have 17 ft ground clearance, two 40 ft driving wheels with rims 13 ft wide, and a 40 ft steering tail-wheel with a 5 ft rim. In January 1915, it was calculated that it would weigh nearer 1,000 tons than the 300 suggested, needing 5,000 hp to propel it. The project was turned down as offering too large a target.

The largest three-wheeled fighting vehicle ever built, if the Russians are to be believed, was the "Tsar" tank of 1915. The two front 29 ft diameter rod-spoked wheels were carried on a pair of horizontal girder forks each leading back to a hollow rectangular "hull" across the vehicle at axle height, supported at the back by a small roller at the end of a single "trail" girder at 40 degrees to the ground. Two 250 hp Sunbeam engines in the hull drove one front wheel each, apparently by friction drive to the wheel rims, and the unspecified armament was at each end of the hull where it projected some 10 or 12 ft outboard of the wheels. Tested in August 1915, at a weight of 40 tons, the trail roller dug in. The machine was judged too big a target, and the project was abandoned. The only prototype was broken up in 1923.

THE FIRST TANKS

The Tritton Trencher was originated in March 1915 at Foster's of Lincoln, based on the commercial Foster-Daimler tractor. It had a long chassis extension in front carrying two wide wheels in tandem to allow it to nose across a trench. It then winched a pair of planks across for the back wheels to use, and then towed the planks over. By reversing the back wheels over the planks, they were positioned for carrying forward to another crossing at the next trench. The machine was too cumbersome, and was dropped after trials in June 1915.

The 15 ft Big Wheelers. Several 8 ft and 15 ft Big Wheelers were designed as alternatives, none of which were built because their ground pressure was too high and they were too big a target. The wheeled landship idea was abandoned.

The Holt tractor, a half-track, with a broad iron steering-wheel at the front, was in commercial production in 1914. Some 800 were with the B.E.F. in France by mid-1915, and Holts were also available in many European capitals.

Mr. W. S. Churchill's (First Lord of the Admiralty) steam-rollers. The War Office went back to building armoured troop-carriers on London bus chassis. Meantime, the Admiralty experimented at Wormwood Scrubs, where the Armoured Car Division of the Royal Naval Air Service was forming in the Daily Mail Airship Shed placed at its disposal by Lord Northcliffe. At Churchill's direction, they tested and found quite ineffective in January 1915, two steam-rollers linked side by side running astride a trench to crush the ground flat and bury the troops in it.

Tritton

Tritton No 1 with Bullock tracks, on trial in 1915.

The Diplock Pedrail landship. In February 1915, a Pedrail 1-ton tracked load-carrying trailer was tested as a possible way of mounting a wide armoured shield behind which infantrymen could advance against machine-gun fire. Two of these tracks might become the basis for the 24-ton landship which the Director of the R.N.A.S. had planned in January 1915. As a result, twelve Pedrails were ordered, as well as six 15 ft Big Wheelers for trials. The shield project was examined by the War Office later, and turned down; the German General

Staff did the same for a similar idea in 1916. By April 1915, the landship had crystallised into a tandem-track hull astride very wide single tracks, each mounted on a turntable with its own Rolls-Royce Silver Ghost engine and transmission. It was to carry a 12-pdr or two 6-pdrs at an all-up weight of 25 tons.

During development, the first rigid 44-footer was articulated for steering. Various schemes to carry between 66 and 90 men mounting weapons from machine-guns to 12-pdr guns on chassis lengths up to 60 ft were tried out. Two imported Giant Creeping Grip tractors were used to test the articulated joint. But by 7th May 1915, the original twelve Pedrails had been reduced to two, one of which was to be on "Creeping Grip", otherwise "Bullock", tracks, so complex had been the problems. In June, the Big Wheelers were dropped. Further progress dwindled ultimately into projects for self-propelled guns, none of which found favour. Finally, the whole idea was given up on 2nd July, and no Pedrails were ever built. Plans and materials already ordered were handed over to the War Office, and months later one machine was completed to carry a powerful flame-thrower. It, too, was never used.

The Killen Strait tractor— an experiment in 1915 at Wormwood Scrubs with an American-type track.

The Giant Creeping Grip tractor, the Killen-Strait, and American influence. At the end of April 1915, after trials of the two Giants, a pair of specially long Bullock tracks was ordered from the U.S.A. By June 1915, dissatisfaction with the apparent lack of progress with landship development had grown. A comprehensive demonstration was therefore run at Wormwood Scrubs on 30th June in order to engender confidence in the work and still criticism. An imported Killen-Strait three-track tractor was among the equipment shown, and some weeks later the same machine was tested carrying the turretless body from a Delaunay-Belleville Admiralty-pattern car. In this form it may have represented **the first tracked armoured vehicle**, but it was not the first tank. It was too heavy, and the scheme abandoned. The Killen-Strait, like the Creeping Grip tractor and the Pedrail landships played no further part in the direct development of the tank; but its American manufacturers suggested "angularising" whatever tracks were used, by raising idler or sprocket to afford greater climbing ability, as had also been suggested by an officer of the R.N.A.S.

The first tank—"Little Willie". As the wheel and the half-track had proved unsuitable for cross-country work, a full-tracked "one-piece" machine was ordered from Foster's on 29th July, to incorporate the long Bullock tracks obtained from the U.S.A. The design was based on an armoured hull supported between track frames on one transverse axle. Pitching of the hull was restricted to a few inches by rubber stops on the short vertical slides and slipper-blocks at fore and aft ends of the hull. For motive power, the Foster-Daimler tractor unit was used, a double sleeve-valve Daimler six-cylinder 105 hp engine, cone clutch, two-speed gearbox and worm-drive differential. Tail-wheels were fitted for wide-radius turns and as counterweights to the machine's point of balance. A wooden mock-up was inspected on 26th August 1915, and that evening, at a meeting in the White Hart Hotel, Lincoln, the revised performance characteristics of 15th June, only then received from the War Office, were discussed. The Tritton-Wilson (or No. 1 Lincoln Machine, otherwise "Little Willie") would not meet these requirements, and something better was wanted. Meanwhile "Little Willie" continued. **It first ran** in Foster's yard on 6th September 1915, with local tests on 19th September. It soon became clear from constant trouble with the Bullock tracks that a major redesign was required. After unsuccessful experiments with Balata belting for the tracks, a new pressed steel plate track proved satisfactory on 21st September. With new track frames and rollers, the revised machine ran on its Tritton-Wilson tracks on 22nd November 1915. There were no further troubles.

"Mother", alias "Big Willie" or H.M. Landship "Centipede". Mr. Tritton and Lieutenant Wilson R.N.A.S. already had a scheme in mind for a vehicle to meet the War Office's revised characteristics, and it was this design which was selected on 26th August. By 25th September, a wooden mock-up was ready, and the actual vehicle ran for the first time on 12th January 1916. After preliminary trials locally at Lincoln, official tests of "Mother" and "Little Willie" were held at Hatfield Park in great secrecy on 29th January and 2nd February. A large number of V.I.P.s attended the second of these, including Lord Kitchener. King George V had a demonstration run on 8th February, **the first with a reigning monarch**.

The first fighting tank—Mother.

The first shot ever fired from a tank came from "Mother"'s starboard 6-pdr in Burton Park, Lincoln, on 20th January 1916. The layer was Major T. G. Hetherington. It was a misfire, and when the breech was about to be opened half-way to see if the cap in the cartridge-case had been struck—as laid down in Misfire Drill—the round went off. Hetherington was uncertain where the shot had gone; he and Major Stern, his loader, spent two hours searching before it was found. (Round and case are preserved in the R.A.C. Tank Museum.)

The first armament planned for "Little Willie" was a 2-pdr pom-pom and 800 rounds, but in the event, nothing was ever fitted, a weighted-up turret being used for the trials. For "Mother", the 75 mm mountain gun was first proposed, but mortars were also discussed. As all weapons were scarce, the Armstrong-Whitworth 6-pdr 8 cwt 40-calibre gun, to be provided by the Admiralty, was used. The shorter-barrelled 23-calibre Hotchkiss 6-pdr 6 cwt replaced it in some Marks II and III, and from Mark IV onwards it was standard.

Two types of ammunition were issued; steel shell with a small explosive filling with either time-and-percussion nose fuse for airburst, or instantaneous base fuse for armour piercing; and common shell, cast iron with a filling, for use as H.E. Soon afterwards a time-and-percussion nose-fused phosphorus smoke round became available, and also a case-shot. The thin steel case, stiffened for passage up the gun bore, carried 500 steel balls embedded in sand and resin. The case collapsed on leaving the muzzle, and the balls spread out over a 15-degree cone. Effective range for case-shot was up to 200 yd—at 100 yd one round would produce an average of 68 hits on a 9 ft by 4 ft target.

The 6-pdr muzzle velocity was 1,350 ft/sec, being sighted with range-drum and telescope every 25 yd up to 2,000 yd. Maximum range was generally accepted as 2,500 yd, although fighting ranges were normally considerably shorter. Each sponson had a 100-degree arc, and plus 20 to minus 15 degrees of elevation.

Machine-gun ammunition was ball. Some armour-piercing tracer was available in late 1918.

An elementary form of fire control was in use in Mark V tanks from late summer 1918, to indicate to sponson gunners from the tank commander the range and bearing of targets by means of coloured lights on a board, powered by the tank battery.

BRITISH TANKS

Wilson

Mark I. The first tank ever used in war was the Mark I heavy tank. Directly based on "Mother", 100 were ordered on 12th February 1916, raised to 150 on 3rd April. **First issues were made** in June 1916. Primitive and untried as it was, the Mark I shape and layout remained unchanged for heavy tanks until the end of the war.

Like its successors, the Mark I consisted of an armoured hull about 5 ft wide, 5 ft high and 15 ft long. On each side was a narrow rhomboid-shaped armoured framework round which ran the tracks on unsprung rollers, and in the centre of which was a rectangular sponson carrying the armament, the sponson projecting some 3 ft outboard of the tracks. The engine, clutch, main gearbox, differential and radiator, in that order from front to rear, were mounted on a deep angle-iron sub-frame bolted fore and aft to lateral cross-members. In front of the engine were driver (right) and tank commander (left) each with a hinged port through which to look out forward. In each sponson were layer and loader for the armament. Further back, one on each side of the differential, were the two secondary gearsmen. The drive to the tracks ran outwards from the differential to a two-speed secondary gearbox in each track frame, and then by 3 in pitch roller chain 6 ft back to an intermediate sprocket meshing with the track sprockets. At the tail was a pair of iron steering-wheels on a spring-loaded frame hinged to the rear horns. A hydraulic ram on the hull back plate could lift the wheels off the ground for skid turns. Cables ran on either side of the hull from the bobbin on the driver's steering-column to the tiller on the wheels. As well as providing long-radius turns in ideal conditions, the tail-wheels acted as a counterweight to shift the tank's point of balance when it was poised on the edge of a trench; without the tail, it could cross a trench 10-ft wide, but with it, a theoretical 11 ft 6 in. The wheels hindered manœuvre and were easily damaged; the ram was slow in operation. By Christmas 1916, all tail-wheels had been removed.

Four men were required to drive the Mark I, and also the Marks II, III and IV to follow. The driver could slowly alter course with the tail-wheels if they would grip, but if a sharper turn was needed, he would have to halt. With wheels off the ground, he would bang on the engine casing behind him to attract the attention of the gearsmen. They would engage high, low or neutral in their respective gearboxes as indicated by the driver's hand signals. If one track was to be stationary in order to make a skid turn, the driver would lock the differential by pulling a lever above his left shoulder so that power would be applied to the other track. If one track was to be in high and the other in low in order to make a wider turn, the differential was left unlocked. The driver then moved off, using the main two-speed gearbox and the hand throttle. Once in motion, corrections to course could be made by degrees if the tank commander carefully operated the levers in front of him, controlling the track brakes. The main brakes operated on the transmission shaft drum behind the differential worm pinion, and were usually only needed at extreme angles of descent or ascent.

Two tanks to right and left of the driving cab carried 45 gal of petrol, feeding the carburettor by gravity. On good level going the tank would do 12 miles on one fill; after 70 miles, it would need a workshop overhaul.

The 6-cylinder Daimler double sleeve-valve engine was selected as power plant because it was a well-tried component of the pre-war Foster-Daimler Tractor. There were few, if any, others of the power needed on the market. At a dry weight of 18 cwt for engine, flywheel and clutch, 105 hp was available at a governed 1,000 rev/min. The engine made a great deal of smoke in the exhaust, and the stacks to take this into the atmosphere went vertically up through the roof plate, with metal baffles above to deflect the flames and sparks.

The Male Mark I had a 40-calibre 6-pdr gun in each sponson, with shoulder-controlled elevation and traverse; Females, the man-killers to accompany the emplacement-destroying Males, had two water-cooled Vickers machine-guns with armoured jackets in each sponson. Males were designed to carry 200 rounds of 6-pdr and 6,000 of small arms ammunition (S.A.A.), Females 10,000 of S.A.A.; but it was common to stow 300 rounds for the guns and up to 30,000 for the machine-guns.

Narrow glass prisms were used at first for observation from inside, but these were soon replaced by polished steel mirrors, as the glass splintered too dangerously. Driver and commander had tabular periscopes projecting through the roof above them. For entrance and exit, there was one small door in each rear hull plate; one circular manhole in the roof; and one door in each sponson. A 12 V generator and battery lighted the two small downward-pointing headlamps, a tail-lamp, and six internal festoon lamps.

The tank was too wide for the railway loading gauge with its sponsons in place, so these had to be unbolted and placed on special sponson trailers for rail travel—an eight-hour job.

The Mark I remained in service until April 1917, later being used as a supply tank. Half of the number built were Males, and half Females.

Marks II and III. Fifty of each of these Marks were built as follow-on orders until the Mark IV got into production. Mark II had the first narrower cab to allow track spuds to be used, and Mark III had Lewis guns instead of Vickers.

The Mark IV differed from the earlier Marks in four important ways. First, it had armour impervious to the new German armour-piercing machine-gun ammunition; second, the sponsons did not have to be removed for rail travel, swinging inboard on hinges instead; third, the petrol tanks were at the back, armoured, and outside the hull; and last, but thoroughly disliked, the Lewis machine-gun was used instead of the Vickers. With other minor refinements, including an exhaust silencer, the Mark IV was the quietest of all the Marks; it was also the most numerous, some 1,100 being built, at £5,000 each.

Mr. W. O. Bentley had been the first to design and fit aluminium pistons to a car, his French D.F.P. 12–15 hp in 1913, and with it he had had considerable competition success. While working at the Admiralty as a newly joined Lieutenant R.N.V.R. in 1914, he was the first to introduce the aluminium piston to British manufacturers as a means of finding more power.

When in 1917 Daimler were pressed for more horsepower from their 105 hp engine, they used Lieutenant Bentley's aluminium pistons to make it deliver 125 hp. The last 200 Mark IV tanks built had these engines.

Ricardo

Mark V was the first British heavy tank which one man could drive by himself, and the first to be powered by a specially designed tank engine. Two other virtues distinguished it, a rear "turret" for the tank commander, with swing-up sides to allow the unditching beam to be shackled on without exposure of the crew; and Hotchkiss machine-guns in place of the Lewis guns. These gas-operated air-cooled guns required only a relatively small aperture for the barrel, thus allowing the ball-mounting to give a much greater training angle.

When Mr. H. Ricardo designed the engine, his target was more power and the elimination of the exhaust smoke of the Daimler. By circulating fresh air under the piston crowns through using little-end cross-head guides, and an inlet-over-exhaust poppet valve layout, his 6-cylinder 150 hp engine exceeded all requirements. It was coupled to Major Wilson's new epicyclic steering units, thereby affording much increased manœuvrability.

The Mark V was the first British tank to incorporate a gun-cotton charge below the gearbox with which the tank could be disabled by its crew if it had to be abandoned— the Germans had salved a number of British Mark IVs to use against their original owners.

Four hundred Mark Vs were built.

Mark V* and V**. In February 1918, Tank Corps Central Workshops in France made up the first Mark V* by cutting the hull of a Mark V in half behind the sponsons and inserting an additional 6 ft of length. This increased trench crossing from 10 to 13 ft, and also enabled about 20 men to be carried as well as the crew. The original 150 hp engine thus had another 4 tons to move, the performance suffering. The rear turret was given sloping front and back plates to allow the machine-gun mountings in each to be used against aircraft. A new compound ball-mounting in the side hull doors gave a much enlarged arc of fire along the sides: 632 were built.

The Mark V** came too late for production before the Armistice. It had the new Ricardo 225 hp engine, which restored the performance

Too big and too late for the First World War— (left) Anglo-American Mark VIII (Liberty) and (right) British Mark IX supply and personnel carrier.

Rolls-Royce armoured car— 1920 model.

Vickers Medium Mark II— too thinly armoured but a wonderful machine in the tactical trials of the 1920s and 1930s.

lost in the Mark V*. The commander's turret was moved forward to join the driving cab, so that the crew could all be located in an embryo fighting compartment. Twenty-five Mark V** tanks were completed by the end of the war, but none went to France.

A Mark V***, otherwise known as the Mark X, was planned but never built.

*British Mark V** with portable bridge.*

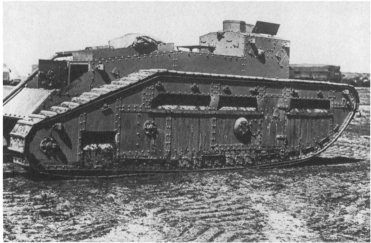

British Medium Mark C (Hornet).

Mark VIII (British "International", American "Liberty") was designed in December 1917 jointly by Great Britain and the U.S.A. for 1919, to be manufactured in an assembly plant at Neuvy-Pailloux in France from British hulls, armament, and armour, and American automotive assemblies: 4,500 were to be made.

In U.S. Army service, the engine was to be the 300 hp V-12 Liberty aircraft type, and in British service, the Ricardo 300 hp V-12. The tank had 6-pdrs in sponsons as before, but it also had the forward fighting compartment bulkheaded off from the rear engine-room. It was designed to cross a 14 ft trench, and since it would work with infantry, it had a two-speed gearbox and epicyclic transmission giving an 8 mile/h maximum speed. Twenty men could be carried in addition to the crew.

Seven Mark VIIIs were completed in the U.K. with Ricardo engines by December 1918, and one with a Liberty in the U.S.A. The assembly plant in France was well under way at the Armistice, but was never finished.

A Mark VIII* was planned but never built, to cross 18 ft trenches. Over 40 ft long, it would have weighed 42 tons.

The Medium Mark A (Whippet) was developed from the Tritton Chaser, designed as a private enterprise project in December 1916. Two hundred of these tanks were built by Foster's. Mr. Tritton's completed design coincided with the need for a faster tank as a result of the Cambrai battles of November 1917. Low-profile tracks were used to keep the weight down, with engines and transmission encased in armour separate from the three-man crew compartment at the back. Twin 45 hp side-valve Tylor JB4 London bus engines were used, one driving each track through a common cross-shaft, to the usual chain-driven sprockets. Steering was accomplished by a turn of the driver's wheel, accelerating one engine while throttling back on the other. **This was the first British tank to be drivable by one man.**

Unlike the original Tritton Chaser, with its single machine-gun in a rotating armoured-car-type turret, the Whippet had a fixed super-structure, the four Hotchkiss machine-guns which were reckoned by users to offer a readier means of engaging targets than the rotating turret.

The Medium Mark B, a "light" tank, designed in June 1917, was the first to have the forward fighting compartment bulkheaded off from the engine-room. It had a flatter run of track to improve climbing power, and a single Ricardo 100 hp engine to reduce complexity. With epicyclic steering, the tank was handier than the Whippet, but greatly underpowered. The original armament included a forward-firing 2-pdr pom-pom and four Hotchkiss, all in ball-mountings, but the pom-pom was dropped in March 1918. None of the forty-five tanks built ever saw action, as they were poor performers.

The Medium Mark C (Hornet) was the successor to the Whippet. It was designed in March 1918 to meet users' requirements for an ideal tank. It first ran in August 1918, and twenty-five had been made by the time of the Armistice; but none ever went to France or saw action.

This was the last British tank with unsprung suspension, and it had several significant features. In its Male form—never built—it would have reverted to the long 40-calibre 6-pdr of the old Mark I because the blast of the 23-calibre weapon might have endangered the driver; it had a rotating commander's cupola; and it was the only Mark to take part in the Victory Parade through London in 1919. This machine was the link between the wartime rhomboids and the Vickers mediums of 1923.

The Ricardo 150 hp Light Six, so named for its use of aluminium pistons and crankcase, driving a Halley four-speed gearbox and Wilson epicyclic steering made the Hornet the equal in speed to the projected Mark VIII, with greater manœuvrability. These two tanks would have been used in very large numbers in 1919 had the war continued.

THE EXPERIMENTAL MACHINES OF 1916 AND 1917

"Flying Elephant" was the heaviest British tank, and the first ever 100-tonner, originated in June 1916 from a requirement for a tank immune to field-gun fire. It was to carry 76 mm front and 50 mm side armour. Designed by Mr. Tritton at Foster's, a special feature was a pair of tracks between, and shorter than, the main tracks, but clear of the ground by 10 in. If the tank sank on soft ground these centre tracks would also take the weight. The Daimler Company made up a V-12 engine from two sets of their standard 105 hp double sleeve-valve cylinder blocks on a common crankcase to produce 240 hp. There were to be mountings for six machine-guns, and a dome-topped casemate for a 6-pdr in the nose.

Although due to complete in September 1917, "Flying Elephant" was cancelled because of cost in January 1917. The machine was scrapped.

The 1917 experimentals and Mark VI and VII. After production of the Mark IV had begun thought was especially given to increased engine power. Mr. (later Sir Harry) Ricardo, a leading engineer, designed a 150 hp engine at the request of the Tank Supply Committee. It took up less room than the Daimler 105 hp, and eliminated its tell-tale exhaust smoke. Despite misgivings, it went into successful volume production off the drawing-board before the tank it was to power had been selected.

Meanwhile, on 3rd March 1917, a well-attended test was run to demonstrate seven possible power train arrangements in comparison with a standard Mark IV, a Mark I Gun Carrier, and a Medium Mark A. Simultaneously, a wooden mock-up of a proposed Mark VI tank was available, having a Ricardo engine offset to port to afford a clear central fighting compartment without sponsons. Instead, a forward-firing 6-pdr was mounted with a 45-degree arc of traverse between the front horns. Among the test vehicles was the hull of "Mother", fitted with a 125 hp petrol-electric transmission unit.

In the upshot, the Wilson epicyclic transmission and Ricardo engine were adopted, but not in the projected Mark VI, for that would have meant retooling. After considerable delay due to doubts about the future of tanks—this was before Cambrai—it was decided to use as many stock components from Mark IV as possible, incorporate improvements, and fit the Ricardo-Wilson power plant. Thus the Mark V, already schemed out at the time of the tests, was drawn up in October 1917 in preference to the Mark VI. The latter was dropped.

The Mark VII, of which three were made, was designed in December 1917, really as a lengthened Mark V to increase trench crossing. It was to have a Williams-Janney hydraulic transmission to reduce driver fatigue and to increase manœuvrability. This design was also abandoned because of expense and complexity.

FRENCH ARMOURED DEVELOPMENT

Tanks. The first of 400 Schneiders were built at Le Creusot as a result of the tenacity of Colonel Estienne. Estienne at first failed to persuade Louis Renault to accept manufacture, but then succeeded with Eugène Brillié of Société Schneider. An order for 400 followed in February 1916. Like Swinton, Estienne saw the value of using tanks in large numbers for surprise.

The St. Chamond was the April 1916 riposte to the Schneider by the French Army's design department, in conjunction with La Société des Forges et Acieries de la Marine et Homecourt. It carried a standard 75 mm gun, unlike the

Schneider's 350 yd range low-velocity 75 mm howitzer. It had an electric drive for its 90 hp Panhard engine. Four hundred of these machines were also built.

Louis Renault came into his own in January 1917, with the decision to go into volume production of a light 6-ton tank, the FT 17. With the assistance of Berliet, Delaunay-Belleville and Schneider, Renault turned out nearly 3,000 of this type by the Armistice; production was at 75 a week from the middle of 1918 onwards. **This was the first tank used in action** to have a 360-degree turret traverse. The Male had a 37 mm gun designed at Puteaux Arsenal, and the Female a standard 8 mm Hotchkiss machine-gun.

As early as 1916, Estienne had proposed heavier tanks, and on 10th December 1917, the first of these began design. The concept of Char 1A, by Forges et Chantiers de la Méditerranée, was close to the layout of the modern tank, its rear engine bulkheaded off from the fighting compartment, with an all-round traverse turret. But owing to changes of specification, and Renault's troubles with the engine, it was never built. Instead, new requirements were agreed for the Char 2, including the crossing of 17 ft trenches.

GERMAN ARMOURED DEVELOPMENT

The first German tank, the A7V, came into service in February 1918, some ten months after its design had begun, and eighteen months after the first British tank attack at Flers-Courcelette. Although a tank had originally been suggested in 1913, it had always been German policy to avoid a war of *matériel*. They built tanks four years later, reluctantly and half-heartedly, in response to considerable pressure from the front line.

The A7V, for all its size, speed and protection, went very badly across country because its hull overhung the tracks front and rear. Top-heavy and ungainly, even the unhandy Mark IV could outmanœuvre it. Lack of team-work between the different arms of service of the eighteen-man crew contributed to its inefficiency.

Developed by a consortium of manufacturers, the A7V was based on the Holt tractor suspension unit, of which three each side supported the hull on a long pair of tracks. **It was thus the first German machine to use sprung suspension.** Armament tested during design included 20 mm cannon, short 75 mm howitzer and low- and medium-velocity naval 50 mm guns; but the 57 mm Sokol, a captured Russian gun, was used as a last resort because of the supply position of the alternatives. Even so, only one gun per tank could be provided. The gun and its ammunition were later manufactured in occupied Belgium.

By the summer of 1918, when the Germans really began to appreciate the urgent need for tanks, their industry was too stretched for manpower and resources to build them. Only twenty A7Vs were made.

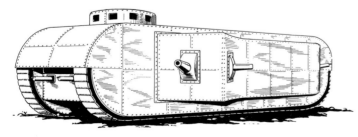

*The biggest German tank of 1918—
the uncompleted 126 ton K Wagen.*

The K-Wagen was the first German 100-tonner (126 tons). Only one prototype was begun, by Steffens and Nolle, in April 1918, and that was later blown up in uncompleted form at the Armistice to prevent it falling into Allied hands. It would have had four 77 mm guns, nine Maxim guns, and a crew of twenty-eight. Twin 250 hp Daimler engines were to have been used, with the A7V transmission.

LK I and LK II. The experimental LK I light tank of the summer of 1918, and its successor LK II never reached production. The concept was to encase available heavy car and lorry chassis in armour and carry it on continuous-track frames each end of which supported the front and rear wheel hubs. An armoured compartment at the back contained the crew. LK I carried a Maxim gun in a modified Ehrhardt armoured car turret above the crew compartment, while LK II had fixed superstructure like the British Medium Mark A, but with a forward-facing 57 mm gun in a casemate.

The A7V-U was designed in spring 1918 to rectify the A7Vs' shortcomings, while using most of its components, all based on the rhomboidal shape of the British heavy tank. But the Holt-type track was no better at remaining in position, while the greater weight, 40 tons, was too much even for the higher powered engine of the A7V-U. Production was ordered in the autumn of 1918, but it was too late.

U.S. steam tank—a failure.

AMERICAN TANK DEVELOPMENT

Tanks. The U.S.A. had developed an extensive tracked S.P. gun programme in the summer of 1917, based mainly on the Holt tractor. In September that year it was decided to adopt the French Renault FT, and also the Mark VIII, jointly designed with Great Britain. In January 1918, after an imported French sample had served as a pattern, assembly of the Renault began at three plants in Ohio: 4,400 were ordered at $11,500 each, but only 64 had been accepted by the Armistice. The Mark VIII was also to be built in the U.S.A., at a cost of $35,000, and one was completed by the end of 1918.

During the summer and autumn of 1918, the Ford two-man, 3-ton, machine-gun-armed tank was also adopted, to be built at a rate of 100 a day from January 1919, at $4,000 each. Of the initial order for 15,000, 15 had been made by the Armistice. Plans were also made to build a three-man version of the Renault FT, with a 37 mm gun and a machine-gun, but the war ended before it was begun.

Experimental armoured vehicles. Three machines stand out among the several varieties produced by private enterprise. These were the Holt Gas-Electric, **the first true tank built in the U.S.A.**; the three-wheeled Steam Tank with one wide roller for steering at the front; and the tracked Steam Tank, built in Boston primarily for use as a flame-thrower.

      Of a number of ingenious ideas, one of the most interesting was the Skeleton Tank (Pioneer Tractor Co., Minnesota), intended to be assembled on the battlefield. Skeleton track frames of standard pipe-work of sufficient length to cross 6 ft trenches were used to support a small box hull in order to keep the weight down to 8 tons.

SPECIAL DEVICES

The first time that unditching gear was used, to give tracks some grip while revolving on a motionless tank bellied in mud, was in the First Battle of Arras in April 1917. Two "torpedo spuds"—4 ft 6 in lengths of oak pole 7 in in diameter —were shackled at their midpoints by short chains to one of the plates of each track. If left shackled on for subsequent revolutions of the tracks, they bumped their way over the various projections on the roof of the tank and went round again. The later single 15 ft length of 9 × 7 in ironbound oak unditching beam—weighing 9 cwt—was first used in the Ypres Salient in July 1917. It was shackled by short chains in the same way, and was kept clear of obstructions while passing over the roof by fixed rails bolted lengthwise.

"Spuds" were first adopted on the Mark II tanks for increasing the bearing area of the track plates. Semicircular flat end-pieces connected by a bar were bolted to every alternate track plate. These were later superseded by projecting oak bars held in pressed steel boxes bolted to the track plates for the Medium Mark A in April, and the Mark V in July 1918, to provide greater grip. They offered no greater bearing area.

The first use of supply tanks was at Messines in June 1917. They were old Mark Is and IIs converted at Tank Corps Central Workshops on the Hesdin–St. Pol road to carry either locally made mild steel sponsons without armament, or normal sponsons with blanked-off mountings. Each supply tank could hold 3 to 4 tons of stores, which otherwise would have required 160 men at 56 lb per man to transport. So useful were these machines for dumping forward refills of tank petrol, water, oil, grease and ammunition, that the initial allotment of two per tank battalion was increased soon afterwards to six. The system was expanded into five companies, each with four sections of six supply tanks each; and the Marks I and II when they wore out were supplemented or replaced by older Mark IV tanks similarly converted. Stores for every purpose were carried.

Wooden supply sledges were first tried out in September 1917. Proving a success, as three could be towed by any fighting tank from a shackle at the back of the roof plate, some 110 were made at Central Workshops for use at Cambrai in November.

The first special supply tank, the Mark IX, was designed in the autumn of 1916 to meet an urgent need to get infantry and machine-gunners forward in safety, with their equipment, ammunition and stores. The tank was in fact **the first armoured personnel carrier**; but owing to labour troubles and production difficulties in the U.K. the first Mark IX did not reach France until October 1918, by which time the need for infantry carrying was partly met by the Mark V*, and in any case was much reduced. Only thirty-six machines were ever made, only a few of which left England.

The first British self-propelled (S.P.) guns were the forty-eight Gun Carriers Mark I built in the last six months of 1916. These could carry a 60-pdr or a 6 in howitzer and 60 rounds of ammunition; the weapons could be fired from the carrier, or "landed" over the loading ramp. To provide for the gun, driver and commander had separate single-seater cabs over the front of each track, the power train and crew being in the box over the back of the central hull. A normal Daimler 105 hp engine was placed behind the differential. A winding drum for loading and landing the gun was fitted on each inner side of the track frames midway along the hull. The tracks had the low profile resembling those used on the Whippet. Gun carriers were first used in their designed role at Third Ypres in July 1917, with Tank Corps drivers and Royal Garrison Artillery crews; but except for a few subsequent actions, they were thereafter relegated to supply carrying. At Hamel on 4th July 1918, four gun carriers brought 24 tons of stores up to within a few hundred yards of the final objective half an hour after its capture. This represented the work previously done by 1,200 men—or two infantry battalions—in anything up to ten hours of struggling through shell-swept ground.

Three further gun carriers were built in 1917, one for the 20-ton steam Priestman grab crane, and two for salvage of knocked-out tanks, with a 3-ton lift from a jib, or 10 tons from sheerlegs.

A Gun Carrier Mark II, resembling the mock-up of the Heavy Tank Mark VI, was made in mock-up form in early 1917, but was never pursued.

British Gun Carrier Mark I—it was mostly used for carrying supplies.

Tank radio 1918—120 watt CW.

The first tank wireless sets at two per British Company were delivered in July 1916. They were 200-m spark transmitters of 3-mile range. But it was then thought that the sets might interfere with existing installations in France, and everything was returned to Woolwich Arsenal.

When tank wireless trials began again in May 1917, there were some 540 ground stations and over 300 aircraft with wireless operating in the B.E.F. area. In July, six stations were available in tanks for the Ypres operations. They were unsuccessful, serving instead as anti-aircraft warning stations. At Cambrai in November 1917, one wireless tank per battalion was used.

Carrier wave sets were first introduced in early 1918 to replace spark transmitters, being more compact, with greater range for the small tank aerials. Both the French and Americans were also to adopt special wireless tanks.

The first half-track armoured car in service was the Russian "Austin-Kégresse" armoured car, based on the Austin armoured cars supplied during the First World War to the Russian Army. The rear driving-wheels were replaced by the Kégresse rubber-track suspension system, chain-driven from the axle-trees of the former wheeled vehicle. In order to improve trench-crossing ability, the car was further fitted with pairs of rollers on pivoting arms in front of and behind the steering-wheels, as well as in front of and behind the tracked suspension. The car weighed between 5 and 8 tons, and mounted two turrets each armed with a machine-gun.

The Kégresse suspension was developed in Russia from 1915 by M. Kégresse, a Frenchman who worked in the Tsar's garage, and orders for the Austin armoured car to be so modified were issued before the Revolution in 1917. A number of these armoured cars were completed after the Revolution and were used by the Soviet Army in the Russo-Polish War, 1919–20. Some were captured and later used also in the Polish Army.

SECTION III

The Formative Decades
1919–1939

It occurred to some of those who stood in silence when an Armistice was signed on 11th November 1918, that there was a strange unreality about the situation. Battle still raged in a great many localities away from the Western Front. This particular cessation of hostilities, in fact, was only local for it ushered in a decade of turmoil and revolution linked to a period of dire financial crisis. Under these conditions fighting went on throughout Russia and on her periphery, minor guerilla warfare abounded within the frontiers of the Central Powers, clashes occurred along the Indian frontier with Afghanistan and, in due course, there would be conflict in Ireland, the Middle East and the Far East besides a full-scale, if unsuccessful, campaign directed by the Russians against the newly created state of Poland.

Post-war struggles between soldiers and politicians revolved around the necessity to reduce the strength of armies while retaining cheaper forces in the world, ostensibly, dedicated to eternal peace. Nations with great tank stockpiles (in addition to orthodox weapons) found only limited use for them, beside an incentive to convert them into scrap metal. Armed forces under economic pressure endeavoured to readjust to new conditions, some merely attempting a reversion to 1914, others facing the future by accepting that submarines, aircraft and tanks had radically altered the balance of martial effectiveness. New philosophies of war, tuned to fresh frequencies of mechanisation, filled the air. Men such as Fuller and Estienne were to convert their practice of war in 1918 into theories of total, mechanised warfare for the future. General Hans von Seeckt, who was to reform a truncated German Army, took this opportunity to inject a theory of mechanised mobility into that organisation, taking the advantage of the 1922 Rapallo Treaty to forge links with the Russian technical forces.

How these theories were implemented depended upon national experience. It was predictable that revolutionary Russia might adopt a radical post-war tank policy, though a surprise that conservative Britain should opt for a unique, independent Tank Corps. When the time came Germany, too, would grant her Tank Arm independence. But in the majority of armies, strongly influenced by France, it was the rule that tank forces fell under strict infantry domination. Consequently it came to pass that the most fruitful tank experiments occurred in Britain, Russia and Germany, the creation by the British, in 1927, of a fully motorised experimental force of all arms setting the fashion and style of all such forces in the future.

Nearly every important industrial nation experimented to some extent with armoured forces in the 1920s. They built a wide variety of prototype vehicles in their endeavours to improve both hitting, defensive and mobile ability, besides overcoming the inherent problems of unreliability. Value was demanded and that meant tanks which could run for longer periods than had been normal in 1918. The intercommunication problem by radio was also tackled and merged with exploration of the technique of command. Strategic and tactical philosophies, which envisaged a tank force as an arm of decision in its own right rather than a subordinate auxiliary of the infantry, were expounded. In a decade of struggle for stability the apostles of strife were constantly at work.

Diametrically opposed to a campaign for disarmament, rearmament started again in the early 1930s. It was led at the outset by Italy and Japan, taken up by Russia and followed through ruthlessly by Germany, then France and, finally, Britain and the U.S.A. The sort of whirligig which had led inexorably towards the First World War made progress towards the Second, yet provided false warnings of its coming shape. For while the pre-1914 wars had accurately foretold the advent of the trench stalemate, those prior to 1939 suggested failure by tanks and yet another trench imbroglio. The appearance of numerous small high-velocity anti-tank guns compelled the prophets to underrate the tank's future: they gave it no better chance than unarmed men against machine-guns! Even Elles, who had once led the British tanks, and Captain B. H. Liddell Hart who, in the late 1920s and early 1930s, espoused the cause of high tank mobility, by the end of the 1930s were denying the tank's original promise.

The doubters—who were in a vast majority—based their conclusions upon lessons learnt during the Japanese invasions of China and Manchuria, the Italian conquest of Abyssinia and the struggle going on between Republican and Nationalist forces in the Spanish Civil War. Tanks, as the hand-maiden of infantry, had shown their worth, but when operating in isolation had been neutralised. Tribesmen fired rifles through vision slits, and anti-tank forces, in the more sophisticated Spanish War (where Russian-built tanks fought against Italian and German machines), held the upper hand. Yet the prophets overlooked forthcoming technological advances and failed to realise that the machines which had faltered were already an outmoded generation lacking good armoured protection and cross-country performance. They also lost sight of the power inherent in a tactical technique of penetration by massed tanks working in close co-operation with artillery and aircraft. Hardly at all had these been attempted. Only Fuller and a German élite under Colonel Guderian, stood by their convictions.

The technique of ubiquitous assault by combined all-arms mechanised formations, which based their ascendancy upon the tank, had been tested by the British, Russians, Americans and French in the early 1930s. But it was brought to perfection by one nation alone—Germany. Here the ideas of von Seeckt were most ably put into practice by technologically inclined officers of the calibre of General Lutz and Colonel Guderian. Against the aggressive background of the Nazi revolution the problem was tackled scientifically. Since an armoured force was strictly an offensive weapon, the outcome was likely to be aggression, and so the first German armoured (panzer) divisions which had come in being in 1936 were the spearhead which brought Poland to her knees in less than a fortnight in September 1939. They began the Second World War which was to be a conflict dominated by tanks.

PART ONE—FEATS & ACHIEVEMENTS

The most important tank operations immediately to follow the First World War were those fought in Russia and on her frontiers—not because so very many tanks were involved, but because they foreshadowed the creation of the largest tank force the world has ever known. Tank battles on Russian soil —such as they were with so few machines involved—took place either internally between Red and White forces or externally when the Russians invaded Poland in 1920.

The counter-revolutionary White armies were provided with tanks by the British and French—quantity is uncertain but it seems likely that some 67 British Mark Vs and 19 Whippets plus 100 French Renault FTs were sent. Mostly manned by Russian crews they fought several scattered actions in the summer of 1919 —the most celebrated being the assault by four Mark Vs on Tsaritsin on 29th June. The event was of interest because this place was later to become famous as Stalingrad. The tanks, led by a British crew, were largely responsible for its capture—one of the few occasions when British crews actually went into battle in addition to acting in their true advisory role.

The Red Army gradually acquired all the tanks that had been sent to the Whites because the counter-revolutionary armies, with no heart for the fight, gave up. At this time the Reds had large numbers of armoured cars of various makes and they were studying the possibility of making their own tanks, but the chaotic state of the country's economy gave little hope of making anything, let alone tanks.

An unsuccessful war against Poland in 1920 convinced the Russians that they were unready for serious operations against a well-equipped foe, for **the Poles had formed their armoured forces** in June 1919 with 150 Renault FTs and 5 German A7Vs. Supplemented by deep-raiding armoured cars they played a tentative part in repelling the Russian invasion.

The first Russian tank unit—*Avtotanki*—was formed of British Mark Vs in January 1920, but it would be many years before any great expansion took place.

A fairly successful anti-guerilla war was waged by British armoured cars and tanks in Ireland between 1919 and 1922, the armoured vehicles used for patrolling, counter-ambush and convoy protection—often helping combat guerillas who themselves operated in motor cars. Tanks were also used by the British and French occupation forces to control riots in Germany—as were a few German-crewed, specially converted German A7Vs and old British Mark IVs, **probably the first such use of tanks for crowd control**.

The implementation of the Versailles Treaty in January 1920 deprived Germany of the right to possess tanks, aircraft or submarines. With Germany's fangs now drawn, this was the signal for the Allied Powers to reorganise their armoured forces. Though they diverged in their methods, they mostly followed the example of the French.

> **France** transferred responsibility for her tanks from the Artillery Branch to the Infantry. The motivating influence was that of Marshal Pétain, the victor of Verdun. A lone cry in opposition came from Colonel Estienne who called for fully armoured forces—armoured divisions, in fact. Yet in Syria in July 1920 a mixed force of infantry, artillery and Renaults fought a successful mobile action against Arab guerillas, demonstrating the potential of such an organisation.

> **The U.S.A.**; burdened with $32,000,000 worth of tanks that had never seen service, rejected General Rockenbach's plea for the retention of a separate Tank Corps and, by Act of Congress in 1920, made the tanks a responsibility of the Infantry Corps. It has to be recorded that those few voices which rose in support of tanks in the U.S.A. sounded only a low note. Pershing dominated, Rockenbach would not fight, Brett, Patton and

Major Eisenhower, who at one time had run the Tank School, were gagged by officialdom.

Italy formed her first tank detachment in December 1918 out of a couple of Fiat 2000s and six Renault FTs, but not until 1926 was a serious attempt made by the Mussolini regime to develop a fighting arm. They were largely manned by the Cavalry but came under firm Infantry domination. At the same time evolution with machines and tactical doctrine was very slow.

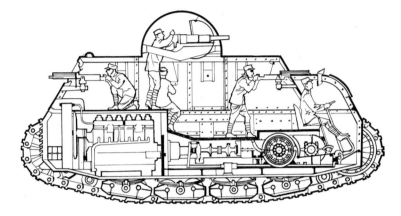

Italian FIAT 2000—only two built.

Japan bought some British Mark Vs and Medium Mark As in 1918 to act as the nucleus of a force that, later, was expanded by Renault FTs. But a policy of reduction in the armed forces withheld further progress until 1925 when expansion began again in earnest. Then two tank companies were formed at the same time as preparations for a home-based manufacturing capability were being made. Japanese tanks also lay firmly under Infantry control, while little in the way of original thought as to their employment appeared.

Great Britain alone formed an effective independent Tank Corps, after much inter-departmental strife, in 1923. The guiding lights were Elles and Fuller—the outcome a force operating for some years on a shoe-string with antiquated machines, its main effort directed to manning armoured car forces in Iraq (later performed by the Royal Air Force), India, Shanghai and any other place where guerilla warfare threatened. Its secondary purpose was to experiment with new vehicles in different climates and with fully armoured forces for use in Europe should a major war occur again.

The first experiment with tanks in a hot climate took place in India, 1922–23. Then in 1925 two of the new Vickers Medium tanks were taken there and run over 1,000 miles in the hottest weather and across some of the most rugged country— the prime purpose an intention to persuade the Indian Government to buy some. Though the machines passed their tests they were rejected on the grounds of expense.

The first post-war tank collaboration between nations came about in 1922 as the result of the signing of the Rapallo Treaty between Russia and Germany. Since these two defeated nations were deprived of help from the West—the former by reason of their Bolshevik regime, the latter by the terms of the Versailles

Treaty, they agreed to pursue mutual aid in the development of aircraft and tanks, both in the industrial and tactical field. Subsequent to the Berlin Agreement of 1924 the partnership ripened until a combined Tank School and Experimental Station was set up near the Karma River. Here, subject to certain reservations, the participants experimented with their prototype vehicles and trained the cadre of soldiers and designers who were to form the next generation of armoured forces. Not all secrets were shared. For instance both the Germans and Russians withheld information about their latest automotive inventions—but enough was done to make both sides think it worth while and to warn the Germans of serious Russian competition to come.

British tanks of the 1920s on parade—left to right: Carden Loyd Mark I tankette, Independent, Morris Martel 2 man, Carden Loyd 2 man.

The most important tactical experiment of the 1920s was that undertaken by the British on Salisbury Plain in 1927. Gathered together for just a few weeks' exercise, the experimental all-arms force clearly showed the way into the future. It was composed of:

(1) A mixed battalion of armoured cars and Carden-Loyd tankettes.

(2) A battalion of Vickers Medium tanks.

(3) A machine-gun battalion carried in unarmoured cross-country wheeled vehicles.

(4) A motorised artillery regiment, plus a battery of howitzers.

(5) A motorised engineer company.

(6) An assortment of R.A.F. reconnaissance, fighter and bomber squadrons.

In one important respect, however, it was lacking: there was no radio communication within the force, hence its reactions to orders and circumstances were slow. Starting with the establishment of basic tactical drills this force worked itself up, under Colonel R. J. Collins, to the pitch at which it could out-manœuvre a numerically superior horse and foot army. The exercises were witnessed by foreign observers and fully reported in the Press, notably by the able pen of the Military Correspondent of the London *Daily Telegraph*, Captain B. H. Liddell Hart. Enthusiasm was lit in Britain, even if her military leaders then refused to adopt the new organisation as a permanency. Overseas a great impetus was given to armoured forces so that, in 1928, the Russians, Germans and Americans were eagerly digging out old or experimental machines, forming them into new formations and endeavouring to copy the British. But lacking in quantity a tank like the Vickers Medium, with its longer range and superior speed, they had to await new equipment that was slow in coming.

The growth of a forward-looking armoured forces philosophy stemmed from the writings of Fuller who produced books and articles which developed the concept of his original plan of 1919. Always caustic about official delay, he was gradually pushed aside from the main stream of progress. Nevertheless the 1920s were distinguished by the mass of pro-tank literature which emanated from all the principal nations. Fuller, however, looked deepest of all into the subject and dreamed what he called "substantial dreams" of the future. In 1932 he published his *Lectures on FSR III* which postulated fully armoured forces composed of tanks, mechanised artillery and infantry working in close co-operation with aircraft. His was a concept of élite mobile formations working in flexible battle-groups ahead or to the flank of the firm base provided by the main infantry army. He foresaw sweeping manœuvres with cut and thrust between armoured forces and, thinking back to the days in Ireland, envisaged motorised guerillas co-operating in depth with the armoured élite. The book was hardly read in Britain, and probably not in France either, but in Germany they understood it and paid attention, while there is little doubt that the Russians also took careful note.

Fuller

De Gaulle.

In France, in addition to Estienne, there were writers like Colonel Romain who could write of tanks: "It is up to the High Command to make them operate in mass and, as much as possible, by surprise wherever it has been decided to make a decisive attack." Later he would be countered by such historians as General Narcisse Chauvineau with "like little mice which run into their holes when threatened, infantry can evade tanks by taking cover and striking the monsters in rear when they passed by". And Chauvineau had the support of the main body of the French General Staff. Later in 1934, Colonel Charles de Gaulle would publish his book *Vers l'armée de métier*, in which he would sponsor all-armoured mobility.

German 6 wheeled armoured car (SdKfz 231) on parade before the war. The overhead grid is a radio aerial.

In Russia philosophy grew out of a bureaucracy which tended to submerge the individual. From published records we obtain fleeting glimpses of the principal creative characters (depending upon who was in favour when they were being written) and from these there appears a concensus of opinion that Leon Trotsky, when People's Commissar for Military Affairs in 1921, played his part in encouraging participation with the Germans; that the Germans had a strong influence; that Mikhail Frunze, who took over from Trotsky in 1923, added impetus, and that each successive Five Year Plan pushed technical progress along, even if it was only loosely attached to tactical ideas. The cavalry influence was strong within the Army itself and here General Tukhachevsky did important work in fostering tank doctrine and relating it to cavalry methods of old. At the same time the concept of strict tank support of infantry prevailed. With enormous resources the Russians could experiment wholesale in all fields.

Chaffee

In America viable doctrine was slow to appear and empirical in formulation. The U.S.A. produced no great philosopher of its own but drew upon the ideas of others—notably the French, then the British and finally the Germans. Their own experiments were carried out chiefly at the will of Colonel Adna Chaffee—a cavalryman who sought to give tanks to the cavalry. American progress, in fact, was largely dictated by this struggle for control between the Infantry and Cavalry arms. Hence, as in Russia, infantry and cavalry techniques moved forward in parallel, but much more slowly since money was short and successive chiefs of staff, from General D. MacArthur onwards, were lukewarm to the tank idea.

Guderian

Germany started with a concept of strict infantry support, but this gradually collapsed under the driving influence of Guderian who, under the tutelage of Seeckt, Lutz and others, arrived at the conclusion that the tank, as a dominant weapon, should receive full support from the other arms instead of vice versa. This concept was opposed by the traditionalists but supported by a significant number of army officers as well as, after 1933, the new Reich Chancellor, Adolf Hitler, who had a nose for the bizarre, the dramatic and the enormous. Yet, as Guderian admitted in 1937, when he published his far-seeing *Achtung! Panzer*, they based their ideas upon those of the British, above all the ideas of Fuller. Hitler merely ensured that the offensive weapons proscribed at Versailles should be given priority, but he put tanks below aircraft in order of precedence for industrial effort.

An extraordinary flashback to the past occurred in 1928 during the armoured force experiments in the U.S.A. at Fort Meade. A hotch-potch of vehicles of First World War vintage were controlled by flag signals from their leader, Major Sereno Brett, as he accompanied his vehicles on foot. It was not that Brett was deliberately emulating his feat at St. Mihiel, simply, that for lack of a better system and, above all, radio, he had no option but to signal visually. The tanks employed were bad signalling platforms while so slow that they went little more than walking pace.

The first full-scale experiment with radio control of a complete British tank formation was launched on Salisbury Plain in the summer of 1931. Under Brigadier Charles Broad a force of eighty-five medium and ninety-five assorted light tanks were put through manœuvres and tactical exercises in which all orders were given by voice radio (the MB/MC set) to individual medium tanks. Pre-operational briefing was kept to a minimum and hand or flag signals resorted to if the radio broke down or for passing instructions to the light tanks, none of which had radio. A special procedure for speaking over the air was devised as well as a simplified system of flag signals—all of which had to be used by commanders from their turrets.

The first radio-controlled tank formation—Vickers Mediums on Salisbury Plain in 1931.

The first Russian experiments with a tank brigade took place in 1931 but, owing to the shortage of radio, progressed no further in exploration of command and control techniques than had the 1929 manœuvres. They bore a formidable look, however, and gained in incentive because the Russians were disturbed by the Japanese invasion of Manchuria in September. From this moment onward the pace of Russia's experiments and production accelerated.

The first exercises by a French joint tank and infantry force began somewhat tentatively in 1932 when motorised cavalry and infantry co-operated as a temporary formation. In 1933 a complete division was tried out at Reims and this led to the creation of **the first ever genuine mechanised division** in 1934 —the *Division Légère Mécanique* which consisted of a mixed battalion of armoured cars and motor cyclists, a brigade of tanks and a brigade of motorised infantry plus an artillery regiment and engineers. There were 220 tanks altogether.

The first German armoured (panzer) division soon followed, mostly modelled on the British system, influenced by the French, but also incorporating much original German thought. Three were founded in 1935, organised as follows:

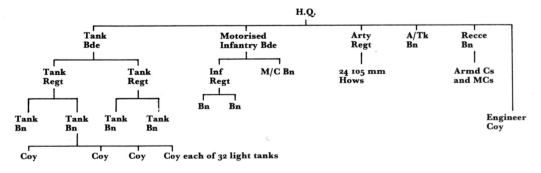

The greatest controversy surrounding the advent of all the new armoured forces was generated by those who saw a need to found mechanical armies upon an élite and countered by those who saw in such an élite a threat to the inviolability of conventional armies. The argument in favour was defined by Broad when, in 1928, he proposed the formation of a British armoured corps made up of selected tank, cavalry and infantry units. The counter-response came later from General Maxim Weygand when the French Army was under examination: "Two armies? Not at any price." Much additional confusion was caused when the litigants presented their cases, by the imprecise use of the word "tank". Though "a tank" was, strictly speaking, a specialised capital vehicle designed to take a direct part in the fighting with its crew mounted, Fuller and his like tended to refer to tracked self-propelled artillery and infantry carriers as "tanks". Hence the term, "All Tank Army" came into use when all that was intended was an "All Armoured Army". To talk of an "All Tank Army" in Britain, rather more than other countries, meant a take-over bid by the independent Royal Tank Corps and this could never be allowed by the vested interests of the older established arms. And even in Germany, where the Tank Idea prospered best, the traditional arms kept the new Tank Arm under strict surveillance, ensuring that cavalry, infantry and artillery maintained their identity within the panzer divisions.

French Panhard 178— taking over from the cavalry in the 1930s.

If Japan started a strong trend of aggression in 1931 and Russia was to take it as good reason to begin serious, large-scale tank production, Italy went ahead by laying down production of a new "tank" fleet in 1932 by manufacturing a number of light machine-gun carriers. The arms race was started by a kind of spontaneous international ignition, the spark provided by mutual suspicion in an unstable climate of opinion.

Russia had examined the Vickers and Christie designs, developed them and, by 1932, was reaping the benefit of such large-scale production that they were able to form a Mechanised Corps of about 500 tanks and 200 armoured cars. In addition there were various tank battalions set aside for infantry support and a special Supreme Command Tank Reserve for use in breakthrough operations either in co-operation with infantry or horsed cavalry, or even independently.

Germany threw off the bonds of the Versailles Treaty in 1934 and began rearmament. At the same time she withdrew from co-operation with Russia, salvaged the prototype tanks from Karma, brought home her specialists and launched her own tank-building programme. She—or rather Adolf Hitler—saw Russia as the threat and eventual target, though nations to the west could not be ignored.

France, frightened by what she saw happening in Germany had already begun tentatively building a new tank fleet in 1931. Not until 1935 did large-scale production begin and then it was mainly to build tanks that were strictly related to close support of the infantry, while those for the cavalry-orientated D.L.M.s were given lower priority. Thus a second D.L.M. did not appear until 1938 even though its predecessor had proved valuable in 1935, and the third would not appear until the eve of war in August 1939.

Britain and the U.S.A. fell furthest behind of all. In fact there was no such thing as a tank-production programme in the U.S.A. until 1939 while the British, like the Americans, continued to experiment, to debate whether or not they wished to follow the French example or put their money on the type of armoured division they had pioneered in 1934. British expenditure on tanks tells its own tale of indecision and delay:

1931 £357,000—the year Japan invaded Manchuria.

1932 £309,000

1933 £315,000

1934 £501,000—the year Germany began rearmament.

1935 £772,000—the year Italy invaded Abyssinia.

1936 £842,000—the year the Spanish Civil War started and Germany reoccupied the Rhineland.

1937 £3,625,000—when the threat became too obvious to ignore any longer.

Although the Japanese invasion of Manchuria in 1931 can be taken as the starting-point for the arms race and her invasion of China in 1937 the beginning of the Far Eastern War, the activities of the European Powers were the most significant of all.

The first doubts on the viability of light tanks were caused by the experience of a few Vickers 6-tonners and Carden Loyd Mark VI machine-gun carriers during the war between Bolivia and Paraguay in the Gran Chaco in the period 1932 to 1935. Bolivia alone had tanks, under the command of a German, Major Wim Brandt, and used them for infantry support on three occasions in 1933. In the prevailing close country they proved highly vulnerable to artillery and armour-piercing small-arms fire, without having the opportunity to riposte in mass and exploit their own firepower.

A provocative land grab was perpetrated by Italy in 1935 when she invaded Abyssinia, fighting ill-armed tribesmen with bombing aircraft, gas and light tanks. For all the paucity of the opposition the Italian Army made hard work of it and many a light tank was knocked out by Ethiopians firing their rifles through tank vision slits. But the intrinsic value of tank support was demonstrated by their ability to give assistance, even in rugged mountain country, and the importance that was attached to building roads adjacent to the battle-front so that mechanised forces could manœuvre more freely.

British A9 firing.

Japan's first tank—the Type 89, based on a British Vicker's design.

Czechoslovakia's LT 35 t taken over by the Germans in 1939 and called PzKpfw 35 t.

The fastest tank— capable of over 50 mile/h— Christie's 1938 Model at speed.

The first major tank actions involving the latest machines took place during the Spanish Civil War, coming from small beginnings in the summer of 1936 and leading to much larger battles as the Russians shipped in tanks to support the Republican cause and the Germans and Italians rushed to the aid of General Franco's Nationalists. The Russians mostly provided their Vickers-type T 26s, along with some early Christie-type BTs—about 730 all told. The Germans shipped in PzKpfw Is and the Italians the little Fiat Ansaldo C 33.

Thus the Republicans acquired a more formidable force and, in addition, were the better disposed to let their Russian advisers try out the theories of independent tank action. General Pavlov occasionally tried deep tank raids—with fifty tanks at Esquivas on 29th October 1936 and with a still larger force in an improvised counter-offensive against the Italians near Guadalajara in March 1937. He failed in his missions because inadequate arrangements were made to back the tanks with equally mobile infantry and artillery and because fuel resupply broke down.

The Germans and Italians were hampered by General Franco in their attempts to act independently and, in any case, their thinly armoured tanks were far too vulnerable and poorly armed to make much impression. A consensus of military opinion thought the lessons learned pointed to the failure of the tank as a weapon of decision in its own right. The French concept of subservience to infantry seemed to have been vindicated and so all the armies—with the exception of Germany, and to a lesser extent Britain—happily went on integrating their tanks with marching infantry or using them merely like cavalry patrols of old.

The first British armoured divisions—or "Mobile Divisions" as first they were called—were formed in 1938 despite opposition from those in the British Army who wished only for an up-to-date motorised version of the 1918 Army. One division was formed in Britain, the other in Egypt under the duress of the Italian threat (against Egypt) from Cyrenaica. Both were made up of obsolescent medium and light tanks and armoured cars, the artillery and infantry content drawn or carried by a miscellany of tracked or wheeled vehicles. The organisation reflected the "All Armoured Idea" and was heavier in tank content than that of any other nation.

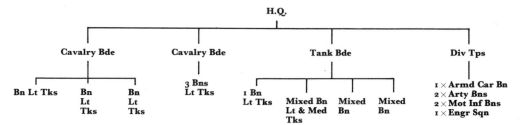

```
                              H.Q.
        ┌──────────────┬────────────┴──────────────┬──────────────────┐
   Cavalry Bde      Cavalry Bde              Tank Bde              Div Tps
        │                │                       │
 ┌──────┼──────┐    3 Bns          ┌──────┬──────┴───┬──────┐    1 × Armd Car Bn
Bn Lt Tks  Bn   Bn   Lt Tks      1 Bn   Mixed Bn  Mixed  Mixed    2 × Arty Bns
           Lt   Lt              Lt Tks  Lt & Med   Bn     Bn       2 × Mot Inf Bns
           Tks  Tks                     Tks                        1 × Engr Sqn
```

Even in Germany, where Guderian had forged the new Tank Arm, there was perpetual opposition to his demand for strengthening the panzer divisions at the expense of the rest of the army. His case was weakened when tank enthusiasts, such as Colonel von Thoma, returned from commanding in Spain to report the shortcomings of the new machines and, among other things, to decry the need for each tank to have its own radio.

Now **the tank philosophers turned coat**, for while men like Chauvineau rode a crest of the wave in opposition to the tanks, Liddell Hart published his doubts that the tank held the promise for which he had once given it credit.

Liddell Hart

U.S. Cavalry's "tank"—Combat Car M1 of 1938.

The niggers in the woodpile were the increasing number of small, easily concealed, high-velocity anti-tank guns with which the infantry were arming themselves and with which tanks were also being armed. Every armament manufacturer turned his attention to these weapons after Cambrai with the result that, by the 1930s, a score or more of different calibres, mostly firing solid armour-piercing shot were on offer throughout the world. Typical were the following:

Nation	Make	Calibre (mm)	Muzzle velocity (ft/sec)	Wt. proj.	Wt. mounting (lb)
U.S.A.	Browning	12·7	2,725	1·83 oz	163
Swiss	Oerlikon	20·1	2,681	4·5 oz	242
British	Vickers	47	1,600	3·3 lb	559
Czech	Skoda	37	1,510	1·81 lb	442
U.S.	M 1	75	1,850	4·45 lb	900

In 1931 almost every one of these weapons had the capability of penetrating the armour of existing tanks (which was rarely thicker than 30 mm at the strongest point and usually only between 8 and 20 mm) at ranges of 300–500 yd. This highlights the critical balance that always dominates the gun armour competition. Governments, and therefore designers, had to minimise costs and therefore there could be no great leap forward either in armour protection or striking power. Therefore ranges of engagements were necessarily low so that more space for tactical manœuvre was available.

Pre-eminent of the discoveries among anti-tank weapons was the Germans' realisation in Spain that their 88 mm flak anti-aircraft gun possessed first-class potential as a dual-purpose weapon—one that could be used against high-flying aircraft and, because of its accuracy, could hit and destroy tanks at ranges well in excess of 1,000 yd—that is more than three times as far as any other anti-tank gun. This was to be a potent factor in the coming Second World War.

The advent of so many deadly threats to the tank led general staffs to think mainly along lines of protection either by great increases in speed or of armour thickness. The Russians tended towards the "fast tanks", the British and French towards "heavily armoured tanks" while the Americans, lacking a clearly defined policy, went for lightly armoured machines armed with several machine-guns in the hope that a deluge of preventive fire would "neutralise" anti-tank guns.

Unique were the Germans who designed tanks to accord with a tactical doctrine which dictated that highly mobile, all-arms formations must manœuvre for vital ground from which to fight battles of decision. Their tanks were given just enough armour to deflect small-arms fire and near misses by shells. Penetration by high-velocity weapons was accepted in the belief that saturation of the enemy's defences by the surprise use of tanks in mass would open a gap through which whole formations could pour, irrupting deep into the enemy rear to paralyse his thinking and break his supply line.

An important, though little publicised, tank battle was fought on the Manchurian border between Japanese and Russian forces in August 1939. The Japanese had provoked the Russians who mounted a counter-offensive. Both sides employed tanks in the close support of infantry but the Russian commander, General G. Zhukov, also used an independent tank brigade to plunge into the enemy rear and establish blocking positions while his main force broke the Japanese by a frontal assault. If this was an example of Fuller's ideas it also introduced a leader who was to prove among **the greatest exponents of tank warfare**.

The first great tank invasion began on 1st September 1939, when the German Army, supported by heavy aerial bombardment, crossed the Polish frontiers using panzer divisions to both smash fortifications and then break away in pursuit of a beaten enemy. Thus began the Second World War, a struggle which was to be dominated by armoured fighting vehicles and aircraft.

The tank strengths of the nations which eventually were to be involved stood approximately as follows in 1939, but would be rapidly expanded as wartime production rose to its peak.

Russia: 10,000. A very rough estimate since no exact figures are available. Mostly they were of the light Vickers types or BTs, though quite large numbers of the heavy T 28s and later large machines were available.

Germany: 3,200. All but 300 were light tanks.

France: 2,200. A good mixture of various modern types (the vast reserves of older machines are excluded from this figure) with about 300 of the heavy Char Bs.

Japan: 2,000. The great majority light machines.

Britain: 1,150. Nearly all light tanks.

Italy: 1,000. All light tanks.

Poland: 700. All light tanks, including many obsolete types.

U.S.A.: 300. All light tanks.

Russian BT 7s of the Christie type.

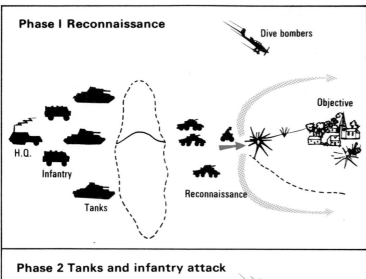

Phase I Reconnaissance

Dive bombers

Objective

H.Q.

Infantry

Tanks

Reconnaissance

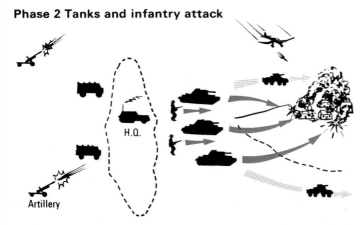

Phase 2 Tanks and infantry attack

H.Q.

Artillery

The Panzer Division technique. Reconnaissance elements find the enemy, fire from aircraft, tanks and then artillery is brought to bear. Swiftly the armoured cars and motor-cyclists infiltrate: inexorably tanks and infantry move to the assault. The enemy is overcome and the advance flows forward. All this could happen in a matter of a few hours.

The balance of forces between Germany and Poland not only showed a great disparity in numbers of armoured vehicles but was reflected in their allocation to formations and units.

Germany: 6 panzer divisions of high tank content.
4 light divisions of low tank content.

Poland: 1 armoured brigade plus 1 forming.
13 battalions of low tank content.

This demonstrated the difference, in philosophies—the clash of concentrated armour with diluted armour.

The crushing of Poland took fifteen days, plus another fortnight to subdue Warsaw and one or two outlying isolated garrisons. Apart from stiff resistance on the frontiers in the first two days, German armoured forces enjoyed a free run until they became enmeshed in the urban complex of Warsaw. In the first nine days the average advance was 11 miles per day, in the last five Guderian's XIX Corps moved 125 miles, though by then it was against negligible resistance. Yet success was magnified because he followed the least line of resistance and struck at the rear of the Polish political nerve-centre.

Losses in tanks were heavy on both sides. The Polish forces were wiped out mostly in isolated actions, though in the case of an armoured brigade, it was encircled complete and annihilated by battle. German losses for the entire campaign were 217 tanks of which the worst single experience overtook 4th Panzer Division when on 9th September it lost 57 out of 120 in the suburbs of Warsaw. The light tanks were easily overwhelmed by infantry and artillery at short range.

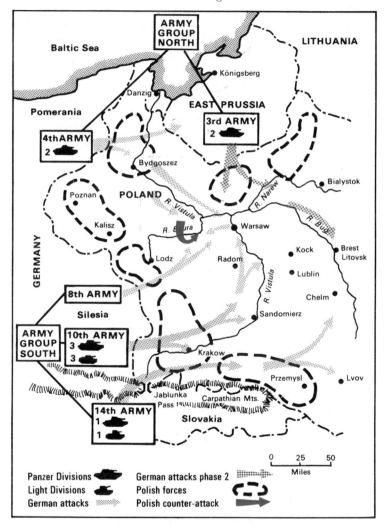

Battle of Poland in September 1939—a hard-fighting nation overrun by the tank technique in a bare fortnight.

The most striking German success was in their encirclement of the main Polish counter-offensive on the River Bzura when panzer divisions were made to converge rapidly from all sides upon the concentrated Polish force. **This was the first great tank victory by annihilation**—and it was to be the model of many more to come.

The striking lessons from Poland did not entirely fall on deaf ears in other countries, even though there was a tendency in France and Britain to dismiss the German success as a product of Polish weakness rather than German strength. The Russians, who had invaded the eastern half of Poland in the latter part of the campaign, were bent upon establishing buffer states between their own territory and that of Germany. As part of this westward expansion they invaded Finland on 30th November and this led to:

The first tank war fought in Arctic conditions. The Finnish Army was all but innocent of tanks and had only 112 37 mm anti-tank guns. The Russians had merely to commit a small part of their strength to crush such puny opposition—or so it seemed. Of their tank force they sent a full selection of operational types, including some of the real giants, such as SMK and T 100, and the first models of the KV series.

Of the many elements which at first defeated the Russians the weather was pre-eminent. With temperatures 25 degrees or more below zero, wholesale mechanical failures occurred. Specially treated fuel proved useless and so the mechanised army stalled in open country while the Finns held out in the fortified Karelian Isthmus. Tank destruction was shared by infantry anti-tank gunners and special stalking parties who tackled the tanks at close quarters in the forest rides, setting them ablaze with petrol bombs that were given the name of "Molotov Cocktails". In four months' fighting (before the Finnish Army became exhausted) something like 300 Russian tanks had been disposed of—some finding their way into the Finnish order of battle. As in Spain, Russian tank units, which dashed off ahead of the infantry and cruised ineffectually behind the enemy lines without striking at important objectives, fell victim to daring tank-hunting parties. But if the Russians complained that the armour protection of their tanks was inadequate it was also to their organisation, training and tactics that they had to pay attention. All were woefully inadequate.

A sweeping reorganisation of Russian tank forces was initiated at the end of 1939 when General P. Rotmistrov was appointed Marshal of the Armoured Forces. He rejected the so-called lessons of the Spanish Civil War and those of Finland and pointed to what the Germans had achieved in Poland by surprise and concentration. It would take several months for his ideas to be accepted and put into action and by then the whole vista of modern tank fighting would have been made crystal clear in battle.

British Medium Mark D—ahead of its time. Note "snake" track.

PART TWO—THE VEHICLES

MEDIUM TANKS

The fastest tank built from the designs of the First World War was the British Medium Mark D, which featured in plans for the large-scale use of tanks in 1919. Weighing 20 tons and having a speed of more than 20 mile/h, it was envisaged as capable of striking deep and fast at headquarters and communications in the enemy's rear. This was a concept of armoured action far in advance of contemporary ideas for the use of tanks only in direct support of the infantry assault. Despite a promising start, technical difficulties and financial stringency after the war stopped further development of the Medium Mark D when the Tank Design Department was disbanded in 1923.

Britain's "too costly" Medium Mark III.

The first British tank to go into quantity production after the First World War was the Vickers Medium Mark I (known at first as Vickers Light Tank Mark I). About 160 of the Vickers Mediums were produced between 1923 and 1928, and remained in service until 1940. With an official speed of 18 mile/h, they were faster than any others in service in the 1920s, and they provided the framework for developing new methods in armoured warfare as well as being the basis for new vehicles in Britain and abroad.

Vehicles in service were Marks I and II, all with a five-man crew, but variations weighed between 11·7 tons and 14 tons, armed with a 47 mm gun (3-pdr) and up to six machine-guns. The main experimental versions were:

(1) Mark III. Only three were produced in 1930–31, based on the A 6 "sixteen-tonner", with two machine-guns in forward sub-turrets.

(2) Medium C. A Vickers private venture based on a Mark II chassis, mounted a 57 mm (6-pdr) gun. Pilot models only, supplied to Japan and Eire.

(3) A 7. The Woolwich competitor to A 6.

The first British medium tanks to get into production in the 1930s were the A 9 and A 10. Both were called for in 1934, the former as a cruiser tank (Mark I), the latter as an "infantry" tank but it proved too light and so was adopted as a "heavy cruiser" (Mark II). There were many variations of these tanks which formed the first components of the British armoured divisions which fought in France and the Western Desert in 1940. Their armament and armour were sufficient unto the day and the strong articulated suspension would do excellent service both for those types and the later, far more successful Valentine. But track life was short and caused many breakdowns that led to high losses in battle.

The A 9 was used for **the first ever experiments in deep wading** whereby a "schnorkel" tube was connected to allow breathing while the tank, wholly sealed at all joints and hatches, motored submerged along a river bed.

The first American medium tank was the Medium A of 1921, an experimental machine of 21 tons mounting a coaxial 37 mm gun and machine-gun in the turret, with a machine-gun in an upper turret. Another version appeared in 1922, and another as the Medium T 1 in 1925. The series ended with a new design produced as T 2 in 1930.

The first convertible wheel/track tank in service was the American Medium T 3/Combat Car T 1, accepted as experimental models for trials with infantry and cavalry in 1931. The tank was designed on the basis of the Christie M 1928 and nine models of the Christie M 1931 were built—five for the American Army and two each for Russia and Poland, but the Polish order was taken over in America. The tank weighed 10·5 tons with three-man crew; three were allotted to the infantry as the Medium T 3s armed with a coaxial 37 mm gun and machine-gun, and four to the cavalry as Combat Car T 1 armed with a ·5 in machine-gun.

Further development led to production by 1936 of sixteen Christie-type T 4 mediums with four-man crew. The project was then abandoned for lack of funds and interest.

The only convertible wheel/track tanks produced for service in action were those of the Russian BT series (*Bystrokhodnii Tank*—fast tank). Production started in 1932 following the purchase from America of two models of the Christie M 1931; early versions of the BT closely resembled the original Christie tank, and all models used the Christie suspension with ability to run on wheels or tracks (speed on wheels up to 70 mile/h, on tracks 40 mile/h). Four basic models were produced for service, all with a three-man crew, and these led, through the experimental BT-IS and T 32 medium tank, to the design of the T 34 which surprised the Germans in 1941.

Cruiser tank Mark IVA (A 13) based on the Christie suspension.

The fastest British gun tanks before the Second World War were the A 13 Cruisers Marks III and IV, which had an official, governed speed of 30 mile/h but were capable of over 40 mile/h. Armed with a coaxial 40 mm (2-pdr) gun and machine-gun, and weighing 14 to 14·75 tons, they were developed from a Christie M 1931 hull purchased in 1936 after Major-General A. P. Wavell and Colonel G. le Q. Martel had seen the performance of the Russian BT Christie-type tanks while attending the 1936 manœuvres. Unlike the American Christies and the Russian BTs, the A 13 was designed for all-track operations (not convertible wheel/track).

First production models of the Cruiser Mark III appeared in 1938; Mark IV was similar with more armour, remaining in service until the end of 1941. They led to development of all subsequent cruiser tanks up to the Comet in 1944.

The first Japanese medium tank in service was the Type 89, which appeared as a prototype in 1929, armed with a 47 mm gun and two machine-guns. Design was based on the Vickers Medium C bought from Britain in 1926, and production started in 1931 as Type 89A Medium. Performance during operations in China was not satisfactory, but modified versions known as Type 89B or 94 remained in service until 1942. In 1937 it was already obsolescent and was replaced by the Type 97 *Chi-ha* of 14 tons.

The first Russian medium tank in service was the T 28, which was introduced in 1932 and closely resembled the smaller British A 6 "sixteen-tonner" with two sub-turrets forward. T 28 mounted a 76·2 mm howitzer with one (or two) machine-guns in the main turret and two machine-guns in sub-turrets. Improvements in later versions up to 1940, with more armour, increased the weight from 28 to 32 tons. It was in action in the Finnish War, 1939–40, and against the Germans in 1941.

First of Germany's production tanks— PzKpfw I of 1934.

The first German medium tank was the *Grosstraktor* (large tractor) of which only two prototypes were built about 1929 and tested in secrecy at the Russian tank centre at Karma River. It was developed from experience with the German A7V(U), and weighed about 21 tons, but had the unusual features (like the French Char 2C) of a forward main turret, with a 75 mm gun, and a sub-turret at the rear with a machine-gun. It was initially designed to be amphibious with screw propulsion.

The most heavily armed German tanks before 1939 were the *Panzerkampfwagen "Neubaufahrzeug"* (PzKpfw "NbFz") types built secretly in 1932 and 1934 as test vehicles. Developed from the *Grosstraktor*, they weighed 24 to 26 tons and followed the multi-turret trend of similar British and Russian tanks. Only six were built, and all had the same arrangement with twin machine-guns in sub-turrets, one to the right of the driver and one at the left rear of the main turret. These tanks were, however, divided into two types and numbered accordingly:

(1) PzKpfw V. With main turret mounting coaxial 75 mm and 37 mm guns side by side, and machine-gun in a ball-mounting. Three of these tanks were landed in the Norwegian Campaign in 1940, but disappeared soon after.

(2) PzKpfw VI. With coaxial 105 mm and 37 mm guns one above the other, and machine-gun in a ball-mounting. These tanks, made in mild steel, were displayed for propaganda purposes in the late 1930s.

German PzKpfw IIs (left) and III (right) in action.

The first German medium tank in service was the PzKpfw III (*Sonderkraftfahrzeug* 141). Prototypes of what were described as "*Zugführerwagen*" (platoon commander's vehicle) appeared in 1936, and production started in 1937. Early models, weighing 15 tons, mounted a coaxial 37 mm gun and machine-gun in the turret, with a machine-gun in the hull front, but in 1940 a short 50 mm gun L/42 was introduced in Type E to replace the 37 mm.

Production of the PzKpfw III in 1937 was followed only a few months later by another medium tank which had started development earlier, in 1935, as a "*Bataillonsführerwagen*" (battalion commander's vehicle)—the PzKpfw IV (SdKfz 161). Armed at first with the short 75 mm gun, it became the main battle-tank mounting a long 75 mm gun L/48, and was the tank in service in the greatest numbers. Production ended in 1945 with a total of about 8,500 built.

The first French medium tank in service was the D 1, a tank of 14 tons carrying a 3-man crew and mounting a coaxial 47 mm gun and machine-gun in the turret with fixed machine-gun in the hull front. It was developed from the 11-ton Renault NC light tank (not accepted in France but sold to Japan). When the D 1 was ordered in 1929 for prototype trials it was classified as a light tank; it was reclassified as a medium after manœuvres in 1932–33, by which time the more heavily armoured D 2 had been produced, armed with the same weapons and weighing 20 tons. Production of D 1 amounted to 180, and of D 2 only 100 when further orders were suspended in 1935; a further 50 of the D 2 were built after 1938.

The fastest French medium tank was the Somua S 35, accepted for the cavalry in 1935 (classified at first as *Automitrailleuse de Combat*). It had a speed of 28 mile/h and was rated as the best tank of its class in its time, being heavily armoured and mounting a 47 mm gun with a coaxial machine-gun. It weighed 20 tons with a three-man crew. About 500 were produced.

Somua S 35—a 20 ton French tank of all-round ability.

HEAVY TANKS

The tank mounting the most weapons was an experimental machine built by the French Schneider Company at the end of the First World War. It weighed 141 tons and was designed to carry a crew of twenty-eight, fighting with four 75 mm guns and nine machine-guns. The project was abandoned after the war.

The heaviest tank in service before 1939 was the French Char 2C, weighing 75 tons. It carried a crew of twelve with one 75 mm gun in a rotating turret at the front, one machine-gun in a rear turret and three machine-guns in hull mountings. An order for 300 was placed in 1918 for anticipated use in 1919, but only ten were delivered before the order was cancelled at the end of the war. These ten tanks remained in service and several improvements were made up to 1933. Six Char 2Cs were in service in 1940, but while *en route* by rail were destroyed by bombing before reaching action.

The heaviest British tank before 1939 was the A 1 "Independent", an experimental tank of 31 tons built in 1926. The tank carried a main turret, mounting a 47 mm gun (3-pdr), and four sub-turrets each with a machine-gun; one of these machine-guns had a special high-angle mounting for anti-aircraft use, **probably the first such example in a tank**. Only one tank was built, but it had a strong influence on later British medium tanks, and on the multi-turret designs which appeared in Germany and Russia.

Russian T 35 Heavy Tank —heavily armed but clumsy; they were failures in action.

The first Russian heavy tank in service was the T 32, which weighed nearly 45 tons and appeared in 1930–31. It carried a crew of ten, mounting a 76·2 mm gun and a machine-gun (or two) in the main turret, with two 37 mm guns and four machine-guns in four sub-turrets. The layout of sub-turrets was similar to that of the British A 1 "Independent" of 1926. The T 32 was followed in 1933 by the more numerous T 35, which was very similar and later mounted two 45 mm guns in place of the 37 mm guns; the sub-turrets were of the types used as light tank turrets. Production continued to 1939, and the T 35 was used in the Finnish War.

The first Japanese tank was one of 22 tons armed with a turret-mounted 70 mm gun, and two machine-guns—each in a sub-turret at front and rear. It was an experimental machine completed in 1927. Development, and more armour, led to a similar heavy tank Type 91 in 1931, followed in 1935 by the Type 95 which weighed 35 tons and mounted a 37 mm gun in the forward sub-turret. None of these was accepted for production.

The fall of France—wrecked Char Bs.

The first tank to have the main armament controlled and fired by the driver was the French Char B1, in which a short 75 mm gun was carried in a front hull mounting that provided movement in elevation only. Sighting of the weapon was controlled by the driver, and corrections for line were effected by moving the tank hull; an advanced form of steering, with delicate control through the Naeder Steering Unit, permitted fine adjustment for line. There was a fixed machine-gun in the front hull—similar to that in other French tanks—also controlled by the driver. Both weapons were served by a loader beside the driver. In addition, the tank carried a turret-mounted coaxial 47 mm gun and machine-gun, handled by the tank commander. Total crew four, including wireless operator.

Under the early direction of General J. B. Estienne, building of the first three prototypes was initiated in 1926 and completed in 1931, when a trials unit was formed. Limited production began in 1936, and three basic types appeared:

(1) Char B 1. With 40 mm armour, weighing 31 tons.

(2) Char B 1 *bis*. With 60 mm armour weighing 32 tons.

(3) Char B 1 Ter. A redesigned hull, 34 tons (75 mm armour) and with additional crew member as engine mechanic. Only five were built.

The Char B was classed as a heavy tank; it was technically advanced and much was expected of it in the *divisions cuirassées*. By May 1940, 337 had been built. In German hands some hulls were modified as flame-throwers or as self-propelled mountings for the 75 mm anti-tank gun.

LIGHT TANKS

The first Swedish tank was the *Stridsvagn* M 21, a light tank of about 10 tons with four-man crew, built in 1921 from components bought in Germany and based on the prototype designs of LK I and LK II. Assembly was supervised by the German designer, J. Vollmer. The new tank incorporated a rotating turret among other modifications, and it appeared in two types—Male mounting 37 mm gun and machine-gun, Female with two machine-guns. Another version with improved armour and transmission appeared in 1929, designated Strv M 21/29.

The first Italian built tank in quantity production was the Fiat 3000 (*Carro Armato* 21), a light tank which was the Italian version of the French Renault FT. Delivery started in 1921, and 100 were eventually built. This tank mounted two machine-guns, but armament was improved in a later version, *Carro Armato* 30, with a long 37 mm gun.

The first Russian-built tank in service was the KS (*Krasno-Sormovo*) light tank, the prototype of which was built in 1920 and was later known as the "*Russkiy-Renault*" or the "Freedom Fighter Comrade Lenin". It was copied from the French Renault FT which was also in service with the Soviet Army, but it incorporated components from other countries and the armament was improved by mounting both a 37 mm gun and a machine-gun. A total of fifteen were made by 1922.

The first Russian-designed tank to go into mass production was the MS 1 (*Maliy Soprovozdieniya*) developed in 1927 and produced in 1928 as the T 18. It was, in fact, an improved version of the KS tank, being a little faster with better engine and suspension. Further improvements were made in later models known as MS 2 and MS 3, and these served as the basis for a light, fast two-man tankette known as T 23. However, the T 18 did not represent any marked progress in performance, and production ceased in 1931 after about 960 had been built.

The first mass-produced Russian-designed tank— the MS I which was used in the Russo-German experiments at Karma River.

Carden Loyd Mark VI towing 20 mm Oerlikon anti-tank gun.

The first "one-man" tank was built in Britain by Major G. le Q. Martel in his garden in Camberley, Surrey. His aim was to build the cheapest tank possible, in order to pave the way for a wider acceptance of tanks in the peacetime Army. Its showing at the demonstration for the British Empire prime ministers in August 1926 led to the construction of Morris-Martel "tankettes" (two-man crew) for use as scout vehicles in the Experimental Mechanised Force manœuvres in 1927 and 1928. The Morris-Martel was not developed further, but the initial publicity drew attention also to the small Carden-Loyd machines.

The first machine-gun carrier to achieve mass production was the two-man Carden-Loyd Mark VI, for which initial orders were placed in late 1927 after trials with earlier models since the Carden-Loyd one-man machine was demonstrated in 1926. Originally conceived as a means of giving mobility to infantry automatic weapons on the battlefield, the early Carden-Loyds were referred to as "tankettes" and were used for reconnaissance. The Mark VI was used more widely in the British Army as a carrier for infantry weapons, and was the forerunner of succeeding generations of Vickers infantry carriers, while the Carden-Loyd Marks VII and VIII were developed into light tanks.

At the same time, the Carden-Loyd Mark VI was supplied to numerous countries and strongly influenced the design of similar machines (frequently called "tanks") in Russia, Poland, Italy, Czechoslovakia, France and Japan.

The most numerous Italian "tank" in service before 1939 was the *Carro Veloce* 33 (later known as L/3), produced in two models of 1933 and 1935. About 1,000 were produced. It was a light, two-man, turretless tank built by Ansaldo of Genoa, based on the British Carden-Loyd Mark VI which had been taken into service as the CV 29. Armed with one or two machine-guns, the L/3 was also modified for flame-throwing and bridging, and some were sold to Austria, Hungary, Bulgaria and Brazil.

The first tanks to be carried by aircraft were the Russian T 27 and T 38, which were slung beneath the fuselage of four-engined bombers during the manœuvres of 1936.

The T 27 was a two-man tankette developed from the British Vickers Carden-Loyd Mark VI, with a driver and gunner side by side, and carrying a machine-gun in a ball-mounting at the front; about 4,000 were built from 1932.

The T 38 was an amphibious tankette with a two-man crew and turret-mounted machine-gun. Production started in 1936. The T 38 was an improved version of the similar T 37 which had been developed from the Vickers Carden-Loyd amphibious light tanks which had been purchased from Britain in 1931.

Bren Carrier Mark I was a
logical development from the
early tankettes, designed to
give armoured firepower and
added mobility to
infantrymen.

Britain's A 10 of 1935
vintage.

A queen of the battlefield—a Matilda Mark III.

The first British light tank with a three-man crew was the Vickers "six-ton" tank, which appeared in 1928 as a private venture by Vickers-Armstrongs. There were two types, each with a three-man crew:

(1) Type A mounted two machine-guns in separate turrets.

(2) Type B mounted a 47 mm (3-pdr) gun and a coaxial machine-gun.

The tank was not accepted for service in the British Army, as there were doubts about the suspension, but it was sent abroad where it was copied and developed, notably in Russia, Poland, Czechoslovakia and studied in the United States.

British Light Tank Mark I.

The first British light tank in service with a three-man crew was the Light Tank Mark V, weighing 4·8 tons and mounting two machine-guns (coaxial ·5 in and ·303 in). Troop trials took place in 1934. It was a development in the series of light tanks produced by Vickers-Armstrongs from the original Carden-Loyds; subsequent versions in this series ended in 1940 with the Mark VIC armed with 15 mm and 7·92 mm Besa machine-guns.

Russian T 26 Bs go to their destruction against the Germans in 1941.

The first Russian light tank with a three-man crew was the T 26, produced in quantity from 1932 until 1939. It was developed from the Vickers "six-ton" tanks purchased in 1931 and, like those, was produced in two basic models:

(1) The T 26A, the early machine, was built with two turrets each mounting a machine-gun, initially, but in later variations carrying a gun up to 37 mm in the right-hand turret. This tank weighed between 7 and 8·5 tons.

(2) The T 26B, the most numerous, carried a single turret with a 45 mm gun, coaxial machine-gun and, sometimes, a machine-gun to the rear. This tank weighed about 9·5 tons.

(3) The T 26S was another version, introduced later, weighing 10·3 tons, with thicker armour, and sloped hull and turret sides.

The first French light tank with a three-man crew was the *Auto-mitrailleuse de Combat*, Renault Type YR, accepted by the Cavalry in 1934 for further trials. In the following year an improved Type ACG 1 appeared, weighing 14·5 tons and armed with a machine-gun and either a 25 mm or 47 mm gun. About 100 were eventually produced, some for service in Belgium, but this tank was soon superseded by the medium tank Somua S 35.

The first French light tank in mass production after 1918 was the Renault R 35 (Type ZM), accepted by the Infantry and ordered in quantity in 1935 as a replacement for the aged Renault FT. It carried a two-man crew and mounted a short 37 mm gun (1918 pattern) with coaxial machine-gun, but weighed 11 tons being heavily armoured (40 mm). An improved R 40 was produced later with long 37 mm gun (1938 pattern).

The R 35 was supplemented later in the infantry support role by the very similar Hotchkiss H 35 which was designed to the same specifications issued in 1933, but rejected at first by the Infantry and accepted by the Cavalry. An improved H 39 was also produced with the long 37 mm gun.

The first British tank designed after 1918 exclusively for infantry support was the Infantry Tank Mark I, produced in 1937 from designs started in 1935 under the security code name "Matilda". It was slow, with a maximum speed of 8 mile/h, and very heavily armoured (65 mm) capable of withstanding all known anti-tank weapons. Weighing 11 tons, it had a crew of two, armed with one machine-gun, ·5 in or ·303 in. Its only real merit was cheapness, and only 139 were built; it went out of service after the campaign in France and Belgium in 1940.

The first German tank produced in quantity was known as an agricultural tractor (*Landwirtschaftliche Schlepper*—LaS) for reasons of secrecy when production began in 1934. It was later named *Panzerkampfwagen* I (*Sonderkraftfahrzeug* 101). It was a light tank of about 5·5 tons with a two-man crew and armed with two turret-mounted coaxial machine-guns. Two types were built, A and B, differing mainly in suspension and engine. A third model, SdKfz 111, with only one machine-gun in a fixed superstructure, was used as a command vehicle. A total of about 1,500 of all types was produced before 1940, and some hulls were later used to mount self-propelled artillery.

The first German light tank with a three-man crew was the PzKpfw II (SdKfz 121), designed to a specification issued in 1932 for a tank in the 10-ton class. It mounted a coaxial 20 mm gun and machine-gun. Production began in 1935 and over 1,200 were made before the start of the German campaign in France, May 1940. There were several variations in engine, armour and suspension, including Types D and E which appeared in 1938 with a Christie-type suspension. The basic vehicle continued in production until 1942, and the PzKpfw II hull was later used for numerous self-propelled artillery weapons from 50 mm to 150 mm.

German experimental PzKpfw II Ds with Christie-type suspension.

The most numerous foreign tank in German service was the Czechoslovakian TNHP-S, produced in 1938 and taken over by German forces when the country was occupied in 1939. Originally a light tank of 10 tons, carrying a four-man crew with one 37 mm gun and two machine-guns, it was classed and used at first by the Germans as a medium tank; it was one of the most modern and effective tanks of its kind. Under the name of PzKpfw 38(t) it made up one-quarter of the tank strength of the Panzer forces in 1940–41. Production continued until 1942, and the hull was then used for mounting nearly 3,700 self-propelled weapons ranging from 20 mm flak to 150 mm artillery.

Apart from the suspension, the PzKpfw 38(t) was very similar to an earlier model produced in 1935 as LTM 35, and developed from the Vickers "six-ton" tank. It was taken into German service as PzKpfw 35(t). The Czechoslovakian tanks were exported to or made under licence in Rumania, Hungary, Sweden, Switzerland, Italy and Persia.

The first Japanese-built light tank was the Type 92, a tankette of under 4 tons carrying three men and mounting two machine-guns. The design owed much to the Vickers

Carden-Loyd. It was produced in limited numbers only and was succeeded in 1934 by the much more numerous 3-ton Type 94, which carried two men in a turretted version mounting one machine-gun. The Type 94 was still in action in 1942.

Japanese T 95 Kyu-go light tanks knocked out in action.

The first Japanese gun-armed light tank was the Type 95 *Kyu-go*, which mounted a 37 mm gun and two machine-guns; it weighed 6·5 tons and carried a three-man crew. The Type 95 was an original Japanese design, developed from a Type 93 light tank and from experience with the tankettes. Production continued between 1935 and 1942, amounting to about 1,300, and the Type 95 *Kyu-go* became the principal Japanese light tank in operations during the Second World War.

The first American (United States) light tank of post-1919 design to enter service was the Light Tank M 1 A1 Combat Car M 1, accepted in similar versions for the Infantry and Cavalry in 1937. Development stemmed from a series of experimental models starting in 1927, and influenced by trials in 1931 with the Vickers "six-ton" tank. The tank had a four-man crew, weighed nearly 10 tons and was armed with up to three machine-guns in the different versions according to its role in the Infantry or Cavalry.

Dutch DAF armoured car. It had a front and rear drivers position.

ARMOURED CARS
The longest-serving British armoured car was the Rolls-Royce, 1920 Pattern, built for the Army to designs which differed little from those of the Admiralty turretted pattern of 1914, armed with a Vickers machine-gun. Similar Rolls-Royce armoured cars were also built for the Air Ministry, for the R.A.F. armoured

car companies in Iraq and Egypt. Another version, known as the 1924 Pattern, with a modified turret carrying a Boys Anti-tank rifle and a Bren type were still in service with the Army in 1939, and some of the 1924 Pattern, with a modified turret carrying a Boys Anti-tank rifle and a Bren light machine-gun, took part in active operations in Libya in 1940–41.

The most powerfully armed armoured car in service before 1939 was the Russian *Bronieauto-mobil* 32, a six-wheeled armoured car with four-man crew which was taken into service in 1930 under the designation BA 10; it mounted a 37 mm gun in a rotating turret, with a machine-gun beside the driver. An improved version designated BA 32-1 appeared in 1932, using a tank turret with a 37 mm gun; in 1934 the BA 32-2 was produced with a 45 mm gun and two machine-guns; finally, the BA 32-3 came in 1937 with the same armament and improved armour.

The first German armoured car to enter service in quantity was the heavy *Panzerspähwagen* (6 Rad) (SdKfz 231), under development from 1929 on a six-wheeled lorry chassis and produced in 1933. Prototypes took part in manœuvres for the first time in 1932, and this was the main heavy armoured car (5 tons) of the 1930s, armed with a coaxial 20 mm gun and machine-gun. Later versions, fitted with wireless and conspicuous aerials, were numbered SdKfz 232 and 263.

From 1938 onwards the six-wheeled armoured cars were replaced by the eight-wheeled PzSpw (8 Rad) (SdKfz 231) which had the same armament but a better cross-country performance with drive to all wheels. They took the same series of identification numbers.

The first French half-track armoured car in service was the *Auto-mitrailleuse* Citroën-Kégresse-Schneider, designed to requirements issued in 1922 for new types of cavalry armoured vehicles, wheeled or tracked. This car was armed with turret-mounted 37 mm gun and machine-gun, crewed by three men, and used the new Kégresse suspension on a Citroën chassis. Sixteen of the first model were ordered in 1923 and gained operational experience in Morocco in 1925. Prototypes of an improved version appeared in 1928, and were accepted with an order for 100 under the name A.M. Schneider P 16.

A reclassification of the types and roles of cavalry armoured cars in 1931 made the Schneider P 16 an *Auto-mitrailleuse de Combat*. It took part in the 1932–33 manœuvres; further development stopped as it was replaced by fully tracked tanks.

Birch gun—an 18-pdr in a casemate on a Vickers carriage.

SELF-PROPELLED ARTILLERY

The first post-1918 British self-propelled artillery weapon was the "Birch gun"—named after Sir Noel Birch, Master-General of Ordnance—mounting originally the 13-pdr and then the 18-pdr gun with all-round traverse on specially designed hulls which had many parts in common with the contemporary Vickers Medium tanks and Dragons. Officially known as Mounting, SP, QF 18-pdr Mark I, the first vehicle was issued for trials in 1925, followed by four more (with varying modifications) a year later, and two more in 1929. Development was stopped in the early 1930s when the Royal Artillery concentrated on towed field artillery.

The first anti-aircraft tank was built in 1930-31 on the British Light Tank Mark I (Carden-Loyd Mark VIII). It was an experimental machine mounting two ·5 in Vickers machine-guns. There was little interest in developing this type of tank and the project was dropped.

The heaviest self-propelled tracked artillery weapon was the German 600 mm Mortar L/8.44 "Karl" (Gerät 040) which weighed 124 tons. The first was made in 1939, and a battery of six was formed for use in Russia against heavily defended positions. Replacement barrels of 540 mm L/11.5 were produced in 1942 to increase the range from 4,500 to 10,000 m, and the equipment was renumbered Gerät 041.

The equipment could move at 6 mile/h and only for short distances. Longer journeys meant some dismantling and use of road transporters, or by rail on two special rail flats, making a total weight of 180 tons. Special ammunition carriers based on the PzKpfw IV hull were built to provide mobile support.

SUPPORT VEHICLES

The first British tracked artillery tractor was the Dragon Mark I, ordered after trials with the experimental Supply Tank in 1922. It was issued for towing 18-pdr field-guns and for carriage of gun crews. Dragon Mark II appeared in 1924, based on the new Vickers Medium tank, followed by the Mark III in 1925 which was designed to tow medium artillery (60-pdr and 6 in howitzer). The final Dragon Mark IV was produced in 1935 and was the only one to see action when a few were taken to France in 1939.

The first armoured half-track support vehicles in service were the German armoured personnel carriers which were delivered in 1939 under the designations SdKfz 250 and 251. Development of the half-track chassis started in 1933 and armoured superstructures were added in 1935, leading to large-scale troop trials of varying models. From 1939 onwards increasing numbers of armoured half-tracks came into service in the SdKfz 250 and 251 series, for a wide variety of purposes, as armoured personnel carriers, communications or support vehicles, as well as mounting weapons up to 75 mm.

The first American (United States) armoured half-track support vehicle in service was the Car, Half-track M 2, an armoured personnel carrier assembled as a prototype in 1939 by using the armoured body of the wheeled Scout Car M 3 on the chassis of a Kégresse-type half-track truck. Development followed with a similar and slightly larger armoured personnel carrier which was standardised as the Carrier, Personnel, Half-track M 3, and mass production of both types started in 1941. Subsequent variations mounted weapons up to 105 mm. With a production of over 40,000 of all models and types, they were used by virtually all Allied forces in the Second World War.

The worst Italian tank—
M11/39.

PART THREE—TECHNOLOGY

The overriding factor in connection with tank technology between the two world wars was the parsimony of governments in granting funds for research and development into new ideas. This was fundamental because the ordinary automotive industry produced little that was of use to tanks: indeed it was the impoverished tank industry, trying hard to devise machines which nudged the frontiers of technology, which produced many useful techniques for the motor industry. Of course, when rearmament began again in the 1930s immense sums were released, but the 1920s were years of famine.

POWER PLANTS

The first tank engine designed as such between the world wars and **the first air-cooled one** was the Armstrong Siddeley 90 hp V-8 air-cooled engine in the Vickers Medium Mark I in 1923.

An air-cooled engine is an obvious advantage for an armoured fighting vehicle, avoiding the danger of coolant leaks and the space to house radiators. However, the space devoted to air-cooling for air-flow, cooling fins and fans can take up so much room in the armoured envelope that their use can be questionable. They are more difficult to manufacture than water-cooled engines. An Armstrong Siddeley four-cylinder version powered the 6-ton light tank in 1928 and one of 180 hp the "Independent" of 1926.

The Russians bought the Vickers 6-ton light tank and developed their T 26 from it using the same Armstrong Siddeley engine and retained air-cooling for all their light tanks until 1940 when they reverted to water-cooling.

The Germans used an air-cooled engine in their PzKpfw I but then, like the British, reverted to water-cooling permanently.

The U.S. standardised on air-cooled engines from the 6-ton M 1917 up to the outbreak of the Second World War.

The first diesel, developed by Ricardo, was a 90 hp type in 1927. In 1928, for the British "sixteen-tonner", he developed one of 180 hp but it never went into production. Although all tank-producing countries experimented with diesel engines, **Japan was first in the field** with a production diesel-engined tank in 1932—in the Type 89B which was also air-cooled. Japan standardised on the air-cooled diesel.

In 1932 the Russians decided to standardise on diesel engines for all tanks. Development went ahead resulting in production of the BT-7M tank in 1938. This engine was developed further and has been used in Russian tanks ever since.

It was a lightweight V-12 engine, liquid-cooled, giving 500 hp at 1,800 rev/min in the T 34 and 600 hp at 2,000 rev/min in the KV series.

The adoption of the diesel engine gave significant advantages. It increased the radius of action by approximately one-third over the petrol engine for a given quantity of fuel. It reduced the fire risk and simplified maintenance, production and logistics.

Among the most successful tank engines were those developed from aircraft power plants. Such for example were some of the Russian tank engines and, later, the British "Meteor"

The most celebrated and first employed of aircraft engines was the American Liberty, 300 hp, first tried in the Anglo-American Mark VIII in 1918 and later developed to power the early Christie tanks in the U.S.A. From this stemmed the use of the Liberty engine in British mediums developed after the Christie hull and suspension was purchased by Nuffield Mechanisation and Aero Ltd., in 1937.

The first radial air-cooled engines were those developed by the U.S.A., examples being the Continental type and the Wright which were put into their light M 2 tanks.

The first "flat" engines were developed for use in high-speed buses on the German *autobahn* by Henschel and exhibited in 1937. These were of immense use to tanks since they permitted a lower silhouette. The British developed different flat engines for the Covenanter and Churchill designs which were to appear in 1940.

TANK ARMAMENT

A modern tank is simply an armoured mobile platform carrying a weapon system so that, in the priorities of tank design, the weapon or gun should always be first priority. Ideally the tank is designed round the gun.

The fundamental formula connected with anti-tank gun performance is: Penetration = weight of projectile × muzzle velocity. It can thus be appreciated that greater penetration can be more easily achieved by increasing velocity^2 than the weight of projectile—but that is not the whole story as later will be seen.

The first dual-purpose gun mounted in the turret of a production tank was the British 47 mm (called 3-pdr). It weighed 2 cwt and fired armour-piercing high explosive (A.P.H.E.), that is a shot containing a small bursting charge which was intended to explode after penetration of the enemy tank had been made. There were ordinary high-explosive and canister rounds made, but these were rarely issued.

The most generally employed tank weapons in the 1920s were machine-guns since it was considered that these were most likely to be necessary in the normal infantry support role expected of tanks. High-velocity anti-tank guns were of secondary, though rapidly growing importance, while larger guns upwards of 75 mm to fire heavy high explosive like artillery were rarities.

Among the most heavily armed tanks was the French Char 2C *bis* with its 155 mm howitzer, 75 mm gun and four machine-guns. Only one was built.

The general run of a great variety of anti-tank guns produced by different manufacturers throughout the interwar years ranged in calibre between 37 and 47 mm for their service tanks, with barrels some 32 to 52 calibres long, firing 2 to 3 lb shot at a muzzle velocity of 2,000 to 2,800 ft/sec.

The interesting French SAU 40 self-propelled gun which had not reached production when France fell in 1940.

The first so-called "close support weapons" mounted in tanks were those put into British and German tanks when it was feared conventional artillery units would be unable to keep up with fast-moving tank formations, thus depriving them of adequate high-explosive and smoke cover against anti-tank guns—the tank's small-calibre anti-tank gun being unable to fire a good high-explosive round itself.

The first close support gun was the British 3·7 in howitzer mounted in the Medium tank. It was to have many successors until the day when all tanks were mounted (by about 1944) with a really efficient dual-purpose gun of not less than 75 mm.

The best early dual-purpose gun mounted in production tanks was 76·2 mm used by the Russians in their T 28s and T 32s.

ARMOUR

The armour on a tank can account for as much as 50 per cent of its total weight. The early tanks had armour of uniform thickness all round, and this policy was retained on the British and Russian tanks until the end of the 1919–39 period. As the demand for thicker armour grew it rose from 8 mm in the Vickers Medium to 14 mm in the Vickers Light and German PzKpfw III and IVs, to 30 mm in the A 10 and 70 mm in the infantry tanks. In the mid-thirties the Germans started to be selective in armour distribution and began to give the frontal aspect of the tank heavier protection up to 30 mm.

The quality of armour was improved by the introduction of homogeneous armour—nickel-chrome-molybdenum steel; but the Germans developed face-hardened rolled plate, which was particularly effective against A.P. shot. Early in the period armour was bolted or riveted. The Germans and Russians started to use welded armour in the mid-thirties. This improved protection, saved weight and cured bullet "splash" through slits. The U.K. and the U.S. still retained riveted armour till the outbreak of the Second World War.

The first cast turrets were introduced by the French in their D 1 in 1931. This was a small turret and presented few problems in manufacture, but it was some years before other countries adopted the practice.

The very slow British Infantry Tank Mark I—Matilda. Proof against all then existing anti-tank weapons.

The A.F.V.s of the interwar period were of "box-like" construction, as was also to be seen in much later tanks—Cromwell and Tiger I being examples. The advantages of sloping armour to give increased ballistic protection had not been considered. For example, if an armoured plate 100 mm thick is sloped at 60 degrees, the horizontal distance through the armour is 200 mm, and it is the horizontal passage which is the route of A.P. shot. In 1937 the Russians developed the A 20 on which they deliberately sloped the armour to take advantage of the cosine law.

The resistance of armour to penetration is as dependent on quality as it is on thickness or slope. Manufacture is carried out either on open-hearth or in electric furnaces where the art of the metallurgist and the foundryman are pre-eminent even in mass production. Just as high-quality armour is needed for protection so it is required for projectiles, and thus battlefield competition really begins in the laboratories and on the factory floor.

The main types of armour available to the British in 1939 were:

Vickers Cemented Armour which was 20 mm plate with the carbon content increased on the front to give a Brinell hardness of 600 while the back was left at 400. Manufacture was difficult and the product was liable to distortion and cracking.

Hadfields Duplex which was two layers of plate rolled together, one layer highly carburised, the other not. Difficult to manufacture there was also a tendency for the plys to separate.

Homogeneous—being plate of even quality, the Hard version of 450 Brinell being non-machinable, the Soft of 380 having an advantage that it could be machined after heat treatment.

Mother

HEAVY TANKS

Char B

Tiger 1

Maus

Conqueror

LIGHT TANKS

Renault FT

Lt. Tank Mk. 1

Locust

Scorpion

Chieftain

MEDIUM TANKS

Whippet

Christie T 3

T 34/76

Panther

M 60 A2

A.P.C.s

Mk. IX

Bren Carrier Mk. 1

A.F.V. Genealogical Tree

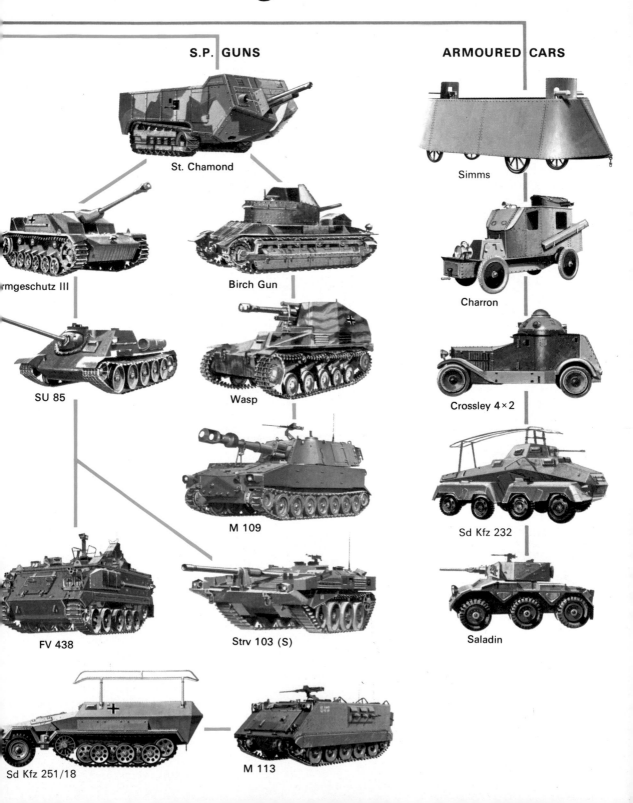

S.P. GUNS

ARMOURED CARS

St. Chamond

Simms

rmgeschutz III

Birch Gun

Charron

SU 85

Wasp

Crossley 4 × 2

M 109

Sd Kfz 232

FV 438

Strv 103 (S)

Saladin

Sd Kfz 251/18

M 113

SUSPENSIONS

The quality of a tank's ride is dependent on its suspension. The smoothness of ride was of particular interest to the British, because they were the only country completely wedded to the policy of firing on the move. To fire on the move with any degree of accuracy requires a smooth ride with minimum oscillations. Cross-country speed was governed far more by the tank's suspension than its power: weight ratio.

Most frequently employed of all suspensions at first were coil springs attached to pivoted bogie wheels, but in many different permutations. Another approach was the quarter elliptical leaf-spring suspension employed on a number of light tanks.

Sturmgeschütz III with short 75 mm gun.

Torsion-bar suspension was first introduced by the Germans in the later PzKpfw II (1936) and the PzKpfw III, and has been adopted in some form by every other country. Perhaps the German lead is attributable to the original Volkswagen design which also had torsion-bar suspension.

The big-wheel Christie coil-spring suspension was first introduced into production by the Russians in their BT range and then T 34, and used on British cruiser tanks from the A 13.

The U.S. graduated through Vickers leaf-spring suspension to vertical volute spring suspension in the M 1 Combat Car. This was a rugged, reliable system which gave a firm ride and was used consistently throughout the rest of the period by the U.S.

TRANSMISSIONS AND STEERING

There is a choice in methods of transmission of power to the tracks: The U.S. and German A.F.V.s used front-sprocket drive, the British had rear-sprocket drive and the Russians changed from front to rear drive in 1937.

The advantages of rear-sprocket drive are to segregate the fighting chamber from mechanical drives; it reduces the distance power has to be transmitted; it can result in a lower front silhouette and is less vulnerable to sprocket damage.

The disadvantage is that the rear sprocket tends to pack with mud, stones and debris from the top track and can result in thrown tracks.

The front-sprocket drive shortens the gearbox and steering control and the tracks tend to be self-cleaning, so eliminating debris packing round the sprocket.

Although various transmissions were experimented with in this period, electrical hydrostatic and hydro-kinetic, none of them reached fruition, and all transmissions were generally mechanical with manual gearboxes.

Clutch and brake steering was normal, but as tanks got heavier, over-heating brake bands became a problem. Consequently the search went on for a regenerative steering system, where one track is slowed down and the other track is speeded up through appropriate gears. Such a system was used in French tanks in the mid-thirties and by the U.S.—called "Cletrac" steering—and in all light tanks entering service from the M 1 Combat Car to the Czech Lt 38 (PzKpfw 38(t)).

A more sophisticated steering system appeared on the French Char B which had a double differential and hydrostatic drive which gave infinitely variable steering. This steering was used for laying the hull-mounted 75 mm gun (which had no traverse).

Yet another type of steering was by "bowed track" in the British Medium D. This type of steering was fitted to the Tetrarch (1936) and on carriers, but only large-radius turns could be made with it.

The great majority of interwar tracks (and those which have followed) were of the flexible pin-jointed type made of metal. It was the Americans who produced the other common alternative, the rubber block linked by external end-pieces. The trouble with rubber was a loss of traction, while the difficulty with the earlier metal tracks was their short life. In the interwar years most British tracks were made of cyanide-hardened, malleable cast iron; these tracks did not wear well. The introduction of manganese-steel tracks, however, gave an enormous increase in life and it was these, for instance, which were mostly used by the Germans and the British as time passed.

SPECIAL EQUIPMENT

The First World War had shown the need for specialised A.F.V.'s and ancillary equipment on tanks. During the interwar years demands for all sorts of aids to enable tanks to cross gaps, minefields and to fight at night were made, but financial stringency withheld progress except in the matter of gap crossing.

The first bridging tank was devised by the British using a Mark V** tank as carrier. The same sort of tank was also tried out with a flexible roller as the means to detect and detonate mines.

An early experiment in the use of searchlights on tanks was made by the British in 1935 when they mounted some on light tanks in Britain and, later, in Egypt.

The first attempt to create a special armoured tank searchlight was begun shortly before the war when a French device was taken up. This was to be a carbon-arc light working through a slit in the turret armour. Its purpose was as an aid to night movement and shooting. It came to be known during the war as Canal Defence Light (C.D.L.) but, although much time and money was spent on it and unfounded claims were made that its "flicker" device could blind the enemy, it was never used as a main battle-weapon. Nevertheless it heralded the host of night-fighting devices which, a generation later, were to become the stock-in-trade of all tank armies.

ANATOMY OF DESIGN

The distribution of component parts by weight in a fighting vehicle is the product of General Staff requirements. For example, if there is a requirement for greater protection by armour, instead of by speed, the weight of armour in relation to power plant is higher than if policy were the other way about. Nevertheless a fairly even weight distribution of components is to be found in each era of tank evolution. The vehicles which went to war in 1939 roughly followed the following proportional percentages:

Armament	5
Ammunition	6
Crew	7
Radio and electrical equipment	1
Power plant	5
Fuel	4
Transmission	8
Suspension	12
Tracks	7
Armour	45
Total	**100**

"Rommel (standing, facing camera) conducts the desert tank battle. All the elements of the control mechanism are here—staff officers, radio truck, staff car, communications aircraft, and an escorting armoured car. On the horizon hangs the smoke of battle." (Major E. R. Andrews.)

SECTION IV
The Era of Domination
1939-1942

If the overrunning of Poland in 1939 was the vindication of all that the tank enthusiasts had prophesied, the next three years' active service were to produce results out of all imagination. Not simply armies but whole nations were to be engulfed and so suddenly that their relapse into a state of shock and coma was to make them quite unable, for years, to reassert their sovereignty. The year 1940 witnessed a cataclysm for Western Europe when Denmark, Norway, Holland, Belgium, Luxembourg and France were eliminated from the Allied order of battle. **The most startling campaign** was that which, in six weeks, encompassed the total destruction of the mighty French Army, with its preponderance of infantry and cavalry tanks, and the withdrawal of the British Army to its own shores, leaving nearly all its equipment in German hands. This triumph was mainly chalked up to the German panzer divisions, for they made the opportunities for a breakthrough, outmanœuvred the Allied armies and pursued them to destruction. They finally completed the encirclement of bewildered hordes of enemy soldiers who had been completely outfought, both morally and physically.

Yet close to the edifice of absolute victory lay the scaffolding of change which, eventually, was to reshape even the modern structure of armoured land warfare. Much credit for the collapse of the French could be given to the German Air Force which had terrified its opponents into surrendering without resistance. But already, towards the end of the campaign, both French and British soldiers were coming to terms with the bomber, realising that its bark was often much worse than its bite. Allied infantry, which had surrendered on call to German tanks, was soon to discover that these machines were highly vulnerable, their thin armour easily penetrable by the existing anti-tank guns. Moreover the resistance of the heavy French and British tanks to German shot, while at the same time they scored kills with their own guns, vindicated tanks that were both heavily armoured and well armed—particularly if they could be thrown into massed action, as happened on a couple of isolated occasions. The Germans recognised these lessons, too. They turned to up-gunning and up-armouring their existing tanks—slowly at first but with increasing urgency as they took the measure of new enemies and a changing situation.

In June 1941 the Germans struck eastward against Russia, having already conquered Yugoslavia and Greece and become involved in the Cyrenaican desert at the side of the Italians whose tanks had been defeated by the British. In Russia the Germans met a massive enemy tank force, but something more besides. They encountered machines which were significantly technically superior to their own, but in the opening encounters completely outmanœuvred the Russians. Thus, although the Germans kept a lead over their opponents in the art of tank combat, they were hard pressed to maintain technical equality. Their tanks were being knocked out by a better-armed and armoured opponent—one who could kill without easily being killed.

Once the myth of tank invincibility had been exploded, the contenders struggled to maintain the credibility of armour—a struggle which revolved more critically around time-consuming technical innovation than rapid tactical development. Each nation competed to keep a jump ahead in the gun/ armour race and to harness the new, more powerful tanks to the original concept of tactical surprise, concentration and pace. As the time between invention and production got longer, battlefield en- counters were liable to be decided in an inventor's mind some two years or more before a shot was fired. The quality of equipment depended upon the availability of natural resources and industrial capability, so while the Axis tried hard to wrest material and industrial centres from the Allies, the Allies hung on, fighting for time to build an irresistible mass of tanks, aircraft and other weapons. Even so the Germans nearly managed to capture the bulk of Russian oil-supplies—the tank's life-blood—and the Japanese, following their entry into the war in December 1941, gathered in most of the Far Eastern oil-wells in addition to so much else, like rubber. Frequently tank production had to be modified to suit raw material availability—it was rarely a case of having only the best.

After 1942 the tide turned in the Allies' favour, with the defeat of the Germans at Stalingrad and their ejection from North Africa, the nature of armoured warfare also changed. Tanks still loomed large in everybody's minds. Wherever they were likely to appear they dictated the planning of battles. But no longer could they win battles simply by their impact on morale. It was not so much that tanks became merged with the other fighting arms—the infantry, artillery, engineers and bombers, etc.—as that the other arms became somewhat more tank-minded themselves. Infantry travelled more frequently in armoured vehicles, only dismounting to fight when necessary: engineers laid bridges and demolition charges from specialised armoured vehicles without dismounting; gunners fought with self-propelled guns that were little different in shape to the main battle-tanks. When an amphibious assault took place or a river had to be crossed it was more than likely that the leading elements which swam or waded ashore were carried in armoured vehicles. But, always they worked in close conjunction, each arm helping the other—that is if they wished to survive against the mounting power of defensive weapons. And gradually, too, armour tried to impose its will during the hours of darkness, adapting technology to help it move and shoot at night.

As the net closed in on Germany, and Japan began to suffer from the constrictions of her weakling economic position, land battles became a story of hammer against walnut, in that the Allies, totally omnipotent in material, bludgeoned the Axis into submission by sheer brute strength. Yet amidst this holocaust, the enormous collisions which took place between armoured forces on the threshold of the German Reich and the awe-inspiring amphibious landings in the Pacific, it became plain that tanks had troubles that could not wholly be solved by increased armour protection. The last months of the Second World War coincided with the appearance of the heaviest tanks yet made—though impotent in battle due to their immobility. Thus when the war ended, even though there were those who claimed the tank had been defeated by anti-tank weapons and that, in any case, the advent of the atomic bomb made all other weapons obsolete, new and sound lessons for the future had been learnt. Already the principal tank nations were producing tanks which neatly balanced protection, mobility and hitting power in one vehicle, though endeavouring always to assure that the gun always outmatched the enemy. These "balanced tanks" were the ones that survived and became models for the future.

PART ONE—FEATS & ACHIEVEMENTS

The most complete of all victories in the Second World War was the more remarkable in that the German Army, when it conquered Denmark, Norway, Holland, Luxembourg, Belgium and France within a period of less than three spring months in 1940 was both quantitively inferior to the sum total of its opponents and, to a lesser extent, qualitatively inferior in terms of tanks and aircraft. While it is true that Denmark surrendered after only token resistance and Norway fell to a surprise assault which depended upon a sea and air descent rather than an engagement by major land forces, other nations in the West—on paper immensely strong—fell victim to an air and tank attack in which the conventional marching forces played little more than a walking-on part.

The victory in Norway absorbed less than 100 tanks—a few light models to lead the assault, where room could be found along mountain roads, and three obsolete PzKpfw V which had never gone into quantity production. The latter were merely paraded for prestige purposes and, by their size made a strong impression on a people which had been winded by the unexpectedness of invasion. Thus the effect on morale of tanks was exploited more adroitly than their actual fighting power.

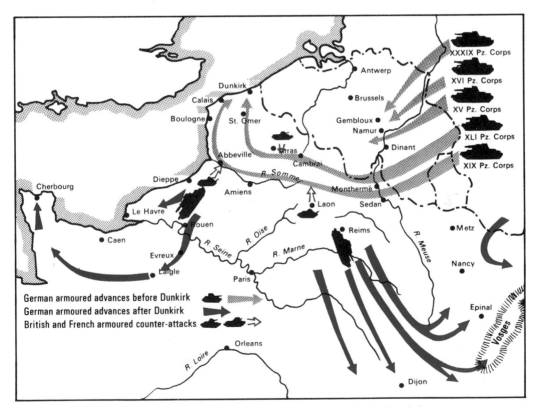

Battle for Western Europe. May and June 1940. Each prong drove remorselessly through the enemy among undefended political and economic objectives. Each was led by tanks.

*A Maginot Line pill-box—
outflanked by Rommel's
tanks in 1940.*

The balance of armoured and air forces available for battle between Germany and the Western Allies on 10th May, 1940 when Germany struck westward, was approximately as follows:

	Light	Medium	Heavy	S.P. guns	Aircraft
Germany	2,770	609	—	12	2,800
France	2,700	500	300	—	575
Britain	300	300	20	—	350 (plus a strategic force in U.K.)
Others	50	—	—	—	100

The truly formidable performance of the panzer divisions overshadowed all else, for while the German Air Force eliminated its opponents in the air and largely paralysed ground forces by intensive dive-bombing upon military objectives (in addition to attacks designed to terrorise the civilian population) the panzer divisions concentrated their entire strength against a relatively narrow front between Namur and Sedan while the rest of the German Army attacked on a wide front to distract Allied attention from the central tank thrust.

The vital statistics of the 1940 campaign were those of rates of advance. The performance of two formations in particular reflect the achievements of the whole. After three days spent penetrating the thick Ardennes countryside and closing up to the River Meuse:

● General Guderian's XIX Corps covered 151 miles to the Channel Coast in 8 days at 19 miles per day (best performance in one day, 56 miles).

● General Rommel's 7th Panzer Division covered 110 miles in 8 days at 13·75 miles per day.

On the debit side had to be recorded a breakdown and loss rate of about 30 per cent along with confirmation that lightly armoured and under-gunned tanks (even the PzKpfw IIIs and IVs) were no match for the heavy French Char Bs and British Matildas. The latter, striking the German flank at Arras on 21st May had so jolted the assurance of the German commanders that they hesitated in their drive to Dunkirk and this let slip the opportunity of encircling the British Army.

On the credit side stood the total elimination of the French tank force, the absolute disruption of their command system and the complete removal of British forces (plus the loss of most of their equipment) from the Continent. Air power could claim equal credit with the tanks, not so much for the physical as the damage to morale it had caused. The real triumph lay with team-work—team-work at all levels of command (despite squabbles brought on by astonishment at the scale of the victory), within the tank forces and each tank itself whose crews combined like one machine.

Hotchkiss H 35—a light tank but better armoured than its German opponents in 1940.

Rommel's 7th Panzer Division advances through France.

The first ship versus tank fight took place as German tanks were entering Boulogne Harbour and were engaged by the guns of a Royal Navy destroyer—with unfortunate results for at least one tank.

This disaster from the British point of view amounted to the loss of most of her best equipment, the threat of immediate invasion and the realisation that her industry was hardly capable as yet of building sufficient heavy and medium tanks with which to combat the German tank force.

The great delusion of 1940 was a belief that the Germans had far outnumbered as well as outmatched the Allies and the assumption that German production was far in excess of the British—whereas, in fact, the British built 1,399 to 1,460 German tanks in 1940—and in succeeding years would easily overtake the Germans in quantity even if not in quality.

Another grand delusion concerned a belief that there had been heavy tank-versus-tank fighting whereas, in fact, most tank losses were inflicted by anti-tank guns and, in the case of the British, 75 per cent of all losses had been due to mechanical failure. These were to be recurring themes as the war progressed.

International reaction to the German triumph led to an elevation in importance of the tank to one of pre-eminence in every army—an exaggerated swing of the pendulum.

In Russia they tried to speed up the Rotmistrov reorganisation by creating special tank and mechanised divisions—the former composed of two tank regiments, one infantry regiment and an artillery regiment, the latter reversing the tank and infantry component. A doctrine that said tanks must be used concentrated was propagated, but the whole business was slow starting and handicapped by having need make do with the older generation of tanks before the next came into being.

In Britain there was a double demand for ten armoured divisions that were even more tank-heavy than the 1938 Mobile Division with, in addition, infantry support tank brigades. A maverick bid by Hobart to create a real armoured army in which tanks, infantry, artillery, engineers and aircraft were to be trained and put into battle as an élite was rejected. But British tank production rapidly gained in pace and volume, aiming at a total of 10,000 tanks in service as quickly as possible. Even infantry units were to be converted to tanks.

Russian heavy BA 10 armoured car in Persia, 1941.

In Germany the success of the panzer divisions led to a demand for a doubling of the number of these formations. But since tank production remained virtually static this could only be done by cutting in half each division's tank content—though with more medium tanks available it was possible to use them as replacements for the lights and thus increase the actual striking power of the tank element.

In the U.S.A. the German victory acted as a spur to come to the aid of Britain and, at the same time, an urgent jog to rearm in haste. The collapse of France coincided with tank exercises in Louisiana during which the U.S. Tank Force showed its paces—though with outmoded machines. Cavalry and Infantry insistence on maintaining separate possession of their own tank fleet was now subverted by the new Chief of Staff, General George Marshall. He ordained the birth of a new branch—the Armored Corps—and he told Chaffee to take over all the armoured forces and begin the formation of two armoured divisions in addition to providing special infantry support (G.H.Q.) tank battalions. In league with this the Americans set in motion a vast tank-building programme of machines some of which hardly existed in prototype. Yet this, too, was only a small part of the massive American rearmament—called the "Victory Program" —which finally eradicated the economic slump of the 1930s.

In Canada, under the insistent impulse of Colonel F. Worthington, an armoured corps was formed, its ranks filled by keen volunteers but its equipment a strange assortment of obsolete Renault FTs and old Liberty Mark VIIIs, bought at scrap value from the U.S.A., plus some British light tanks. This force was to expand into two armoured divisions and two armoured brigades.

The real acquisition for the future that came from the French Campaign, besides the booty won by the Germans, was the unchallenged establishment of a new way of making war whereby command was exercised from the forefront of the battle, through radio control. All arms were combined into teams as integrated (even if informal) battle-groups. Yet though the Germans had concentrated all their tanks in ten selected panzer divisions they had also begun to dilute the armour by giving an armoured element to the infantry formations, allocating armoured self-propelled artillery as a means of deploying direct artillery support among the leading elements. This process was to be extended, as time went by, when it was realised that the S.P. gun had a wide variety of uses as a sort of poor man's tank.

Italian M 13/40s under bombardment in the desert.

The greatest demonstration of sheer tank virtuosity took place in the Cyrenaican Desert when a 31,000-man British army, 275 strong in tanks, under General Richard O'Connor, annihilated completely an Italian army of about 240,000. The statistics for a two months' campaign from 6th December to 8th February speak for themselves:

- British losses—500 dead, 53 missing and 1,373 wounded.
- Italian losses—some 100,000 casualties plus 130,000 prisoners; 845 guns, 180 medium tanks, and 200 light tanks.
- British rate of advance at one period, for a 30 per cent mechanical failure rate was, 250 miles in 30 days (including a pitched battle and a siege) an average of 8·3 miles per day with as much as 50 miles in a single day.
- Exchange rate in tanks at the grand finale of the campaign—the all tank and gun Battle of Beda Fomm from 5th to 7th February: British 4—out of a total of 32 mediums and about 50 lights. Italian 101 M 13/40s—their latest machine and their entire remaining force.

The most shattering riposte was to follow in the desert less than two months later when a combined German-Italian force under General Erwin Rommel (with the Afrika Korps as its spearhead) swept the British back to the Egyptian frontier. British tanks fought badly and broke down at the rate of one per 10-miles run. In the absence of O'Connor they were outgeneralled. Again statistics speak for themselves:

- The Axis, 150 tanks strong advanced 500 miles in 14 days—an average of 35·7 miles per day.
- The British lost nearly all their 100 tanks—their numbers subject to wild fluctuations due to mechanical failure.

A crescendo was now being reached in tank warfare. Five panzer divisions—about 1,000 tanks—were launched into Yugoslavia and Greece on 6th April and within three weeks had overrun both countries and ejected the small British and Anzac force (with only fifty-two medium tanks) sent to aid them. With opposition so slight it could hardly be counted a feat, tanks had achieved a resounding success in mountainous terrain, yet **this was the first time** a really large tank force was employed under those conditions and it said much for their agility and the expertise of their supply echelons that were able to maintain the normal momentum of advance. At the same time there were big tank battles on the Egyptian frontier where the Afrika Korps repelled successive offensives by British tanks.

The importance of co-operation between tanks and artillery was repeatedly demonstrated in two British desert operations—"Brevity" in May and "Battleaxe" in July. Thrusts by British columns were made in the direction of Tobruk and were repelled with heavy tank losses, the damage being caused more by anti-tank guns than tanks, whenever the tanks attempted to charge an unshaken defended locality. What success the British won in "Brevity" came as the result of their Matildas withstanding the fire of Axis tank-mounted guns and the obsolete 37 mm guns. The Matildas were conquered during "Battleaxe", however, by 88s hidden in emplacements which were quite undisturbed by a preliminary bombardment. Yet when British tanks and artillery fully co-operated in harrying various German tank thrusts they, too, were instrumental in causing the Germans heavy tank losses. Tank losses for the two sides during "Battleaxe" were: British eighty-seven—of which the majority were due to mechanical failure in the new Crusaders; German twenty-five.

A climax was to be reached on 22nd June when the Germans invaded Russia. Here in **the greatest tank battles of all time**, between over 20,000 tanks, there occured a struggle that was to decide the outcome of the Second World War. The enormous disparity between numbers of tanks on either side was as dramatic as the difference in their employment. Estimates of Russian tank strengths vary between 15 and 24,000. German strengths are more exactly known—3,200 plus about 200 armoured self-propelled guns. **The Germans** used their tanks concentrated into seventeen panzer divisions with the armoured guns spread among the infantry divisions. **The Russians** used their armour in all manner of ways—sometimes concentrated into great unwieldy masses which thundered about rather aimlessly against the German thrusts, at others spread thinly among the infantry. Either way they suffered crushing losses, and for the following reasons:

● Three-quarters of their tanks were of the light Vickers or Christie BT types and therefore both outgunned and out-armoured by the Germans who, by now, fielded 1,440 PzKpfw IIIs and 517 PzKpfw IVs.

● The German tanks were under comprehensive radio control, whereas the Russians possessed few radios and hardly any below battalion level. Therefore they were unresponsive to quick changes in situation.

● The Germans had practised battle drills: the Russians had not—and moreover they were caught in the middle of reorganisation and were thus in two minds about command and tactics.

● German tank crews were well trained: the Russians were not. For instance their drivers tended to follow crest-lines and presented themselves as easy targets.

● On 22nd June 29 per cent of the old Russian tanks required total overhaul and a further 44 per cent needed routine servicing.

● The German Air Force rapidly gained superiority and thus was able to provide excellent information to their army (plus bombing) while denying these valuable assets to the Russians.

PzKpfw IV A in action in Russia.

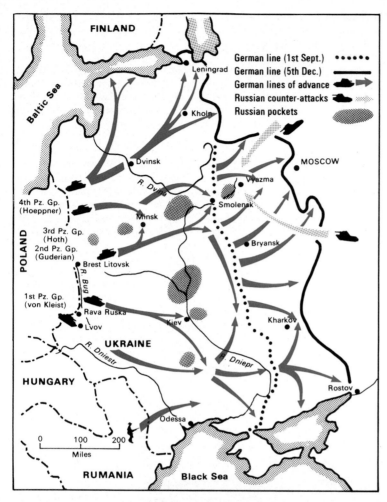

Russia 1941
*Panzer Division power at
its zenith against the
numerically superior
Russian tank force. Each
became exhausted from
immense losses. The
advance halted for lack of
supplies.*

Yet the Germans failed to knock Russia out of the war even though they accounted for 17,000 Russian tanks in 5 months' fighting for a loss of only 2,700 of their own. The reasons were:

● Inability of the German tanks to sustain intensive operations beyond six weeks before they needed a prolonged halt to carry out maintenance.

● Their fundamental lack of a strong tank reserve—nearly everything was "in the shop window" while captured French tanks were unsuitable for front-line service.

● Difficulty of maintaining supplies over long ranges across roads that broke up in wet weather. The Germans had no good cross-country supply vehicles.

● An inability to complete the capture of great enemy hordes, after several superb encirclement operations, without at the same time halting and losing momentum. Again this occurred for lack of adequate reserves needed for so gigantic a task as the subjugation of Russia.

● Above all the sheer impossibility of overwhelming so big a nation as Russia with German Army resources of 1941—itself **the best army the world had ever seen** in matters of organisation and ability.

Prodigious feats were performed by German armoured forces in 1941, though rates of advance were lower than in France—the best was by Guderian's 2nd Panzer Group which covered the 413 miles from Brest Litovsk to Smolensk between 22nd June and 16th July at an average of 16·5 miles per day. But in this period they fought many more battles than in France and had to deal with the absorption of thousands of prisoners, often having to wait for infantry divisions to catch up. The best single advance in a day was 72 miles on 28th June—a quite remarkable performance since it was against local resistance and in face of flank counter-attacks in forest terrain.

The most devastating anti-tank weapon now proved to be the German 88 mm flak gun, whose potential had been realised during the Spanish Civil War, and confirmed in scattered engagements during the Polish and French campaigns. But against the heavily armoured Russian KV 1 tanks, and to a lesser extent the British Matildas in the desert, this was the one weapon which could be certain of achieving penetration. The gun's disadvantage was its high silhouette and size which made it vulnerable if it was not well dug in.

The worst enemy of armoured forces in Russia was the weather. In summer there was dust which not only choked the crews but also overcame air-filters, thus causing a significant reduction in engine life. In autumn the heavy rains reduced the countryside to a quagmire and stifled mobility—the tank force's chief asset. In winter temperatures dropped to -32 °F, freezing and cracking crankcases and radiators, immovably fixing vehicles in suddenly frozen mud—frequently causing hundreds of vehicles to be abandoned to the enemy. Both sides suffered, but the Germans worst of all because they had made few preparations for winter and the new Russian tanks had a marginally better cross-country performance.

The principal enemy of armoured forces in the Western Desert was also dust and heat, but whereas the British forces which faced the Axis forces had a good supply of tanks building up after their latest defeat in June 1941, the Axis were invariably hard-pressed for new tanks and spare parts, as well as fuel supplies.

A jolt for the Germans— the heavily armoured Russian KV 1.

The least important war, in German eyes, was the desert war. At first they committed only two divisions and kept them a quarter below normal establishment. The purpose of the Afrika Korps' presence was political and not strategic—to prop up the failing Italians, not to win military laurels or take Egypt. But in British eyes the desert theatre of war was **the most important** since it was their one point of contact with the German Army as well as a shield to the vital Suez Canal and the Iraqi oilfields beyond.

The great tank battles which flared up in response to the British offensive "Crusader" on 18th November 1941 involved cut and thrust over a period of six weeks by 756 British tanks (backed by a 50 per cent reserve), and 569 Axis tanks almost totally lacking in reserves.

The key to the great defensive Axis successes in the early stages of "Crusader" could be found in their technique of concentrating all their strength in time against individual British formations that became separated in desert space. Thus the Germans managed to knock out individual British armoured brigades in turn, often compelling battle by using their tanks as bait to lure the British tanks on to a line of anti-tank guns. At one moment, for instance, the British 7th Armoured Brigade was reduced from 141 to 28 serviceable tanks—and this was no unique experience.

The subsequent Axis collapse occurred because they were unable to consolidate their primary success, partly because Rommel abandoned the decisive point on the battlefield in order to take his tanks on a wild-goose chase into the British rear (thus giving the British breathing space to recover and repair tanks), and partly because his fuel supplies were run down. True, the drive against the British rear unnerved the British commander (General Cunningham) and caused his removal from command, yet Rommel was forced by General Auchinleck to withdraw into Libya at the end of the year, abandoning much material and several thousand men.

The first tank Victoria Cross of the war was won by Captain Phillip Gardner of the Royal Tank Regiment on 23rd November 1941 during the British attempt to break out of the beleaguered fortress of Tobruk in an effort to link up with the main forces advancing from Egypt. Gardner left his tank to rescue the crews of two armoured cars. He tried to tow them back, but this failed. So he carried out his task while under heavy fire and himself wounded, holding a wounded man on the back of his tank while it was driven home in the face of intense shellfire.

Rommel was able to make a startling recovery when, on 21st January, having received a shipment of new tanks, he unexpectedly riposted and drove the British back to Gazala, sweeping up the best part of the tank force which ineffectually sought to block his way. **This was of the true essence of tank warfare's** cut and thrust.

The overriding worry for the Germans as 1942 began seemed to be the looming threat of oil shortage as their increasingly mechanised armies used up tons of fuel in ever more mobile battles at the end of insufferably long lines of communication. Hitler laid down that the campaigns of 1942 must lead to the taking of the Caucasian oilfields, with the seizing of the far-distant Iraqi and Persian oilfields as a long-shot bonus. This was to compel the thrust into the Caucasus and the extension of flank protection to Stalingrad on the River Volga. It was to be the climax of Germany's tank power in aggression —yet experience was to show that so long as the Rumanian oilfields and synthetic plant were working for Germany she had sufficient for her needs.

The strain of fighting on the Eastern Front was to be maintained in defensive offensive battles throughout the winter of 1942, culminating in the rebuff of Russian armies in a spring campaign in which their tanks were used almost as unimaginatively as in the previous battles.

The curtain-raiser to the German summer offensive was the defeat of the Russian spring offensive after 12th May 1942 when a pincer movement, either side of Kharkov, was blunted after initial penetrations and then countered by a series of successful German pincer movements which cut the Russian forces into several small pieces. The Russians had an overall numerical superiority of 2 to 1 in tanks but, where the Germans chose to strike back, the ratio was reversed to 4·4 to 1 in the Germans favour. This was the measure of German tactical prowess and led to the destruction of the best part of a 1,200-strong Russian tank force—the Germans put the Russian losses at 14 armoured brigades out of 15 and took 240,000 prisoners.

The ratio of Russian to German tanks in 1942 was lower than it had been in 1941. Furthermore, during their drive into the Caucasus the Germans could frequently outnumber the Russians—in places by as much as 2 to 1, while employing just 3,000 tanks plus armoured self-propelled guns.

The decline in rates of advance continued. Fourth Panzer Army under General Hoth could manage only 250 miles between 28th June and 20th July (an average of 10·6 miles per day) even though the Russians were taken by surprise at the outset near Voronezh and pursued without restraint to Bogutschar.

The quality ratio remained much the same however, for while the Russians had far more of the superior T 34s and KV 1s the Germans had also improved their armoured striking power by introducing many of the more powerful PzKpfw IIIs and IVs besides up-gunned assault guns in quantity. Moreover the trained élite of the panzer force remained intact while Russian crew and commander quality deteriorated. **The Russian tank crews** were never to match their German opponents.

Tank forces, unlike the air forces, did not encourage the building of personal reputations into the "Ace System". If it was difficult to confirm a fighter pilot's real score it was well-nigh impossible to examine a tank crew's claims of kills registered. Fighter pilots frequently fought personal duels: tank crews were teams which only occasionally found themselves in individual combat against a solitary opponent. Often tank kills were the joint work of several tanks, anti-tank artillery, infantry and engineers. So when the German S.S. attempted to make heroes out of selected members of their private army—the Waffen S.S.—they did so at random and without sufficient knowledge to certify their claims. Thus the great names in tank history are the force commanders who dictated the shape of campaigns and battles.

All tank crews like front-line soldiers everywhere were heroes. Their deeds are numberless and perhaps typified by the stories of a German armoured car gunner at Arras on 21st May 1940. He impotently went on pumping 20 mm shot at a British Matilda even though both his vehicle and himself were on fire. And the British Matilda gunner who, a mile further off, was continuing to man his gun after a strike on the turret by an 88 had broken his arm. Then there was the Russian crew whose KV tank sat astride an important road for forty-eight hours defying all attempts by German tanks, anti-tank guns and even demolition parties to blow it up—the crew kept supplied with food by near-by partisans.

Valentines of the 11th Armoured Division being inspected by Winston Churchill in a Daimler Scout car. General Hobart sits beside the Prime Minister.

Yet the really important people were the commanders of battle-groups and tank formations who took or made their opportunities and, by skill in manœuvre, placed their tanks and guns in such a position that they either throttled the enemy or made him fight at a gross disadvantage.

The best tank leaders avoided head-on clashes and sought to fight as from an ambush. They used their armour to help their units reach key places in safety, unlike a knight of old who used it as a means to deflect blows in solo combat. Those who offered a stand-up fight suffered the heaviest losses, for the penetrative power of guns almost invariably maintained superiority over the resistance of armour at battle ranges.

Sturmgeschütz IIIs in action.

Effective battle ranges were higher in 1942 than 1941, having risen from 600 to 1,000 yd, making it possible for a single tank to cover a greater area of ground by fire, thus further raising the defensive quality of tanks.

The significant failures in 1942 on all sides continued to be tank breakdowns (rarely less than 30 per cent unserviceable) and supply breakdown. It was unusual for an advance to be sustained for much more than 300 miles without the need for a pause to repair tanks and restock supplies at the point of the spearhead. In the confines of Western Europe this had been relatively unimportant. In the depths of Russia it could be catastrophic since it gave the defender time in which to recuperate while avoiding utter defeat.

A fundamental German error was connected with their system of tank repair. At first it had been their policy, after a campaign, to withdraw tanks to Germany for over-haul. This worked well while campaigns were short in duration, but the long Russian war enforced improvisations in repair at the front—using an inadequate organisation. A notorious mistake once took place when spares for a certain type of tank in southern Russia were sent, by an oversight, to the northern front. This was by no means an isolated occurrence in the years 1941 and 1942.

In the year 1941 the Japanese, by striking in the Pacific at American, British and Dutch territory, brought themselves and the U.S.A. into the war.

The first action by U.S. tanks took place in the Philippines, but their counter-attack was a failure due to poor co-operation with infantry and good Japanese anti-tank measures.

Japanese Medium T 97 (Chi-Ha).

The emphasis of the war in the Far East was on maritime operations in which land forces mostly exploited initial amphibious landings. The Japanese used a relatively small number of obsolescent tanks—some in the van of a landing and all in the strict infantry support role.

There were no armoured divisions employed whole in the Far East even though the Japanese formed three tank divisions in 1942. In practice they were to be employed piecemeal.

The first major jungle war with tanks took place in scattered localities from Bataan to Malaya and the Dutch East Indies. Mostly the Allies used obsolete pre-war light tanks and armoured cars, though in Burma there was a brigade (7th Armoured) of British-manned Stuarts in action. In such close country the tanks could hardly operate far from the roads and tracks, hence they were easily ambushed and often cut off by parties of Japanese infantry with guns moving through the jungle to set up defended road-blocks in their rear. Thus the tanks fought without the initiative—a quite unnatural state for machines of aggresssion. By the time the Japanese had conquered Burma and pushed their island possessions as far south as New Guinea, by May 1942, there was nothing left of the Allied tank force which had begun the campaign in December 1941.

Lanchester Armoured Car Mark I of 1931 which was to see action in Malaya in 1941–42.

The small initial contribution the U.S.A. could make on land was to be offset by her production which was already rising fast in 1941. Like the other combatant nations by the end of 1942, it was turning out vast numbers of all kinds of machines.

World tank production in 1942 looked something like this, the bulk of the new machines leaving the factories in the second half of the year:

Germany	5,056—nowhere near peak but including self-propelled guns
Italy	700—falling from its 1941 peak of 1,500
Japan	500—below peak
Russia	24,500—rising to an annual peak over 30,000
U.S.A.	20,000—rising to a 1943 peak of 29,500
Britain	8,611—at peak

PART TWO—THE VEHICLES

It was a fundamental fact that the tanks which fought in the initial campaigns of the Second World War had to be the products of pre-war philosophy and financial parsimony. Therefore the first tank battles were tests of largely unconfirmed theory, the many failures to be laid at the door of false economies.

Yet it was a something of a paradox that, even after the Germans had proven the practicability of their theories in 1940, money for tank research and production remained either short or misdirected. In the case of the Axis Powers this was because priority was given still to aircraft production and because it was optimistically believed that the shooting war had been won. In the case of the British, after the French had been knocked out of the war, it was because they decided to concentrate entirely on the production of existing types in order to compensate for their alarming deficiency of tanks; they postponed the development of more powerful machines and thus forfeited what little technical lead they had.

The first practical deep-wading tank—Germany's special PzKpfw III with snorkel and float.

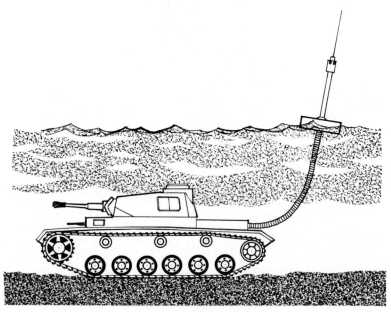

The first practical deep-wading tank was produced by the Germans early in 1940 when they sealed all joints in a PzKpfw III, connected the engine air-inlet to a floating buoy by a tube, and thus permitted the machine to travel submerged on its tracks. It took twenty minutes for the crew's air to run out, yet there was only one disaster. This vehicle was intended to lead troops ashore in the invasion of Britain but eventually was employed in the invasion of Russia, crossing the River Bug and River Dneiper.

Another vital infusion into German armoured forces during 1940 was their **first self-propelled anti-tank gun**, the PzJag (SdKfz 101)—a PzKpfw I aimed with a Czech-made 47 mm gun in a frontally facing, limited-traverse mounting. It was the forerunner of a prolific breed.

Winston Churchill and General Horrocks review tanks standing on a Covenanter.

A most unfortunate tank from the design point of view was the British Covenanter cruiser which reached armoured divisions in the summer of 1940. **It was one of the fastest medium tanks produced.** A complex steering system led to unreliability and a tendency, under certain conditions, to reverse steering —going left when the driver pulled the right stick. There was a lot of plumbing connecting the frontal radiator to the rear engine and other complications, too. This tank was relegated to training and never used in action, though 1,100 were built.

A highly successful tank, built in great numbers and possibly the largest variety, was the British Valentine—so named because its designs were accepted on St. Valentine's Day 1938. It was meant as an infantry support tank but also saw service in armoured divisions. As a tank it appeared in eleven different Marks of which 8,275 were built either in the United Kingdom or in Canada. Its armament was to rise from the 40 mm 2-pdr gun to one of 75 mm, its chassis' uses to vary from self-propelled anti-tank gun, self-propelled field artillery, mine-sweeper, swimming tank (DD), flame-thrower, bulldozer, command vehicle, bridgelayer, and mortar carrier. After the war it was converted into a rather poor agricultural tractor. Its engine was usually of the London bus type. It fought in North Africa, in Russia, Sicily, Italy, the South-west Pacific, Burma, Madagascar and from Normandy to the Baltic, in the armies of a great many nations.

Italian M 13/40s surround a Churchill Mark III knocked out at El Alamein. Only three Churchills were present at the battle.

The first Italian medium tank to go into action in Cyrenaica in June 1940 was the M 11/39—a poor fighting machine in all respects and notably because its 37 mm gun was mounted in the hull and thus restricted in traverse. It was to be replaced by the better M 13/40, with its 47 mm gun, in a fully rotating turret. Neither were good across country since their Vickers-type suspensions were poor and they were also under-powered. Such a machine as M 13/40 was never a match for its British opponents. Over 100 were taken at Beda Fomm, it never won a battle and was obsolete by 1942.

The heaviest tank built by the British was the 80 ton TOG—meaning *The Old Gang* in the persons of its promoters, the early tank design team headed by Wilson, Tritton and Ricardo. This monster, of which two experimental versions were produced, was to weigh as much as 80 tons and designed to cross shell-torn ground of the First World War type. It contained many novel features, but was basically at variance with the tactical requirements of its day. It also had difficulty in steering because its track length was too great in relation to its width. It was abandoned.

The most battleworthy heavy tank put into production by the British was the Churchill, begun by Harland and Wolff in 1940 as the A 20, produced off the drawing-board as the A 22 by the firm of Vauxhall (who had no previous experience of tank manufacture) and christened after the Prime Minister who was disturbed to have so unreliable a tank take his name. It first saw action with Canadian crews of the Calgary Regiment in the amphibious raid on Dieppe in August 1942. Eventually it was to be produced in fifteen different Marks, Marks VII and VIII representing a radical change in construction to all the others. It was to prove a robust tank which fought on many battle-fronts, last seeing combat during the Korean War in 1951. It was still in service with the Irish Army in 1967.

Churchill Mark I exiting from a Landing Craft Tank.

The most praiseworthy attempt to produce a balanced force of armoured fighting vehicles all at once was made by the U.S.A. in 1940 when, lacking modern weapons of any sort, they perforce had to build in quantity and haste. When they formed the Armored Corps in July 1940 they specified combat teams composed of certain basic vehicles:

A medium tank which, in 1940, was envisaged as a vehicle mounting a 75 mm gun in a rotating turret. Since this ideal could not be produced before 1942 an interim model was devised by packing the 75 in a side sponson of a modified existing experimental tank, called "T 5". The end product was the M 3 (called "General Lee" by the British and "General Grant" in modified form). Both tanks also had a 37 mm gun in a rotating turret. They were to receive their baptism of fire in North Africa in 1942 and act as a serious check to the Germans.

U.S. Combat team in Tunisia—left to right: M3 Light, M3 Half-track, M3 Medium.

A light tank, called "M 3" ("General Stuart" by the British who also nicknamed it "Honey") which was founded on pre-war designs and proved fast and highly reliable though outgunned with only a 37 mm weapon. **It first fought** in North Africa in November 1941 during Operation "Crusader", but was misused and outclassed as a battle-tank and soon relegated to its correct reconnaisance role. Throughout the war, and long after in six different Marks, it was to appear in nearly every theatre of war, finishing life in the British Army, as a turretless tractor for 17-pdr anti-tank guns.

Self-propelled field artillery, of which various types were engineered, the most famous being the M 7, based on the M 3 tank chassis and armed with a 105 mm piece. The British took it up, called it "Priest" and used it at El Alamein. They renamed it "Sexton" when armed with a 25-pdr gun.

An armoured infantry carrier which turned out the celebrated M 3 half-track (see page 97). It is in service to this day at its original task, with the Israeli Army among others.

The easiest type of armoured fighting vehicle to produce continued to be the armoured car because existing automobile production lines could be readily adapted to its manufacture. Every nation, less the Americans who were late in the field, acquired a large number—the Russians building on their pre-war

*Marmon-Herrington
Armoured Car Mark II—
note variety of armament
with 1 Vickers MG,
1 Boys anti-tank rifle and
2 Bren light machine-guns.*

models, the Germans doing the same, but starting to adapt existing models
to carry heavier guns, and the British making them more enthusiastically
than anybody else when invasion threatened in 1940 and the desert war
came to the boil in 1941. Chief among the wartime British designs into
service were the Humber (almost identical to the pre-war Guy Wheeled
Tank) and the Daimler. Of the latter 2,694 were eventually built. South
Africa also built 3,630 cars of the Marmon-Herrington type in eight
different Marks: their weight remained roughly between 6 and 10 tons
and speed about 50 mile/h, but their armament varied greatly from all
sorts of British weapons, such as the 2-pdr gun and the Boys anti-tank
rifle, to locally mounted captured Italian Breda 20 mm and German
37 mm guns. The components for these vehicles were imported from
America and assembled in South Africa. These cars all found extensive
employment across the excellent desert terrains of North Africa.

Germany's most useful tank
—a PzKpfw IV with the
longer 75 mm gun.

A typical German
adaptation—Marder III.

Hanomag. SdKfz 251/18
was an observation-post
version of the basic German
Second World War APC.

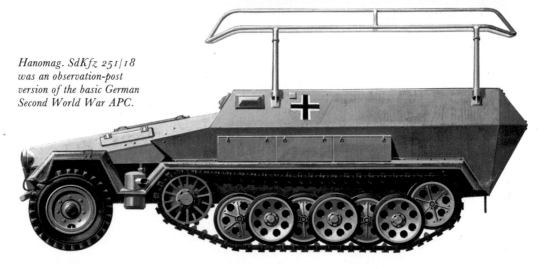

The most astonishing range of light armoured cars, appeared in Britain as the result of the invasion threat—such as the little Beaverettes (2,800 built and based on the Standard 14 hp motor chassis), the Humberette (based on the Humber Super Snipe car) and the Canadian Otter with its General Motors 104 hp engine. Few were really battleworthy and most reverted to airfield protection or to the Home Guard who, fortunately for them, had no need to use them in anger.

The first purpose-built German self-propelled assault gun was the Sturmgeschütz III of 1940 with its 75 mm L/24 gun. Devised primarily as an infantry support vehicle based upon the PzKpfw III chassis, it was to proliferate into a number of versions that were, increasingly, to assume a strong anti-tank role as well.

The first Canadian devised and built tank was to appear in 1941—the Ram I, a by-product of Canada's desire for national independence and a good amalgamation of the U.S. M 3 chassis with a Canadian-built turret housing a British 2-pdr gun. As a tank it was never to see action, though, in 1944, the hulls were to be used as armoured personnel carriers called, ironically, "Kangaroos".

A British Tetrarch entering a Hamilcar glider.

The first practical airborne tank—the British Tetrarch—was introduced into service in late 1940, but did not partake in an airborne operation until 6th June 1944 when seven were carried to Normandy in giant Hamilcar gliders. **They first saw action**, however, during the seaborne invasion of Madagascar in May 1942 and they were also to see service with the Russians.

The most extraordinary-looking fighting vehicle was the British Praying Mantis—an elevatable machine-gun post incorporated in a Universal Carrier chassis and intended as a means to fire over hedges and into upper-floor windows. The idea never progressed beyond experimental models.

One of the most attractive production cruiser tanks was the British Crusader which first saw action during Operation "Battleaxe" in June 1941. Its good looks and crisp engine note belied its incipient unreliability and the fact that it was on the verge of being outgunned as it entered service—and lacked the facility of being easy to up-gun. Given a 57 mm gun in mid-1942, its operational life as a tank was extended by another year, but thereafter it saw service only as a gun tower and, with a special turret, as an anti-aircraft tank with two 20 mm guns or one 40 mm.

The great revolution in tanks, which had taken place in Russia during the late 1930s, and which had gained them experience with heavy tanks as well as the light BTs, now became linked to inspired specifications and design, and led to the production of the KV (*Klim Voroshilov*) and T 34 tanks. Their soldier's demand for a vehicle that was proof against the 37 mm anti-tank gun, and armed with a dual-purpose gun, firing anti-tank and high-explosive projectiles, was answered by the heavy KV 1, which was resistant also to 50 mm shot. This tank, designed by Kotin, was needed for the assault on heavily defended localities and tried out against the Finns in December 1939 before going into production. It broke the Russian penchant for multi-turreted tanks because it gave better protection and mobility at reduced weight. An artillery version, the KV 2, was also produced, but this was a tactical monstrosity whose enormously tall turret presented far too big a target.

T 34/76 passing a knocked-out PzKpfw III.

The best tank ever built, in the opinion of many experts, was the Russian T 34—the brainchild of the team of Koshkin and Mozorove of the Tank Design Office. Incorporating the best features of a wide-tracked Christie suspension, a fine lightweight diesel engine (of Italian derivation), good sloping armour and the

76 mm gun, it was superior in some respects to the German tanks of 1941 since it could out-range them in every department. The fact that the Russian crews' ability was unworthy of it (and inhibited by the two-man turret) detracted nothing from the tank's virtue, which rested its many claims for excellence on the advantage of being robust, easy to operate and maintain. Nearly 45,000 of the principal Marks were made. It dominated the Eastern Front by sheer numbers and manœuvrability, acted as a model for the principal Russian tanks to this day and, in fact, is still in service with several armies.

The most effective weapons against these new Russian tanks were the new German 50 mm anti-tank gun, PAK 38, on its field mounting and the 88—although even the former could be defeated by the frontal armour of the KV at 500 yd. The 88 was fairly sure of killing a KV 1, however, at 1,000 yd and beyond.

A tank force in the doldrums was that of Japan which produced nothing of importance in the way of new vehicles during the Second World War. They experimented a little in 1941 with **their heaviest tank ever**, the 120-ton *Oi*, but during the opening phase of the war were more content to develop new light tanks and improve and up-gun the existing Type 97 Mediums. For example *Chi-He*, which appeared in 1940, had double the armour of the original *Chi-Ha*, a more powerful engine and a better gun, though of smaller calibre.

The most imaginative Japanese tanks were the amphibious kind, built in response to her maritime requirements. Type 2 *Kamisha* was a light version of 11 tons floating on detachable pontoons, fore and aft, and swimming in the water at a speed of 6 mile/h. The Navy experimented with a 26-ton heavy amphibious tank—*Kachisha*—while the Army also tried out *A-Igo* which was a light tank propelled by water-jets.

P40—Italy's last tank, which never reached full production.

Another tank force in the doldrums was Italy's which, throughout the war, failed to do better than modify its 13/40 design and tended rather to turn to Germany in the unfulfilled hope that they could buy or build German tanks. Projects such as these fell through, more through Italian industrial opposition than German intransigence. In the meantime the Italians produced Semovente M 42, a self-propelled gun with a 75 mm gun on the M 13 chassis, and P 40 which was to be the next generation of tank but which, when it appeared (only in prototype in 1943) was already far inferior to American and British tanks in service in 1942.

The gun/armour race began to hustle vehicle design as soon as the Germans came up against the Russians in 1941. The Germans at once up-gunned their PzKpfw III with a long 50 mm L/60 gun and their PzKpfw IV with the longer 75 mm L/43 gun. At the same time they practically doubled the thickness of the frontal armour and thus significantly increased weight, though without making compensating improvements to the power plant. Vehicle weight could be kept within manageable proportions, however, if the turret was discarded, and so several vehicles were developed as tank hunters by being given a high-velocity gun in a self-propelled mounting. Final examples of this were to be the Jagdpanzer IV of 1943 and 1944 when the successive L/48 and L/70 75 mm guns were mounted on the PzKpfw IV chassis with 80 mm of frontal armour. Another example of the German desire to increase the fire-power of light vehicles was the mounting of a short 75 mm gun (L/24) on the hull of the SdKfz 233 armoured car. Thus a whole vast range of fire-support vehicles came into being in addition to the conventional tank force which, in 1942, **actually declined in number and influence** as Hitler began to visualise turning from offensive to defensive warfare.

Self-propelled field artillery also began to appear in far greater quantity—the Germans leading in practice by mounting 105 mm and even larger calibre guns on PzKpfw II, and on different captured French chassis such as R 35 and Chenillette Lorraine.

The German Wasp—a 105 mm piece on a PzKpfw II carriage.

The practical crystallisation of armoured warfare seriously affected the Russian light tank force. Their latest T 60 and T 70s were never happy on the wide open steppes and were shot to pieces in the forests. Hence the chassis of T 70 followed the popular trend and became the vehicle for **the first practical Russian self-propelled gun**—the SU 76.

Serious trouble afflicted British tanks from 1941 onwards. Having fastened on the idea of using two types of tank—heavies for infantry support and mediums for armoured divisions—they virtually dismissed the concept of self-propelled artillery though converting a few Valentines into 25-pdr mountings called "Bishops". As the infantry-support Matildas and Valentines began to fall behind in the gun/armour race the Churchill was meant to take their place and in 1942 the Mark IV appeared with a 57 mm (6-pdr) gun. The successors to medium Crusader fell much further behind, however, because the breed, hard enough to adapt to the 57 mm, was impossible to convert as the carrier of a still larger weapon.

Lack of British foresight in 1940 projected a breed of medium tanks which would still be incapable of accepting guns larger than 75 mm. Meant to appear in 1942, but in fact delayed by specification, design and production difficulties until 1944, the new range of Cavalier, Centaur and Cromwell tanks came slowly into being. Only the latter, in fact, was ever considered fit for active service, while the others were relegated to training and subsidiary operational tasks.

One of the most versatile, perhaps one of **the most reliable** and certainly **the most prolific tank** ever made (49,000) was the American M 4 (called "General Sherman" by the British) in all its many Marks. It first appeared in action with British crews at the Battle of El Alamein in October 1942 and has been present in one form or another on the majority of tank battlefields ever since. Specified in the summer of 1940 as a fighting vehicle that had to be armour-proof against existing anti-tank guns and with a dual-purpose gun of 75 mm, a start had to await the building of manufacturing plant. Eventually built by Ford, Chrysler, General Motors and other companies, it was to evolve into over twenty different Marks before the end of the war. It became still further varied in the post-war years, using at least four different types of power plant (both petrol and diesel), acquiring another half-dozen or so different kinds of gun and proving adaptable to just about every conceivable battlefield role of armoured fighting vehicles. Among its many virtues were ease of production (whether with cast or welded hull and turret), simplicity of crew maintenance and the replacement of components. It was also **the first tank to be fitted with a gun stabilised in elevation**, though it has to be admitted that the Westinghouse device was anything but stable in action. Shot flew all over the place! The Sherman became the standard medium tank in the U.S., British and all Allied armies in 1943. The Americans, so keen to maintain mass production, deferred a successor (the T 20) and thus risked falling behind in the gun/armour race, though both they and the British undertook extensive up-gunning and armouring of Shermans in 1943.

The heaviest U.S. tank in production was their M 6, devised in 1940, prototype in 1941 (accepted the day after Pearl Harbor) and in limited production (forty made) in 1942. But the U.S. General Staff took the view that though this 56-ton tank was a match for anything then in existence, there were too many difficulties in shipping: they could transport two Shermans overseas for every M 6. So M 6 went into mothballs and never saw service. As time went on, Allied crews fought the Germans at a disadvantage.

SECTION V
The Era of Struggle, 1942–1945

PART ONE—FEATS & ACHIEVEMENTS

The most protracted tank battle, engaging the greatest number of machines yet employed, broke out at Gazala on 26th May 1942 when Rommel's Axis Panzer Army with 560 German and Italian tanks attacked the British Army with its 849 tanks. This battle was to rage in the vicinity of the Gazala Line until 20th June, shift to a quick siege and reduction of the British fortress of Tobruk on the 22nd, rush headlong in Axis pursuit of the British to Mersa Matruh on the 26th and arrive (both sides rather out of breath) at El Alamein on 1st July. There the British were able to stand within the confines of a narrow frontage, to rebuild their strength for a counter-attack. Close-locked battles for the Alamein position went on until the end of July. There occurred a constant succession of dramas throughout this great Axis advance of about 400 miles in thirty-six days (with intensive battle during much of the time).

(1) The crisis of 24th May when, for lack of water, Rommel, cut off by the British, was within twenty-four hours of abject surrender.

(2) The utter collapse of British armoured forces—138 tanks lost before midday on 13th June and only 75 fit for battle by that evening.

(3) The loss of Tobruk in twenty-four hours of battle.

(4) The premature British retreat from Mersa Matruh on 26th June even though the Axis had shot their bolt.

(5) The hopeless Axis struggle to overcome the British artillery defence of El Alamein—their fifty-odd tanks never up to the task even though British armour had been reduced, temporarily, to impotence.

THE DESERT WAR IN MAPS

1

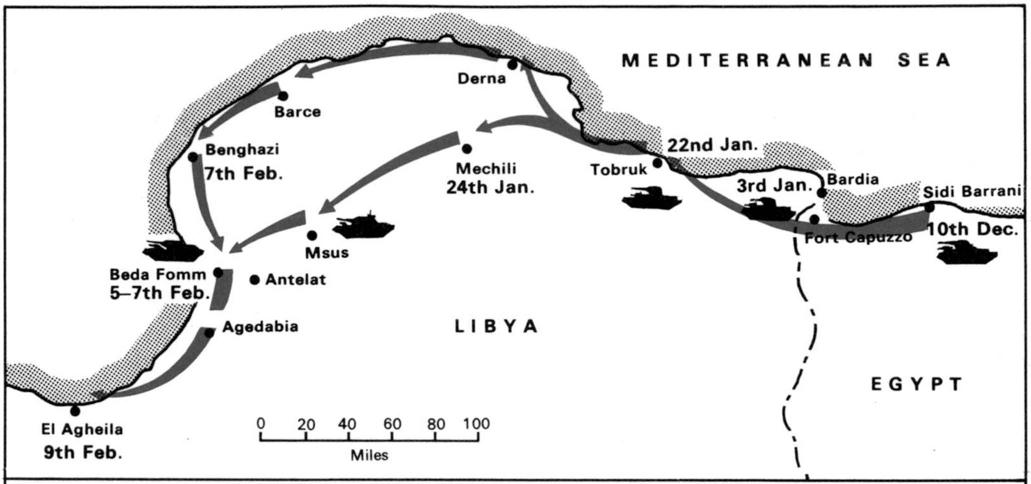

MEDITERRANEAN SEA

Derna

Barce

Benghazi
7th Feb.

Mechili
24th Jan.

22nd Jan.

Tobruk

3rd Jan.   Bardia

Sidi Barrani

Fort Capuzzo   10th Dec.

Msus

Beda Fomm
5–7th Feb.   ● Antelat

Agedabia   LIBYA

El Agheila
9th Feb.

EGYPT

| 0 | 20 | 40 | 60 | 80 | 100 |

Miles

2

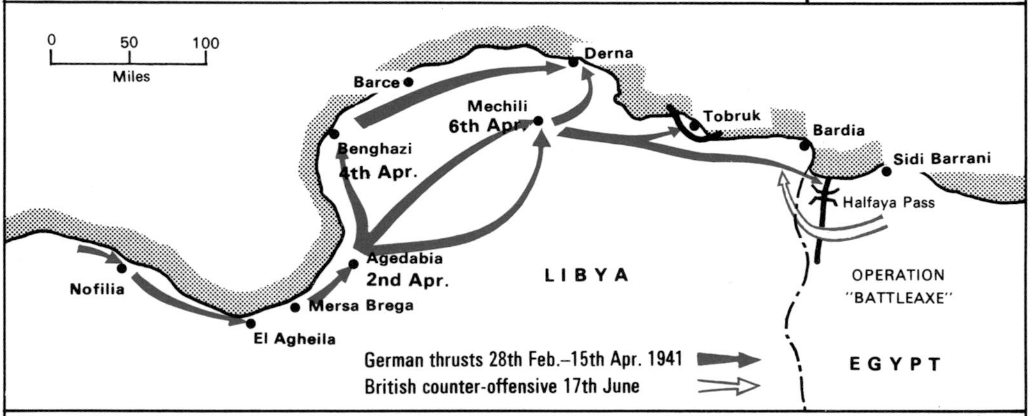

| 0 | 50 | 100 |

Miles

Derna

Barce ●

Mechili
6th Apr.   Tobruk

Benghazi
4th Apr.   Bardia

Sidi Barrani

Halfaya Pass

Agedabia
2nd Apr.   LIBYA

Nofilia   OPERATION
"BATTLEAXE"

Mersa Brega

El Agheila   EGYPT

German thrusts 28th Feb.–15th Apr. 1941
British counter-offensive 17th June

3

Derna

Barce
23rd Dec.

Mechili
18th Dec.   Tobruk

Benghazi
24th Dec.   Sidi Rezegh   Bardia

18th Nov.–
7th Dec.

Bir el Gubi ●   Halfaya
Pass

Msus   18th NOV.
OPERATION
CRUSADER
STARTS

LIBYA

Agedabia

Mersa Brega

El Agheila
6th Jan.

EGYPT

27th DEC.
AFRIKA KORPS
LOCAL
COUNTER-ATTACKS

| 0 | 25 | 50 |

Miles

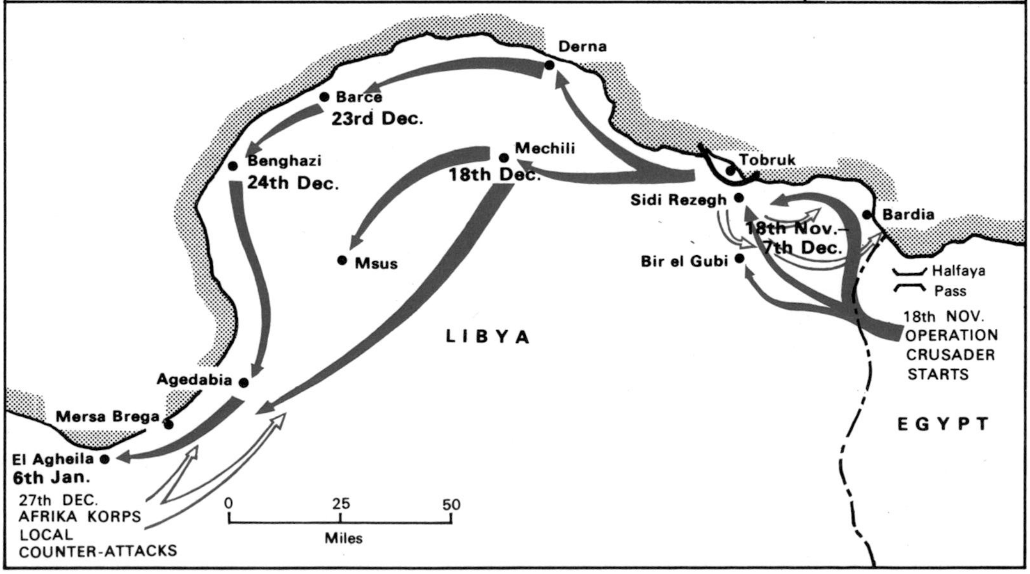

continued overleaf

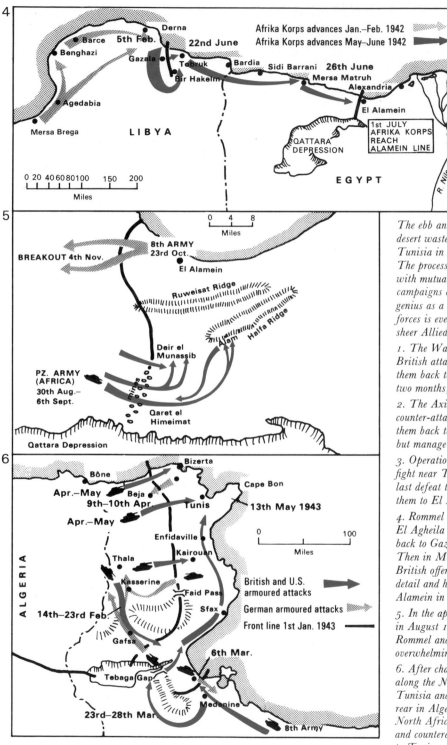

4

Afrika Korps advances Jan.–Feb. 1942
Afrika Korps advances May–June 1942

Derna
5th Feb.   22nd June
Barce
Benghazi
Gazala
Tobruk   Bardia   Sidi Barrani   26th June
Bir Hakeim   Mersa Matruh
Alexandria
Agedabia   El Alamein
Mersa Brega   LIBYA   1st JULY
AFRIKA KORPS
REACH
ALAMEIN LINE   CAIRO
QATTARA
DEPRESSION
EGYPT
R. Nile

0 20 40 60 80 100   150   200
Miles

5

0   4   8
Miles

BREAKOUT 4th Nov.   8th ARMY
23rd Oct.
El Alamein

Ruweisat Ridge

Alam   Halfa Ridge

Deir el
Munassib
PZ. ARMY
(AFRICA)
30th Aug.–
6th Sept.
Qaret el
Himeimat
Qattara Depression

6

Bizerta
Bône   Beja
Apr.–May   9th–10th Apr   Tunis   Cape Bon
Apr.–May   13th May 1943

Enfidaville
Thala   Kairouan   0   100
Kasserine   Miles
Faid Pass
Sfax   British and U.S.
armoured attacks
14th–23rd Feb.   German armoured attacks
Gafsa   Front line 1st Jan. 1943
6th Mar.
Tebaga Gap
Medenine
23rd–28th Mar.   8th Army

The ebb and flow of war in the desert wastes between Egypt and Tunisia in the years 1940 to 1943. The processes of cut and thrust with mutual exhaustion in campaigns dominated by Rommel's genius as a leader of armoured forces is eventually decided by sheer Allied numerical superiority.

1. The Wavell Offensive—the British attack the Italians, drive them back to El Agheila and in two months, destroy their army.

2. The Axis under General Rommel counter-attack the British, push them back to the Egyptian frontier but manage only to besiege Tobruk.

3. Operation Crusader: in a dog-fight near Tobruk the British at last defeat the Axis and pursue them to El Agheila

4. Rommel counter-attacks from El Agheila and drives the British back to Gazala in January 1942. Then in May he pre-empts a British offensive, defeats them in detail and herds them back to El Alamein in June.

5. In the approaches to El Alamein in August 1942, the British foil Rommel and then riposte with overwhelming success in October.

6. After chasing the Axis forces along the North African shore to Tunisia and landing in the Axis rear in Algeria, the last battles in North Africa are staged, by attack and counterattack, in the approaches to Tunis.

ALGERIA

*British version of U.S.
Medium M3—the General
Grant.*

The most important tactical event of the desert war was the clogging of the battlefield by enormous minefields which greatly hampered the mobility of armoured vehicles, slowed down offensive operations and enforced laborious mine-clearing operations, including the development of mine-sweeping tanks. Some idea of vehicle casualties can be gained in the knowledge that one in five of all tanks damaged were mined—a figure which could rise as high as one in three during attacks amid heavily defended localities.

The most significant tank event of 1942 was the revival of Russian tank production (once their new factories had started up east of the battle-zone), and the re-formation of their armoured forces beginning in the summer. Under their new chief, General Fedyunenko, the Russian Armoured Forces were formed into tank armies made up of tank and mechanised corps—a tank corps consisting of two armoured and one mechanised division, a mechanised corps being in reverse order of composition to a tank corps. In numbers each corps was about equal in strength of a British, U.S. or German division. The Tank Corps were intended to break the enemy front in mass, the Mechanised Corps to pursue to a depth of 25 to 30 miles in self-contained operations of 72 to 96 hours' duration. Whereas the tank units of 1941 had included several different types of tank they now specialised in one type only—to the great enhancement of crew training.

The first major operational test of the new Russian organisation came at Stalingrad on 19th November when Russian pincers under General Zhukov closed round the German Sixth Army located in the environs of Stalingrad—894 Russian against 675 German tanks. The resultant battle, which included fierce German attempts to break through the Russian ring and raise the siege of Sixth Army, went on until 31st January 1943. This was the **first major defeat inflicted on the German Army in the Second World War.**

Zhukov

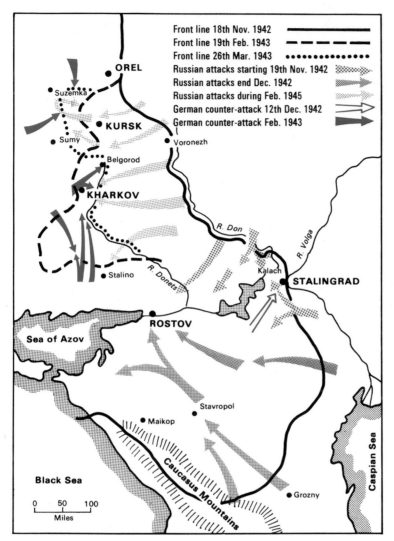

Front line 18th Nov. 1942   ━━━━━━
Front line 19th Feb. 1943   ━ ━ ━ ━
Front line 26th Mar. 1943   ●●●●●●●●●●●
Russian attacks starting 19th Nov. 1942
Russian attacks end Dec. 1942
Russian attacks during Feb. 1945
German counter-attack 12th Dec. 1942
German counter-attack Feb. 1943

The Caucasus Campaign of 1942–43—the Russian armoured riposte under Zhukov cuts off the Germans at Stalingrad in December, and then pours westwards until it runs out of energy beyond Kharkov in February. Then comes the German counter-stroke under Manstein to nip off the Russian spearheads and restore the position.

Stalingrad was to highlight the temporary bankruptcy of the German armoured forces. By the time the Russians had driven them out of the Caucasus, back to the River Donets, the panzer divisions were **at their all-time low** of an average twenty-seven tanks each. At this moment the true meaning of the gun/armour race came home to the Germans, for even though better Russian tanks had yet to appear their first self-propelled guns were in service in January 1943 and making their killing power felt.

A fantastic revival of the Panzer Force began in February 1943. New tanks with better armour and guns had been placed on order in 1941. The up-gunned PzKpfw IIIs and IVs which had appeared in early 1942 had been followed by the first Tiger Is in September that year. Soon the first Panthers would come into service, though they were somewhat more unreliable than the Tigers. Self-propelled guns were coming forward too, in far greater quantities and with ever better guns.

German Pz III with British prisoners, Tunisia, 1942.

The most inspiring event for the German tank men was Hitler's recall of General Guderian to become Inspector-General of Armoured Troops on 1st March 1943, with sweeping powers over all such forces, less the artillery-manned S.P. guns. He was to revive the courage and faith of his men just when General Manstein was in the process of turning the tables on the exhausted Russian tank forces at the Battle of Kharkov at the end of March.

Manstein

German PzKpfw 38 t leaving an Armoured Railway Train.

The second overwhelming defeat of the Germans took place in North Africa. Rebuffed at the Battle of Alam Halfa in his final attempt to break through to the Suez Canal, Rommel was himself heavily defeated at El Alamein by the British under General Montgomery at the end of October. Chased for more than 1,500 miles to the Tunisian frontier, it was the Axis Panzer Army which lay in tatters by the end of January 1943, its retreat into Europe seriously threatened by the Anglo-American landings in Algeria which now moved towards the vital ports of Bizerta and Tunis in Rommel's rear.

Yet a great Axis revival threatened when a reinforced tank corps struck the U.S. 1st Armored Division at Faid and rolled it back in confusion and with heavy losses, to Kasserine in mid-February—the battle ending as a draw only when Anglo-American tanks and guns held fast in the vicinity of Thala.

The final defeat of the Axis was then inevitable. Well over 2,000 Allied tanks backed by many hundreds of guns, overwhelmed little more than 100 Axis tanks. The number of prisoners taken may well have been greater than at Stalingrad and the loss of so expert a panzer élite was **an almost irreparable** blow to the German chances of revival.

The most dramatic rise in German A.F.V. production took place after 1942—in which year it had already risen to 5,096. In 1943 it was 9,372 and in 1944 (despite heavy bombing of the homeland) 17,843—but this could never compensate for the loss of élite crews, since their under-trained replacements incurred still heavier losses due to a decline in skill.

The most decisive tank battles of 1943 were those won by anti-tank forces. While mines cluttered every battlefield and canalised the movement of armoured vehicles, the increased power and range of anti-tank guns, whether vehicle or ground mounted, compelled tanks to fight at a tactical disadvantage until mechanical attrition had worn down one side or the other.

The greatest tank battle of all, at Kursk in July 1943 when over 6,000 Russian and German machines clashed, was decided by guns in defence decimating tanks on the attack. When the German tanks made their initial advance they were hammered by an entrenched anti-tank defence: when the Russians counter-attacked the German guns ruined the Russian tanks.

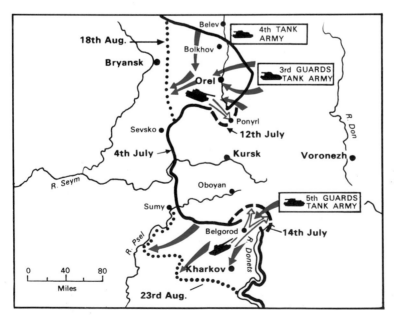

The great tank battle of Kursk in July 1943. The Germans attempt a double pincer at the base of the Russian salient and are held by a well-informed and prepared opponent. Then, the Russians attack in mass and after incurring heavy losses sweep away the worn-out Germans.

The latest anti-tank weapon, said by some Germans to have been used with telling effect, was
cannon-armed aircraft attacking from low level. The most celebrated
German anti-tank ace, Major Hans-Ulrich Rudel, eventually claimed to
have destroyed 519 Russian armoured vehicles in the course of the war—
but it must be said that such claims were unsubstantiated while post-
battle examination of claims by anti-tank pilots, in other theatres of war,
were to reveal gross (and quite unintended) over-estimates.

The first attempts at air anti-tank action had, in fact, been made by the Germans in 1917 at
Cambrai, by the Russians in 1941 and by the British in the desert in 1942.
Never were the actual results very sensational, apart from severely
frightening the tanks' crews.

One of the biggest night tank battles took place after the German rebuff at Kursk when Russian
tanks tried and failed to break the Germans near Kharkov. It followed a
day-time battle, in which 143 German A.F.V.s had destroyed 184 T 34s,
and took the form of a Russian charge to the mouths of the German guns
in the dark. Tank rammed tank, the whole bizarre scene illuminated by
flares and burning buildings and vehicles.

German armour in trouble—PzKpfw IIIs.

The vital controlling factor in tank advances, besides actual losses in combat, continued to be
vehicular reliability and the efficiency of supply organisations. The
following comparative table gives the state of change on the Eastern Front
between 1941 and 1943:

		Tanks engaged	Aircraft engaged	Rate of advance (miles per day)	Distance advanced (miles)	Normal range of tank engagements (metres)
1941	German	3,940	3,000	16·5	413	500
	Russian	8,000	12,000	N.A.	N.A.	400
1943	German	2,100	2,000	N.A.	N.A.	1,000
	Russian	2,400	2,850	6·5	105	1,000

The first British attempt at amphibious tank warfare took place in August 1942 when a squadron of Canadian-manned Churchills landed but was totally destroyed on the beaches at Dieppe.

The first successful landing with U.S. tanks took place in North Africa between Oran and Algiers in November 1942. This was Operation "Torch", a landing opposed only by a few obsolete French tanks.

The first successful Allied tank landing took place in July 1943 on Sicily and led to the quick conquest of the island. The experience of Dieppe, North Africa and Sicily was to be consolidated for the later landings in September in Italy (at Messina and Salerno) and in January 1944 at Anzio. But always tanks came ashore after the first infantry assault wave since they were embarked on ships and could only wade instead of swim on their own.

The most massive build-up of armour of the entire war took place in Britain prior to the invasion of Normandy on 6th June 1944. It is probable that something in the order of 6,000 tanks plus a horde of self-propelled guns and armoured personnel carriers were mounted in readiness for the assault, and behind these, from the factories and the U.S.A., there stood an inexhaustible reserve. Against them the Germans might produce 1,500 or more, depending upon the demands of the Eastern and Southern fronts and the ability of the internal transport system (itself under constant air and guerilla attack) to get them there.

Armour clutters the Normandy beaches on 6th June 1944.

The first specialised armoured division, a force designed to hold and train the crews of swimming, mine-sweeping, engineer and flame-throwing tanks, was included in the Allied order of battle with the purpose of breaching the concrete and steel embattlements of Hitler's Atlantic Wall. This was the 79th Armoured Division under General Hobart whose armour was to land in the forefront of the assault, dominate the enemy guns and clear pathways for the entire invading force to follow. Its success on 6th June was decisive. Only where specialised armour failed—notably in the U.S. Army's Omaha Beach— were there heavy casualties.

Churchill with Bobbin. The carpet laid on the beach helped other vehicles ashore across soft going.

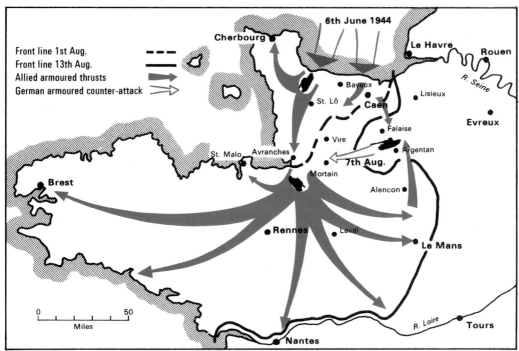

The outward explosion of Anglo-American armour from the Normandy beach-head in summer, 1944. Having built up their strength and worn down the German Army in close combat, the tank deluges pour forth, hardly checked by the ineffectual German counter-attack at Mortain. Within a few weeks the advance was to free most of Western Europe.

Many enormous tank battles were to take place throughout June, July and August in Normandy. The most concentrated in terms of tanks per acre was the British Operation "Goodwood" south of Caen on 18th July when nearly 2,000 assorted A.F.V.s from both sides clashed in an area measuring 8,000 yards square. The British were to lose over 300 machines in three days' fighting.

The most far-reaching, since it opened up the entire campaign and began the destruction of the main German Army with a pursuit to the German frontier, was the U.S. breakout battle, Operation "Cobra", which began on 25th July and started six U.S. armoured divisions, joined by three British, a Canadian, a French and a Polish, flooding through France and Belgium.

An important innovation in the tank versus infantry battle was the appearance, in ever greater numbers, of small, hand-held, hollow-charge, "bazooka"-type infantry anti-tank weapons. The Americans had first used these short-range weapons in North Africa in November 1942. Now the Germans had them in quantity and were making good use of them in the close hedgerows of Normandy. An unusual adventure was that of a British Churchill which, hit and penetrated through the thickest frontal turret armour, had all its hatches opened by blast and the fighting compartment filled by fumes. But to the crew's astonishment nobody was hurt, the tank failed to catch fire—so they closed the hatches and went on fighting.

The most exciting races in short-range tank fighting took place during some chance encounter—when competing gunners endeavoured to traverse faster on to target than each other in order to get in the first fatal shot.

The sheer enormity of Allied tank strengths now became apparent, for in July and August the combined number of Allied tanks operating offensively on the three main battle-fronts amounted to over 20,000 machines, machines which were infinitely more powerful than those which had gone to war four years previously. Included in this horde, as it closed in from all sides upon Germany, were great numbers of self-propelled guns which, used skilfully to make best use of their guns with least exposure of their (usually) thin, side-armour, made some memorable kills.

The first U.S. Congressional Medal of Honour to be won by a tankman in this war was gained by Second Lieutenant Raymond Zussman of the 756th Tank Battalion at Noroy-le-Bourg in France on 12th September 1944. After his own tank had bogged down he dismounted and from then on walked ahead of his other tanks, seeking enemy targets and then directing fire upon them— even though under fire himself at 50 yd range. Repeatedly he sought the enemy at the closest possible range and nailed them down, finishing with a score of eighteen killed and ninety-two captured.

The most celebrated example of German tank commanding was the action by Lieutenant Michel Wittman of 501st S.S. Heavy Tank Battalion near Villers-Bocage in France on 13th June 1944. In his Tiger I he came upon the advance guard of British 7th Armoured Division in a sunken road. Picking his shots he killed the leading and tail vehicle in the British column, thus blocking their escape. Then he engaged the rest in turn, destroying twenty-five vehicles as he was joined by the rest of his company in an orgy of destruction that finally put paid to a complete squadron of Cromwells plus motorised infantry.

Daimler armoured car Mark II (foreground) with a Conqueror looming in the distance.

Gun flash from the 57 mm (6-pdr) gun of a Crusader III.

Jagdpanzer IV with L/48 75 mm gun.

Tiger I with schnorkel for deep wading erect. The little half-track motor-cycle was made by NSU and had a 36 hp Opel Olympia engine.

Great competition motivated the Allied tank forces as they raced from Normandy to the German frontier. Typical are the following rates of advance:

Patton

(1) First U.S. Army under General Hodges 140 miles in 7 days, average 20 miles per day.

(2) Third U.S. Army under General Patton 220 miles in 15 days, average 14·6 miles per day.

(3) Second British Army under General Dempsey 200 miles in 3 days, average 66·6 miles per day.

But such figures are not truly comparative of performance since they stem from different circumstances, times and places.

The most shattering blow to the Germans came with the failure of their panzer divisions to break the American spearhead at Mortain (due more to the superior fighting quality of the American soldier than the impact of air attacks on German tanks), and with the encirclement of their army at Falaise, bringing the loss of men and machines to gigantic proportions. Yet the Germans collected themselves and went on fighting as they reassembled fresh tank forces behind the old Siegfried Line protecting the Fatherland.

The last battles on the German frontiers are memorable for the skill of outnumbered German tank crews despite insuperable odds. Outnumbered on the ground, desperately short of fuel and using tanks that were often terribly unreliable due to too short a development time or production difficulties, they always managed to maintain the shreds of manœuvrability which gave them a fighting chance in battle. Hence their opponents always had to treat them with respect. A single Tiger could hamstring a whole squadron in the open, let alone in a sunken road.

Royal Tigers at range practice.

The penultimate panzer offensive took place in the Ardennes in December 1944 in a futile effort to break through to Antwerp and cut off the Allies in Belgium and Holland. It failed of its own meagre strength and, best reason of all, because German petrol production had been cut to a trickle and the tanks were on half-fuel rations.

The final panzer offensive took place in January and February 1945 when they turned east to counter the Russian invasion of Hungary, to try save the last remaining oilfields as German fuel supplies ran out. This, too, was defeated by overwhelming odds. From now on each battlefield became cluttered as much by abandoned German tanks as those knocked out in action.

Before abandonment became the rule, however, a fair estimate of the reasons for most tanks being knocked out was as follows:

(1) Armour-piercing shot: 40 per cent.
(2) Hollow charge: 25 per cent.
(3) Mines: 16 per cent.
(4) High explosive: 8 per cent.
(5) Air attack: 6 per cent (much lower than claims at the time due to the inaccuracy of the rockets and bombs employed).
(6) Abandonment: 5 per cent.

The majority of hits were scored on tanks' frontal plates, and of these more than half achieved penetration. However, of those tanks hit and ignited the great majority of fires were caused by ammunition catching light rather than fuel. Meanwhile, of those who were in tanks at the time they were knocked out, by one means or another, about half became casualties inside and the rest after they had left the vehicle, being caught by hostile fire in the open. Yet the average loss to every five-man-crewed vehicle knocked out was the proportion of about one killed to a little under two wounded.

In the final collapse of Germany the country was wholly overrun by the thousands of Russian, American, French and British tanks with their accompanying armoured infantry and artillery, shielded by a cloud of aircraft which constantly hunted what few German armoured vehicles remained.

The first crossing of the River Rhine was made when 9th U.S. Armored Division seized the Remagen Bridge by surprise on 7th March 1945.

The greatest river crossing led by armoured forces took place on 23rd March when Anglo-American amphibious tanks went over the Rhine by night between Rees and Dinslaken. As it happened, on 22nd March, General Patton's Third Army had already crossed the river further up its course where it was narrower.

U.S. All Arms Combat Team—left to right: Shermans, Greyhound armoured car, Sherman, M 10 tank destroyer.

The last major river crossing was of the Elbe on 29th April, when Anglo-American amphibious armoured forces were again in the lead. This was the forerunner of the last armoured drives in the war. The Allies in the West struck eastward in the direction of Berlin, and also towards Czechoslovakia and Denmark, while Russian forces moved to join them and also to crush what remained of the German forces in and around Berlin.

The last shots in this, the greatest tank war, died away on 15th May 1945.

Many of the tank leaders who were in top command at the end of the war had started quite low down the rank ladder at the outbreak. Patton was merely a colonel in 1940, but rose rapidly by way of commanding a division, a corps and then an army— all formations which he made fully dependent on armoured vehicles. Von Manteuffel, on the German side, began the war as a battalion commander and finished it commanding a panzer army against the Russians. Comparisons are invidious and there are many more men whose promotion in the whirlwind of war were equally rapid—one can think of men who were corporals in 1939 and who finished as squadron commanders in 1945. For sheer consistency of steady promotion, through a series of highly responsible appointments (all associated with armour) that of Major-General G. P. B. Roberts in the British Army is supreme.

G. P. B. Roberts (known as "Pip") was a captain and adjutant of a tank battalion in the Western Desert in 1939. During the 1940–41 offensive he was Brigade Major of an armoured brigade and was later to command a squadron of tanks, then a battalion early in 1942 and a brigade at Alam Halfa in August 1942—a command he held until the end of the campaign in North Africa, though changing from one formation to another. Finally he was appointed as commander of an armoured division for the Normandy invasion and in this capacity was at the head of nearly every major British advance from Normandy to the Baltic. Before leaving the Army after the war, to join a biscuit-manufacturing firm, he became Director of the Royal Armoured Corps.

Shermans in a cornfield. Second from right is a Firefly with 76·2 mm gun.

The last battles in the Far East, in the meantime, were coming to their climax with the great American amphibious assaults on the islands surrounding Japan (every assault with amphibious armour in the van) and the British retaking of Burma.

The last great Russian tank invasion took place in Manchuria in August 1945, after they had declared war on the Japanese. Here a force of 5,500 Russian tanks, each one of which was technically superior to the 1,000 obsolescent Japanese machines standing in their way, travelled 500 miles in 13 days in what amounted to little more than an exercise in logistic support, so ineffectual was the opposition. This was a sign that the Russians had thoroughly mastered tank logistics, for they managed to achieve their conquest without serious hold-up, using air supply when other methods seemed likely to fail—the entire operation a copy-book example of pursuit with meticulous planning based on vast experience.

PART TWO—THE VEHICLES

The first of the operational big-gun tanks made their appearance in 1942, and the way was led by Germany even though the impulse to build them was inspired by Russian superiority.

The first genuine big-gun tank to go into action was the German Tiger I with its 88 mm gun and thick 110 mm of armour on a machine weighing 56 tons. The heavy tank, first mooted in 1939 by the Germans had been postponed by them in development in the hope that they could win the war without resort to such expensive and clumsy equipment. But the advent of the superior Russian tanks compelled a crash programme of new tank construction, calling for machines that were both much more heavily armed and armoured. Given the go-ahead in July 1941, the firms of Henschel and Porsche competed to produce an acceptable design in the quickest possible time. Henschel won the race and the contract, and the first Tigers were sent on a disastrous battlefield trial to the Leningrad front in September 1942. It was many months before this tank was rid of all its teething troubles. Nevertheless its combination of gun and armour made it supreme where it stood—a domineering weapon which compelled its opponents to stop and think once its presence was spotted. Incidentally, Tiger was also **the first production tank capable of wading underwater** using a built-in Schnorkel device.

The first big self-propelled gun—earlier called "Ferdinand", changed later to "Elephant", but properly named Jagdpanzer Tiger (P) was an offshoot of the failed Porsche Tiger project. They were ready for action by June 1943 and saw their baptism of fire at the Battle of Kursk where they proved too clumsy to survive for long against the more highly mobile Russian forces which took them in flank and rear. Only ninety Elephants were built.

The last German attempt at building a light tank was the Lynx (PzKpfw II L). One hundred were made in 1942.

Panther D. Germany's answer to the T 34.

The best German tank, in the opinion of many experts, was the 43-ton Panther which first saw action in 1943 at Kursk. It, too, came into being as the result of panic measures following the appearance of the Russian T 34. This tank, with its well-arranged armour plate (including a beautifully sloped 80 mm glacis plate derived from T 34) and its excellent, long 75 mm L/70 gun was to become the backbone of the panzer divisions as the PzKpfw IIIs and IVs were phased out of service—though the latter never entirely disappeared.

The rational response by the Allies to the German increases in fighting power could come only from a similar process of up-scaling. In 1942 the Americans had developed their 76 mm anti-tank gun and the British their 76·2 mm (17 pdr), while the Russians were well advanced with their 85 mm. But whereas the Russians were ready to fit the 85 mm into a redesigned T 34—the greatly improved T 34/85—the Americans were chiefly concerned to build the 76 mm into their M 10 Tank Destroyer (with its thin armour and open turret) while the British thought mainly of fielding their 76·2 mm on a wheeled carriage or in the hopelessly clumsy Challenger. The latter was merely a lengthened Cromwell with a tall turret that reached service in small numbers in 1944 and was most unpopular with its crews.

Cromwells of the British Guards Armoured Division.

The falling from grace of the British was symbolised by the Cromwell tank which arrived into service early in 1944, some two years too late to be evenly matched with the new German tanks. Fast it might be, but its 101 mm of vertical frontal armour was of little protection against the long 75s and 88s of the Panthers and Tigers when it had to close the range to strike home with its own puny, short 75 mm. Yet the Cromwell, which equipped six British armoured regiments for the invasion of Europe, had the saving grace of reliability which was to stand it in good stead when the pursuit of the beaten German Army began. On the road to the German frontier it passed many a broken-down Panther and Tiger.

The real saving grace for the British was the mounting of their 76·2 mm in the American M 10 (Achilles) and in the Valentine S.P. (Archer) and, above all, in a modified Sherman V, called "Firefly". The latter was achieved by modifying the turret bustle and making the front-gunner redundant in order to give room for the much larger ammunition. Introduced into service against the advice of the pundits (who at first thought it technically unfeasible) the few made available to supplement the underarmed Shermans in Normandy gave British armour a fighting chance against the German tanks. Firefly's gun could penetrate most German armour at battle-ranges even if the Sherman's armour was quite inadequate against the German guns. The British gave the Americans 300 at the end of 1944 because the U.S. 76 mm gun was so poor.

Russian SU 85 carrying infantry to the attack.

The first big-gun Russian armoured vehicles were the heavy self-propelled artillery pieces that appeared under the nomenclature SU (*Samakhodnaya Ustanovka*). In 1943 Kotin designed the SU 152 which was a 152 mm howitzer mounted frontally in a KV chassis. It first saw action in the Kursk battle that July. It was followed in August by SU 85 (with a T 34 chassis), but this gun (the same as that being mounted on the T 34) was primarily an anti-tank piece as opposed to the 152 which was medium artillery. Hence SU 85 was the first all-Russian equivalent of the German Jagdpanzers.

The first improvements on the early Russian SUs were soon to appear in 1944. On the KV chassis was to be mounted the 122 mm high-velocity gun, SU 122; to improve on SU 85 was to come SU 100 with the new 100 mm gun. Thus the Russians raced neck and neck with the Germans who at this time were also producing ever more powerful self-propelled guns of their own in addition to their new tanks.

The most stagnant backwater in new tank design was to be found in the Far East. The Japanese did little more than flirt with improvements to their basic Type 97, though in 1943, a step forward was taken in the production of *Chi-nu* with its medium-velocity 75 mm gun. This was in response to the American M 4s, but not by any means a solution of the inherent problem of American numerical or qualitative superiority. Japanese mass production could never match that of her opponents, while shortage of basic materials was a constant handicap.

An enormous number of experimental projects appeared in Japan, some conventional gun-tanks like the *Chi-to* and some self-propelled guns such as the 75 mm and 150 mm howitzer versions of *Chi-ha*. Light tanks also abounded and were suited to the terrain in which they fought. But in a stand-up fight they were death-traps.

The first Australian attempt to produce a home-built tank—the Sentinel—made erratic progress as the Japanese threat of invasion got closer. It was intended to build a sort of hybrid tank out of American transmission and tracks, three Perrier Cadillac engines, locally cast hull and turret and British armament. The 2-pdr gun was mounted in Mark I, but in Mark III there was the 25-pdr (there was no production Mark II) and in Mark IV the 17-pdr (76·2 mm). No Sentinels ever saw action.

Valentine with Scorpion flail mine-sweeping device.

The first mine-sweeping flail tank was produced by the British in Egypt by local manufacture as the result of an urgent demand for means to clear gaps through minefields while the men remained under armoured protection. A South African engineer called du Toit improvised a rotating drum with heavy chains driven by two Ford V-8 engines and mounted on a Matilda hull. This was called "Baron". Later from England would come an adaptable kit called "Scorpion" which could be attached to almost any tank. It was used by the British on the Valentine chassis and by the Americans on the Sherman. The Barons were first used during the Battle of El Alamein and were of little use but, subsequently, flail tanks were to be a most effective mine-clearing device and, to a certain extent, remain so to this day—though no army is equipped with them.

The next generation of Allied armoured cars began to enter service in 1943 and 1944. In addition to improvements to the early Humber—Mark IV, for instance, with its 37 mm gun—there came several heavy models. There were the experimental eight-wheeled South African Marmon Herrington Mark VI with the 57 mm gun, the vast American Boarhound (T 18 E2 built to British specification) weighing 23·6 tons and capable of 50 mile/h on the road—perhaps **the most formidable-looking and certainly the heaviest armoured car** ever made—even if it was by no means the most effective and never reached production. There was also the 11·5-ton British Coventry with a 40 mm gun that entered production as the war was ending. The contract was cancelled, though several were built and sold to the French.

Staghound—a highly sophisticated armoured car. with automatic gearbox and gun-stabilizer.

First among armoured cars to have both a stabilised gun and an automatic gearbox was the American T 17 E1 (called "Staghound" by the British). It was used by several armies from 1943 onward, had twin engines, powered steering and turret traverse. But it suffered the tactical disadvantage of no high-speed reverse—a most desirable quality in all armoured cars since their survival depends above all else on evasion by quick retreat.

Largest of the British-built armoured cars was the A.E.C. "Matador", the Mark I armed with a 2-pdr gun and driven by a 105 hp diesel engine. This 11-ton machine had quite a good cross-country performance but took up a lot of room on the roads. In fact it was too cumbersome for reconnaissance work—its role was close support to lighter cars. As Mark II it was armed with a 57 mm gun; Mark III with its 75 mm gun was later to see service well into the 1950s. It also equipped Yugoslavian partisans in 1944.

Russia's answer to the Tiger—the JS II.

The more powerful Russian tanks to reach fighting units before the war came to an end were, in addition to the T 34/85, the new heavies—KV 85 in August 1943 (a KV chassis with a more powerful engine and a cast turret similar to that on T 34/85); JS (Josef Stalin) I which appeared in 1944, a greatly improved KV armed with the 122 mm gun; and then the JS II in late 1944 with a reshaped hull that gave even better protection than did the JS Is. Finally there arrived, in January 1945, the JS III with its tortoise-shaped hull—called "Pike" by the Russians because of its pointed nose plates. There is some doubt whether this tank ever got into action during the Second World War though it has since been in action with the Egyptian Army.

A key to battlefield supremacy in the latter stages of the war, was mechanised artillery, which played an ever expanding role. The Germans modified many old chassis and, besides their own, adapted those of the French and the Czechs to take field guns. There was, for instance, the French Lorraine Schlepper with its Krupp 150 mm gun (of 1917 vintage) and the Wasp—a 105 mm howitzer mounted on a PzKpfw II chassis. The Americans mounted their 155 mm howitzer externally on the Sherman chassis. Thus enabled by tracks, artillery could keep up with a cross-country tank advance and come quicker into and out of action than if it was tractor drawn.

The greatest upsurge in modified vehicles occurred, however, as a result of the demand for armoured vehicles for special tasks. Largely as a result of the need to overcome fixed fortifications—notably the celebrated German Atlantic Wall—all kinds of specialised armour was developed:

Swimming tanks on the Duplex Drive (D.D.) system (invented by Nicolas Straussler) whereby power to the propellers was carried from the main engine, and flotation achieved by surrounding the tank's hull with a collapsible canvas screen which displaced enough water to carry the tank's weight. With the screen down the tank could fire its gun as usual. The Tetrarch D.D. was used as a trial model, then the Valentine D.D. was intended for operational purposes but, in the event, it was the ubiquitous Sherman D.D. which led the way ashore in Normandy on 6th June 1944. The Americans also introduced a special floating, armed carrier called L.V.T. (Landing Vehicle Tracked, originally devised in peacetime for flood rescue), which they first used in North Africa and extensively in the Pacific at Guadalcanal and during the series of island stepping-stone invasions on the way to Japan. L.V.T. 4, was given the name "Buffalo" by the British, who used it in landings near Antwerp in 1944 and to cross the Rivers Rhine and Elbe in 1945.

Sherman DD with screens lowered after swimming ashore in France, 1944.

Detail of a DD propeller on Valentine tank.

Jagdpanzer Tiger (P)
Elephant.

Street battle—a Sherman in action. The artist, a Hungarian called Markos Ludwig, had no tank experience but painted this scene to the directions of officers of the 4th Royal Tank Regiment and by studying photographs and models.

Maus. The heaviest tank ever.

The British Archer—a 76·2 mm (17-pdr) gun pointing over the engine decks.

Successors to the Sherman. The U.S.A.s M 46 (Patton) and M 26 (Pershing) medium tanks.

Mine-sweeping tanks, of which the successor to the Scorpion was the Sherman Crab, with power for the rotating drum taken from the main engine to enable the vehicle to flail forward at 2 mile/h. The Russians mounted one on T 34/76, too. Other mine-clearing devices were Ploughs fitted to Shermans and Churchills, and Rollers which were adopted by practically every nation, except the Germans who, by 1943, were forced permanently on to the defensive.

A Crab flailing.

A Sherman Crab with flail boom raised when in transit. Station-keeping devices are in position at rear.

A Churchill AVRE drops its S.B.G. Bridge.

Bridging tanks, some like the Churchill with a Small Box Girder (S.B.G.) complete bridge that was dropped ahead of the tank, others like the scissors opened out by mechanical means ahead of the tank—and a whole host of assault devices created by all nations to enable tanks and following vehicles to cross narrow gaps without stopping long or exposing engineers to fire.

Flame-throwing tanks—either short-range such as the Germans developed on their PzKpfw III, the Americans on the Sherman, the Russians on the T 34 and KV and the British on the Universal Carrier —or long-range devices of which none were more powerful or capable of sustained "flaming" than the British "Crocodile". The latter was based on the Churchill VII and carried 400 gal of flame fuel (napalm) which it could project to a range up to 120 yd at 3 gal/min.

Night-fighting tanks such as the 13,000,000 candle-power arc lamp mounted by the British on the Matilda or Grant. It was intended as the means to illuminate the battlefield and partially blind the enemy during a night breakthrough and pursuit. Never used in this capacity it was, nevertheless, the first purpose-designed tank night-fighting light, its title of Canal Defence Light (C.D.L.) being only a security cover.

Anti-aircraft tanks, since, with the aircraft of both sides' intervening more purposefully in the ground battle, the need to protect vital positions, targets and supply columns was ever present. Self-propelled armoured anti-aircraft guns (of which all nations had quite a number based on obsolescent chassis) could take post nearer the front line than normal field-mountings and thus provide direct protection.

Airborne tanks which only the British with Tetrarch, Alecto and Harry Hopkins, and the Americans with Locust, took seriously. Seven Tetrarchs were landed by the British from giant Hamilcar gliders on 6th June 1944 in Normandy and on 24th March 1945, with a few Locusts, on the enemy side of the Rhine.

Locust—America's airborne tank.

The dominant armoured fighting vehicles of late 1944 and early 1945 remained the German innovations of 1943 along with the addition of **the heaviest tank ever put into production** by the Germans—the Tiger II (Royal Tiger) of 68 tons with its long 88 mm gun. In company came two great Jagdpanzers —Jagdpanther, with a long 88 mm, and Jagdtiger with the enormous 128 mm gun.

Britain's last attempt to achieve tank parity in the Second World War—the Comet.

The Anglo-American responses to these powerful German machines were the American T 26 (Pershing) with its 90 mm and the British Comet with its 77 mm gun. These tanks were capable of dealing with all opponents at battle-ranges with the exception of Royal Tiger and Jagdtiger, both of which remained almost invulnerable to the end. The new Allied tanks came into service, however, as the deep invasion of Germany began and, therefore, as the

German tank arm began to wilt from loss of its industrial backing. Therefore, although the Pershing and Comet enjoyed successes—one of the former is credited with attacking and killing a Tiger and two PzKpfw IVs in a single action—they were rarely fully extended except to prove their reliability in long-range advances.

The backbone of the Allied armies to the last remained the Sherman, albeit up-armed with a longer 76 mm American gun and given more power, a better suspension and thicker armour in the E 8 version. They were supported, too, by derivations of the earlier equipments—Stuart light tanks, now improved in the Mark V and VI versions, T 36 tank destroyers which were the T 10 with a 90 mm gun and so on in the normal course of the gun/armour race.

The latest American A.F.V.s of original design to join the Pershing as the war came to its end were the M 18 Tank Destroyer and the new Light Tank M 24 (General Chaffee)—a far more powerful fighting reconnaissance machine than the Stuart—almost the equal, in fact, of the original Lee of 1941. In Korea in 1950, the M 24 was to show that it could cope with the T 34/85 under certain restrictive conditions at close ranges. M 18, sometimes known as "Hellcat", depended entirely on its high-velocity 76 mm M 1 A2 gun which could deal with almost any existing enemy tank and the high speed of its M 24 chassis. Its armour was so thin as to be worthless; tactically, therefore, it was a hit-and-run vehicle.

The abortive vehicles of the war's latter years were the truly gigantic projects attempted by the Germans, British and Americans—vehicles which approached and overlapped the 100-ton mark and which defied both mass production and practical battlefield employment. None of the following vehicles saw active service (with one possible exception), but all are monuments to overstatement in the gun/armour controversy:

The German Maus was the biggest tank of all (188 tons) and armed with the enormous 150 mm L/38 gun (**the biggest tank gun ever mounted**) in addition to a coaxial 75 mm gun. Its armour was between 50 and 200 mm thick, its power plant a 1,200 hp Daimler-Benz engine which could drive it at 12 mile/h. It is said that a few prototype machines fought on the Eastern Front but this is unlikely. In any case it was a hopelessly ineffective machine by comparison with its cost. The E 100 was only a little smaller at 140 tons and never got beyond the experimental stage.

The British produced a few prototype, up-scaled Churchills called "Black Prince" which weighed 45 tons. But their **biggest A.F.V. of all** was the Tortoise self-propelled gun with its 94 mm gun—a grossly clumsy vehicle weighing 78 tons with cast armour up to 230 mm thick.

The U.S.A. turned their hands to the construction of a giant self-propelled gun in their 83-ton T 28—a machine with a 105 mm gun and frontal armour of 305 mm—**the thickest ever fitted**.

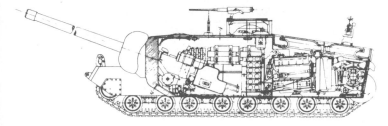

America's monster T 28 self-propelled gun.

The most significant designs to appear as the war came to its end were the Russian T 44 and the British Centurion. Both suffered early teething troubles and the T 44 alone saw action in 1945—and then only of a limited nature. But the T 44 —first armed with the 85 mm and then the 100 mm gun—was a distinct improvement on the T 34/85 and acted as a design bridge towards the next startling improvement in Russian tank design in the post-war years. Torsion-bar suspension was used, an improved engine, and a frontal glacis plate strengthened by being relieved of the driver's hatch.

The best tank ever produced by the British was the Centurion of which six examples of the Mark I version with their 76·2 mm gun were just too late to join in the closing hours of the war. At last the British had made a well-armed tank with good overall sloping armour, a vehicle with enormous potential for up-gunning and up-armouring which was to be sold to many other armies and to make an indelible mark on armoured fighting in the next two decades.

The last battle appearance of the pre-war-designed Matilda was made in Borneo when Australian forces used them in jungle to support their invasion in 1945.

PART THREE—TECHNOLOGY 1939–1945

U.S. M7 SP artillery (105 mm).

The dominant theme of advancing tank technology during the Second World War years was centred upon armament, either in attempts to increase the brute penetrating force of missiles thrown by guns or by raising the penetrative power of the missile itself regardless of its velocity or weight. The many other aspects of tank technology took second place to armament, though that is not to suggest that they were totally excluded from research and development— as anybody reading the foregoing pages must have realised.

Russia's JS III—for years a bogey of great potential. In fact a rather inefficient tank.

ARMAMENT

The first attempts to increase penetrative power resolved themselves into increases in missile size and weight rather than velocity. A glance at the table on page 224 shows how muzzle velocities remained roughly static, in proportion to calibre lengths, while calibres rose from 50 mm to 75 and then as high as 128 mm in 1945. It will also be noticed, however, that, as the war progressed, barrel lengths were significantly extended with higher velocities. The reasons for change were complex, but a moderating influence was always the difficulty of manufacture, associated with metallurgy and scarcity of essential materials. The longer the barrel and the higher the velocity the greater the problems.

There came a point at which it was no longer worth while to increase gun calibre in order to step up velocity. Then more research was applied to increasing velocity either by squeezing the round through the barrel or by applying a normal force against a lighter missile whose core was as dense or denser than that of the original shot.

The first squeeze gun was produced by the German firm of Gehrlich. A tungsten-cored shot was fired through a tapered barrel whose diameter reduced from 28 to 20 mm. The shot emerged at 4,600 ft/sec—which was **the fastest velocity ever achieved** by any production gun in the Second World War. Later the Germans had to give up this method because of shortage of tungsten.

The first attempt to increase muzzle velocity by firing a lighter missile through a normal barrel was attempted by the Germans in 1941 when they encased a small, hard, tungsten carbide core in a light, larger outer jacket. This was called Armour Piercing Composite Rigid (A.P.C.R.) shot. It was expensive and rapidly lost velocity due to its large frontal area.

The first attempt to increase muzzle velocity through a normal barrel by applying normal force to a conventional round was by streamlining the shot with a ballistic cap. The British invention of 1942 was called Armour Piercing Capped Ballistic Capped (A.P.C.B.C.).

The best compromise way of firing a light-weight shot with smaller frontal area was achieved by the British when, in 1944, they introduced Armour Piercing Discarding Sabot shot. With this round the shot was held in a light case (or sabot) which fell off after the round had left the barrel. Velocities of 2,950 ft/sec which had been achieved with A.P.C.B.C. through the British 76·2 mm gun rose to 3,950 ft/sec with A.P.D.S.

The means of a breakthrough, away from the need to use large high-velocity kinetic energy anti-tank guns came with the almost universal discovery, round about 1940, that a shaped charge of explosive packed into a coned warhead and exploded at a distance from or against armour plate would penetrate in a way unlike anything found before. This method usually takes the name Hollow-Charge or High Explosive Anti-Tank (H.E.A.T.). When the round explodes a very high-velocity jet (28,000 ft/sec) blasts its way through the armour and is followed by the debris from the cone. The pressure of the jet can be as much as 2,000 tons/in², though the debris rarely travel faster than 1,000 ft/sec. Performance is erratic, however. The jet can be deflected or dissipated by premature detonation away from the plate. The best performance is achieved at an optimum "stand-off distance", at which, for example, a medium-sized war-head will penetrate 200 mm of armour—far in excess of any armour carried by modern tanks. Again, however, performance can be degraded if the round is travelling at a high velocity, but low-velocity rounds are inaccurate. Furthermore, the terminal effects of the round can be insignificant: a hit does not necessarily imply much internal damage, let alone a kill. Future developments could, of course, increase killing power after penetration.

The earliest weapons to be given hollow-charge ammunition were low-velocity artillery pieces and the first anti-tank rocket projectors. The latter were the short-range infantry weapons which became generally known as "Bazookas". They came into service in 1942 in the U.S. Army and by 1945 were in massed use by all major armies.

The first guided anti-tank rocket weapon was devised by the Germans in 1944 and called X 7. The rocket, armed with a hollow-charge war-head, was guided towards the target by signals sent by the operator down a very thin cable paid out by the missile in flight. X 7 hardly passed the project stage, but the French took it up after the war and then developed the first practical A.T.G.W.— the SS 10—a weapon which has yet to prove its worth in battle.

NIGHT-FIGHTING EQUIPMENT

The increasing power and accuracy of anti-tank weapons made it desirable for tanks to move as much as possible either under smoke cover or by night. Actual night combat, however, was something of a rarity since, for many years, there were no good aids to shooting, the inability to see a telescope cross-wire after daylight had failed being the main inhibition. Later in the war the shining of searchlights on low cloud to produce what was known as "artificial moonlight", partially solved the problem, but the introduction of genuine night sights based on infra-red transmissions was only in its infancy in Germany in 1945.

The other main problems in night-fighting are telling friend from foe and knowing which way one is heading. To this day a foolproof system of identification (one that denies advantage to the enemy) eludes invention. By 1945, however, the rudimentary methods of battlefield navigation in addition to ordinary map-reading by moonlight depended upon:

Tracer illumination: whereby a stream of tracer shots from small-calibre guns pointed the way to the objective. Rather a vague method.

Directional radio beams, which were unreliable and vulnerable to enemy interference.

Homing beacons, which were as two-edged an aid as radio beams.

ARMOUR PROTECTION

The most stable item in tank technology throughout the war was armour plate. For reasons of economic policy nations were forced to stick to the type with which they started—the British staying with homogeneous plate and some cast, the Germans with face-hardened, and the Americans and Russians a mixture of homogeneous and cast. Differences in quality were caused mostly by the need to economise in vital ingredients. For example, a severe shortage of nickel forced the British to reduce its content by 80 per cent along with substantial reductions in aluminium and molybdenum, the final material being kept at a high strength by means of tight quality control.

Britain's most successful tank—Centurion. This picture, taken in Singapore in 1959, was the first time a tank of this size had been put on to the island.

The biggest improvements in tank protection came from changes in jointing and from variations in the layout of armour—methods imposed by the demands of rationalisation in industry. The system of jointing by bolts and rivets gradually gave way to the superior welding as production techniques were developed. It was not an overnight process since large-scale capital investment in the factories was implicit. Changes in armour layout, in addition to increases in thickness, were found in:

(1) **Sloping of armour** by every nation—the British just about last in this field.

(2) **Spacing of armour** to create an air gap between two plates as a possible way of dissipating kinetic energy shot and an even more certain

method of reducing the effects of hollow-charge war-heads. Started by the British in the 1930s this system was copied strongly by the Germans as part of the general up-armouring programme after 1941.

(3) **Shielding of armour** by means of wire net screens to detonate hollow-charge war heads and by sticking cement outside the armour to prevent the hand attachment of magnetic charges.

(4) **Crew modifications**, whereby they festooned turrets and hulls with track links and additional pieces of scrap metal to make up for what they, the crews, thought the designers had omitted. In due course "appliqué" armour was produced and added at manufacture to the original skin—the Americans were particularly adept at this.

The most usual causes of fire in tanks were ammunition and petrol—in that order of risk. Self-sealing petrol tanks were considered but rejected. Late in the war, however, the Americans introduced "wet stowage" surrounding the ammunition bins with ethylene glycol (later only by water) so that, when penetration was achieved, the ammunition was instantly doused. **The first vehicle to incorporate this system** was the Sherman M 4 A3 E8, causing an enormous number of additional modifications as penalty.

POWER PLANTS

The most suitable sort of tank engine is the diesel, and not only because the fuel's fire risk is so much lower than petrol. Nevertheless during the Second World War nearly every country turned over to petrol because this fuel was more easily obtainable and national policies tended to allocate oil fuel to navies. The Russians stuck to diesels, however, and with good results except for the manner in which clouds of exhaust smoke contributed a tactical penalty by giving away their tank positions.

The most powerful tank engine of the war was the 1,200 hp Daimler-Benz developed for the gigantic German Maus in 1943. Generally, however, engines for main battle-tanks produced power of between 350 and 700 hp. The pre-war tendency of adapting aero engines was continued. For example the famous Rolls-Royce Merlin engine, which powered the Hurricane and Spitfire fighters in the Battle of Britain, was derated, called "Meteor" and first fitted in the Cromwell and then several other tanks.

The most interesting ideas for the future naturally concerned greater power from a more compact unit and improved economy in fuel consumption.

The last British armour in India. 7th Royal Tank Regiment's Fox armoured car and Stuart tank by Kim's gun in Lahore, 1947.

The most important fuel-utilisation device was the one demonstrated by General Motors in 1942 when they made their two-stroke diesel run on petrol—the forerunner of today's multi-fuel engines.

The most original way of increasing power was by substituting fuel-injection systems in place of carburettors. In this the firm of Maybach (which virtually possessed a monopoly in German tank-engine work) led. They adopted a system derived from aircraft manufacturers in the 1920s and first used it on the HL 230 700 hp engine which powered the Tiger II: it raised the output to 900 hp. There was also the promise of fuel economy which was to be pursued in the post-war years by most industrial nations.

TRANSMISSIONS

Easily the most important wartime development with transmissions came in the production of tanks with regenerative steering, thus saving power which, before, had been lost through clutch and brake systems. The Merritt-Maybach system, which had appeared in 1938, was adopted both in Britain and Germany by 1941. The British tried it out in an experimental medium tank (A 16) and put the first production version (Merritt-Brown) in the Churchill tank; the German firm of Henschel using it for the first time in the Tiger I.

The first gearbox system to permit a tank to turn on its axis was the Merritt-Brown box. With the gears in neutral, application of a steering-lever made the tracks turn contrariwise, causing the vehicle to pivot.

OPTICAL SYSTEMS

The first fighting vehicle gun-aiming systems were either open sights or simple telescopes fitted with cross-wires. Fire and correction of aim was maintained by watching the fall of shot (or observing the shot's tracer path) and making the necessary adjustments to the point of aim for subsequent engagements of the target. Telescopes rarely had much more than three times magnification and, though they slightly helped to clarify the object, it was difficult to find targets in bad light.

Russian JSU 152s.

As battle-ranges increased, along with more powerful and accurate guns, and ammunition varieties proliferated, a demand for more complicated sighting graticules appeared. Gun-laying, which was a pretty slapdash subject in the hands of the dullest crewman in 1939, turned into a highly scientific matter by 1945. Sighting had to keep pace with accuracy and a tactical requirement for the earliest possible chance of hitting the target before the target could hit back. The demands for a first-round hit were always somewhat optimistic, but a hit with the second round was considered realistic. Towards the end of the war the highly complex German sighting equipments were achieving this object and sometimes did better.

The supreme art in the Second World War gunnery was judgement of distance by the tank commander so that he could give the gunner as close an estimate of range as possible, thus reducing the number of ranging shots required.

The most inhibiting factor produced by the most powerful guns at the war's end was that of obscuration. A gun throws up smoke and dust when it fires and this was found to obscure vision until after the round had arrived at the target. Hence observation and correction of fall of shot, from within the tank, became almost impossible. Therefore the only way of ensuring sufficient data was to post the commander to a flank where he was unaffected at any range by obscuration; by firing at point-blank range where a miss was impossible; or engaging at such long range that the obscuration had subsided before the shot reached the target. At medium ranges—those most commonly used in battle—the problem of ranging was almost insuperable, and therefore many advantages inherent in the latest guns were forfeited.

The sourest remark in comparing German tank technology of 1944 with that of the Allies was that they led in every aspect except that of gun-control equipment. A little severe, perhaps, but there was a grain of truth therein.

SECTION VI
Armour in Limited War
1946 to The Present Day

Post-war tank policies were the brainchildren of the war experiences of the combatant nations. The German tank force lay in ruins, but new tank forces belonging to nations as yet unborn or un-recognised were to rise and soon, too, German armour would be reborn.

It was symptomatic that the Russians, who had fought the most strenuous tank battles against the Germans in the closing stages of the war, should start the peace with confidence in the tank's well-being—even if they were somewhat slow starting production on new types. It was historically characteristic that the Americans should at first turn away from Europe and, therefore, imagine less future demand for the tank than might otherwise be the case: it was equally natural that they and the British should wish to rid themselves of all armaments in the search for peaceful pursuits. In any case there arose, once again, a feeling that anti-tank forces outweighed the tank. But in the unrelaxed political atmosphere of the immediate post-war years there appeared the ever growing shadow of what was interpreted as a threat of Russian world domination. There occurred innumerable outbreaks of nationalist violence in every corner of the globe—outbreaks into which first the British and French, and then the Americans were to be drawn. In two decades of struggles, involving at one time or another nearly every nation, and which saw hot war in Korea, the Middle East and India, the tank retained its importance. Sometimes it merely appeared threateningly at street corners to cow unruly crowds, but time and again its full anger was unleashed to reaffirm its potency—despite the rumblings from pundits who, as usual, foretold the tank's imminent doom.

Yet, try as they might, practical military thinkers could find no alternative to the tank as the means of assuring man's mobility in the face of small arms and shell-fire—the self-same reasons for the tank's origin. Moreover they had now to consider the threat of nuclear firepower, against which armour was shown to give good protection. So the designers went on developing better (and more expensive) armoured fighting vehicles, and the soldiers revised tactical doctrines, helped in their task by improved command and control arrangements, vastly better means of securing and disseminating information, and therefore superior ways of integrating all the battlefield elements within self-sufficient armoured combat teams. Technology was vigorously stirred by intensive research and development programmes which dwarfed those of wartime. New types of armour; better running-gear and more powerful engines of improved reliability; more accurate and harder-hitting weapons (either of the high-velocity armour-piercing sort or of the lower hollow-charge kind), guided missiles, radar early warning systems, night vision devices—all these things were adopted to make the tank a more sophisticated and deadly weapon capable of creating its own environment on the battlefield.

Successive little wars were to raise the tank's prestige above the troughs into which it fell between each spell of intensive action. The anti-tank pundits seemed incapable of remembering how often they had been proved wrong in the past: with each hint of a new anti-tank weapon they leapt in to restate a case against the tank's survival. When hollow-charge weapons were shown to be fallible, the guided weapon was propagated as the panacea solution, and when that failed the armed helicopter became heir-apparent to the tank. Journalists had their day, but the soldiers doggedly stuck to the weapon which had given victory in battle since 1917. So far they have been proved right.

Historically speaking it is not difficult to understand why they are right, for even a rough count affirms how curtailed have been the periods when man has fought lacking the protection of armour. Why should he risk all by going without in the future?

PART ONE—FEATS & ACHIEVEMENTS

British breaching exercise—Crocodiles, Comets and AVRE and Ark.

The last shots of the Second World War—above all the explosion of **the first atomic bomb** at Alamagordo on 15th July 1945 and its **first operational use** at Hiroshima on 6th August and then at Nagasaki on 9th August, sparked off the debate as to the future not only of tanks but of armies in general. There were those who immediately foresaw the nuclear bomb as a totally dominating weapon such as would sweep away all others, while those who thought a little deeper welcomed it as a deterrent to war. And then there were men who recognised that outlawing total war merely opened the door to more limited wars, inclusive of armoured battles that would be little different in form from those which had taken place in the past.

Man's first entry into a nuclear irradiated zone was made by American observers travelling in a Sherman tank immediately after the Alamagordo test.

The first genuine doubts thrown on the future efficacy of armoured vehicles, however, came about as the result of a renewed belief that the latest anti-tank weapons, in infantry hands, would make tank attacks impossible. Hence, while it was admitted that armoured vehicles provided good protection against nuclear effects, it was thought better, by some, to dig underground in safety, rather than go mobile in armour that was highly vulnerable. Therefore, although various nations continued to develop tanks after 1945, they did so against a background of official doubt.

The first day of national celebration specially set aside for tankmen was inaugurated in Russia in 1946—Soviet Tankmen's Day to be recognised annually on 8th September. But like every other nation the Soviets soft-pedalled their enormous armoured army, waiting to see which way the nuclear debate would turn, though rebuilding the tank factories which had been stripped during the German invasion.

T 54 facing a hostile crowd in Prague.

The first employment of armour in action after August 1945 was by tanks and armoured cars in many parts of the world in support of peacekeeping forces endeavouring to curb nationalistic and revolutionary outbreaks which studded the attempts of people of the old colonial nations to assert their independence. In China tanks of Russian design fought for the Communists against tanks of American design with the Nationalists. By 1949 the Communists had captured them all. Armoured vehicles came into action in Dutch Indonesia, in Malaya, in India and throughout the Middle Eastern countries whenever authority was threatened. Inevitably its impact was strong and yet also provocative; it might curb dissidence at first, but, in due course, partisans could learn to cope, when armoured vehicles were ordered to act at less than their maximum performance, tied by political demands to use only minimum force in controlling the populace. The tank is hardly a suitable weapon of minimal force.

The first new tank force of future importance to be formed after 1945 was that of the emergent State of Israel when it came into being in 1948. Composed of a handful of old French H 35, British Cromwell and American Sherman tanks, it **fought its first, quite abortive engagement** against the Egyptians at Lod Airport on 16th October—far more tanks failing from breakdown and bad driving than from enemy fire.

The first sure indication that tanks were as effective as ever, despite the employment of the latest infantry anti-tank weapons (in this case the U.S. 3·5 in bazooka) came in the opening battles of the Korean War. North Korean-manned T 34s swept aside American infantry, artillery and light tanks at the Battle of Taejon early in July 1950. Unfortunately for the North Koreans their supply arrangements fell apart after their tank arm had won a battle. Had they at once driven hard to the south it seems likely they would have conquered the rest of the country before the United Nations—above all American—reinforcements arrived. As it was the North Korean forces were later defeated, as their own tank force declined and that of their opponents, heavily backed by air power, built up to a much greater strength.

The first extensive use of air-dropped napalm (burning jellied petrol) bombs as an anti-tank weapon was made in Korea, with serious injury to tanks when they were found and hit. Thus the aeroplane at last began to have a direct counter-effect on armour by its use of an area weapon.

The first full-scale examination of the effects of nuclear explosives on armour occurred at Bikini Atoll in the Pacific Ocean between the 1st and 25th July 1946. Thereafter crucial tests of nuclear weapons to integrate them with armoured ground forces took place in the U.S.A. as follows:

January 1951: Demonstration in Nevada of a small-field weapon followed by Exercise "Southern Pine" in which the marginal effects on ground troops were demonstrated.

May 1953: Firing of a nuclear shell from a 280 mm gun.

May 1955: Employment of armoured Task Force "Razor" at Nevada in which a tank battalion and other armoured vehicles was deployed only 3,000 yd from ground zero and, after the explosion, driven through the devastated and irradiated zone.

The greatest outpouring of military literature on future global war, since the 1920s, accompanied the early demonstrations of nuclear effects and continues to the present day. Happily, nobody so far has put the literature—or the nuclear weapon—to practical use.

The first major changes in military formation organisation took place with the confirmation that armoured vehicles could survive on a nuclear battlefield. It was appreciated that, with improved radio communication based on the V.H.F. and U.H.F. frequency ranges, deployment and battlefield reaction would become faster in accord with the vast increase in firepower that might give as much a boost to offensive as to defensive capability. The concept of permanently established instead of *ad hoc* battle-groups gained favour. Tanks, engineers, artillery and infantry were brought together in formal teams controlled by more highly sophisticated command centres. This was the European idea. The U.S.A., on the other hand, developed a so-called "Pentomic" Division, organised so that an almost infinite number of tactical combinations could be devised within the formation by slick regrouping on the battlefield of individual units and combat teams. This system was to fail because commanders became dazzled by the sheer delight of arranging different permutations regardless of the essential requirement of battlefield simplicity.

British Combat Team guarding a bridge—left to right: Ferret scout car, FV 432, Chieftain.

The old tyranny of tank predominance was once more demonstrated during the Israeli/Suez Crisis in the autumn of 1956 in Sinai.

The first major tank victory since 1945 was won by Israeli armoured forces in Sinai, even though it was not the original policy of General Dayan, their commander, to fight a predominantly tank war—hardly surprising when it is recalled that many tanks were delivered but a few days before the fighting began and that hardly any of the artillery was self-propelled. The Israeli Army was founded on the original infantry element of Hagana—the underground defence force which had fought for Israeli independence. As in other armies of the past thirty years the armoured element in Israel's army had to struggle for recognition—a somewhat surprising state of affairs bearing in mind that a small nation with such inadequate frontiers was almost compelled to fight an offensive war—and fight it, moreover, in the desert where mobile armoured forces had a clear advantage over the less mobile infantry/artillery type of army.

This first Israeli tank victory was won in eight days at a cost of only 150 killed. In booty it gathered 125 Egyptian tanks among a vast haul of military supplies. Along with the invasion of Suez by Anglo-French forces—**the first large amphibious landing** with armoured force since the Second World War (if one excludes the U.N. landings at Inchon in Korea in September 1950 which was predominantly by infantry)—this tipped the scales against the Egyptians for many years in addition to leading to a world political crisis of the first magnitude.

AMX 13—the arrangement of the oscillating turret is plain to see.

Nothing really new in armoured warfare marked the Sinai Campaign. Gun-tanks dominated, air power played its part in the old proportion, infantry wilted before well-led armoured formations and a strong tank pursuit in depth brought ruin to the defeated. The new anti-tank guided weapons (French SS 11s) though possessed by the Israelis were not used.

The most flagrant, though certainly not the first, attempt to subjugate crowds by tanks was employed by the Russians during rioting in Berlin in 1953. Since it was soon apparent that the Russians were loath to use the tank's full armament their role became emasculated and they were made the target of the rioters' scorn in addition to impudently aimed bricks.

The most uninhibited use of tanks to control rioting occurred in Budapest during the Hungarian uprising of October 1956. Here, after the failure of initial attempts to bring the trouble under control, the Russians drafted tanks into the streets to find them seriously attacked by urban guerillas who set several on fire with petrol bombs or by igniting the external, unarmoured auxiliary fuel tanks. Thereafter the tanks were employed to the full effect of their striking power, causing great loss of life and destruction to buildings, in a police action which paid little regard to the principle of minimum force.

The first genuine rival to the tank as a means to battlefield mobility was the helicopter after it first appeared on the Korean battlefield. In Korea the helicopter was used only as a reconnaisance, supply carrier and casualty-evacuation vehicle. It was for the French **to develop it as a weapon carrier** during the guerilla war in Algeria throughout the mid-1950s.

The first helicopter to be armed with an anti-tank guided missile was the French Alouette, armed with SS 11 missiles. It appeared in 1963 and initiated the theory that armed helicopters could replace tanks in a battlefield role. Trials have been carried out by many armies, including those of the U.S.A. and Britain, the exciting atmosphere surrounding them not unlike that which affected the early tank tactical trials in the 1920s and 1930s. The debate continues though opinion seems to be hardening along the lines that, while the armed helicopter has many roles and is a most useful complement to the tank, it in no way can replace the tank as a battlefield maid of all work. The helicopter may well form "sky cavalry", but strictly in the reconnaissance and light raiding role rather than as a weapon of absolute decision.

M 113 crews watching helicopter attacking in Vietnam.

The first full-scale helicopter war took place in Vietnam with the new weapon system used throughout its repertoire, first in the early 1960s as support for South Vietnam forces and later as the central element in providing the U.S. Army with mobility and firepower—the element of protection being dependent upon the speed of the machine and the pious hope that the guerilla enemy would never deploy sophisticated anti-aircraft weapons at the front.

Buffalo—the U.S. LVT 4 which was first developed for flood rescue.

Armoured vehicles were first used in Indo-China (Vietnam) by the French. They had a platoon of old Renault FTs in Hanoi prior to 1939. The appointment of General Le Clerc to command in Indo-China in October 1945 naturally led to the increased use of armour since Le Clerc had been an armoured divisional commander already—and this theme was uppermost when Marshal de Lattre de Tassigny took command. Much of Vietnam is paddy-field and a great deal forest and swamp. But there are uplands which provide good tank going and the French were to employ all kinds of armoured vehicles as the campaign against the Viet Minh guerillas widened. In addition to armoured cars (M 8s), half-tracks, M 5 light tanks and M 8 S.P. howitzers they used British Humber and Coventry armoured cars, pre-war Panhards and the amphibious U.S. L.V.T. 4s. Later they acquired M 4 medium and M 24 light tanks to replace the M5s and at the same time greatly developed the many techniques for employing armour in country which, at first, appeared totally unsuitable for their use.

The first air-lift of tanks took place in 1951 when ten M 24s were flown, broken-down into bits, by DC 3 and Bristol Freighter aircraft, into Dien Bien Phu where they were reassembled and brought into action. This was the first of several such operations.

The early Viet Minh defensive measures relied upon mines, which accounted for 85 per cent of French tank casualties. They also used anti-tank ditches, hollow-charge bazookas and recoilless guns—but these latter caused few casualties. Ambush was frequently employed—the French counter-measure the practice of constant mobility since the most vulnerable vehicle was the one that halted. The Viet Minh found it most difficult to stop units of L.V.T. 4s which could go most places, carry a heavy weapon plus sections of infantry—the essence in fact of a genuine multi-purpose weapon system. The French armour had many successes before it was withdrawn in 1954. It also laid the foundations of indigenous armoured forces in South Vietnam, Laos and Cambodia.

The first U.S. armour involved in Vietnam against the North Vietnamese Army and the Viet Cong mostly consisted of armoured personnel carriers backed by obsolescent tanks and air power. Over the years as the fighting grew in intensity, the Americans began to acquire the same experience that once belonged to the French. They used tanks more and more. Additionally they virtually converted their armoured personnel carriers into light tanks, fitting them with sub-turrets and with heavier weapons in place of the original un-protected roof-top medium machine-guns.

The first U.S. armoured actions kept tanks strictly within the role of infantry support, but gradually this changed until the day arrived when fully armoured combat teams were to be found advancing in country which, a few years previously, would have appeared daunting. It was extensive engineer support to clear routes linked to constant battlefield improvisation which made these things possible.

The first employment of tanks by the Viet Cong did not take place until 3rd March 1969. Until then tank defence had been by orthodox ambush based on hollow-charge weapons and mines. But at Ben Het in the Central Highlands, overlooking entrances to the Ho Chi Minh Trail, the North Vietnamese committed a number of armoured vehicles, including Russian-built PT 76s, to a night assault. A platoon of four U.S. M 48s was part of the perimeter defence and had detected enemy engines. Later yet track noises were heard as the enemy approached. Then the Americans came under fire. Nothing could be seen through night-vision scopes until a PT 76 detonated some anti-personnel mines, setting itself on fire. A shooting match began in which one M 48 was struck on the glacis plate and some of its crew killed or wounded. The enemy withdrew leaving three vehicles, including two PT 76s destroyed. **This was the first time** in sixteen years that U.S.-manned armour had engaged enemy tanks in battle.

PT 76s swimming, powered by hydrojets.

The first tank war on the Indian subcontinent took place in August and September 1965 between Pakistan and India on the West Pakistan frontier. Border skirmishes escalated into full-scale armoured cut and thrust on excellent tank country between Sialkot and Lahore.

This was the first occasion in which British-built Centurions came into action against American-built M 47s (Pattons). The Indians had the former, with 83·4 mm guns, the Pakistanis the latter with 90 mm guns. On balance the former did much better, confirming not only that the Centurion was the more powerful machine but also that its simpler fighting arrangements gave crews a better chance of success. Yet neither side achieved outright victory and tended rather to resort to a series of head-on clashes which remained unresolved when the war was brought to an end by economic and diplomatic pressures and then a breakdown in supply arrangements.

The first occasion when anti-tank guided missiles were used in anger seems to have occurred during the Indo-Pakistan War; but the results were inconclusive.

The greatest Israeli versus Arab war began in Sinai and on the Jordanian and Syrian frontiers on 5th June 1967—a conflict which has become known as the Six Day War since this was all the time needed by Israel to defeat her opponents utterly.

The Six Day War was dominated by tanks and aircraft. Israeli air power practically eliminated the Arab air forces in the first day and thereafter had a free hand in the land battle to reconnoitre and attack the enemy ground forces, besides preventing enemy air-to-ground attacks in return.

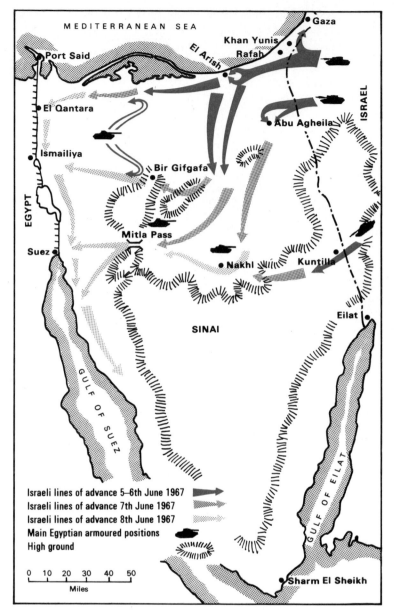

Israeli tank forces repeat the tank triumphs of old by defeating numerically superior forces with better trained and led tank divisions.

Israeli lines of advance 5–6th June 1967
Israeli lines of advance 7th June 1967
Israeli lines of advance 8th June 1967
Main Egyptian armoured positions
High ground

0   10   20   30   40   50
Miles

The opening round of the fight in Sinai comprised an all-out westward move by three Israeli armoured divisions (tank-preponderant but closely supported by armoured infantry and artillery) to cut up the forward Egyptian infantry/tank-held localities. Having completed this in an action which cost the lives of many Israeli tank commanders (thirty-five in one division alone) a mobile battle for the envelopment and destruction of the best Egyptian armour—Russian-built T 54s and T 55s—took place in the approaches to the Suez Canal. In a battle of annihilation 850 assorted Egyptian tanks were captured along with a mass of other military material.

The outstanding success in all the tank-versus-tank engagements was the high-velocity tank gun. Once again this weapon, in the hands of men who understood it and applied simplified techniques, demonstrated its battlefield prowess.

The chief anti-tank failure seems to have been the anti-tank guided missile of which the Soviet types made hardly any impression even though many were fired. Few struck their targets and, of those which did, hardly any penetrated. No conclusive lessons can be drawn, however. It is possible the missile operators were of low calibre or the missiles of the smallest type and therefore ineffective.

French AML 245 carrying ENTAC ATGW.

Inflated claims for knocking out tanks were once more to be heard from the advocates of air power, but as in the past it seems more than likely that, while air power isolated the Israeli battlefields by wrecking and stopping supply columns, it achieved little by direct action against tanks themselves.

Total annihilation was also visited upon the Jordanian tanks which endeavoured to intervene on their front. Lured into frontal attack by Israeli flank pressure they, too, were massacred, but only after they had fought with a lot more élan than had the Egyptians.

The crowning Israeli victory took place at the end of the war when infantry supported by tanks assailed the Syrian Army fortified in the Golan Heights. This caused the fiercest fighting of all, as well as a somewhat nostalgic tank occasion— **what was perhaps the last battlefield appearance** of some old German PzKpfw IVs, dug in, manned by Syrians and shot to pieces by modern tank guns.

A recent clash of armour has taken place on the frontiers of India in 1971. In East Pakistan there was early jousting in which the Indians destroyed and captured some Pakistani M 24s, but the subsequent fighting in this part of the continent was largely between infantry forces supported, at a distance, by tanks. There was sharp though rather half-hearted tank fighting on the Punjab front with claims from both sides of extensive losses inflicted on their opponents.

For the first time two newcomers went into action—the Vickers 37-ton tank (Vijayanta) fought on the Indian side and the Chinese T 59 (a rather low-grade version of the Russian T 54) with the Pakistanis.

The latest reported tank fighting has taken place in Vietnam where it would appear that, in April 1972, the North Vietnamese committed a number of their T 54 type medium and PT 76 light tanks in successful attacks against the South Vietnamese Army. It seems that a general engagement has taken place in which tank versus tank fighting has occurred along with attacks against armour by aircraft and armed helicopters—though whether the latter used guided missiles is not clear.

PART TWO—THE VEHICLES

Probably the most lasting impression carried in the memories of tankmen from the war to peacetime years was the vital necessity to possess superior hitting power in a tank battle. During the lull, after the fighting had ceased and before the Cold War became a recognisable political reality, only the long-term planners and tank designers searched for ways of improving the performance in successive tank generations, devising paper plans for families of vehicles at various weights. Even so, when those on either side of the Iron Curtain decided on rearmament in 1949, it was with modifications to old designs that both sides had to be satisfied. Medium battle-tanks took first priority, with heavy, light tanks and ancillary machines lower down the list.

BATTLE-TANKS

The first reshuffle of design in the U.S.A. occurred when an interim medium tank was needed urgently in 1949. They had planned a new light tank (T 41), a medium (T 42) and a heavy (T 43). They made do in practice with a re-engined and re-turreted M 26 called M 46. From this stemmed the evolution of U.S. medium tanks to the present day. Mainly it transpired as follows, with additional subsidiary changes to hull and components all the way through:

Year	Type	Modifications
1950	M 47	M 46 hull with T 42 turret and 90 mm gun.
1952	M 48	M 47 with new turret and 90 mm gun. T 42 project now dropped.
1955		M 48 A2 had fuel injection engine. M 48 A3 had diesel engine.
1959	M 48 A4	M 48 with modified turret and 105 mm gun. Became M 60.
1962	M 60 A1	M 60 with new turret and 105 mm gun.
1968	M 60 A2	M 60 A1 with new turret, Shillelagh gun launcher, Xenon searchlight and laser range finder.

The only post-1945 U.S. heavy tank to go into limited production was the M 103, with its 120 mm gun, evolved from the T 43. But the Army kept insisting on modifications to this 54-ton vehicle until, eventually, they rejected it and only the Marine Corps took a few. It was soon phased out of service as the M 60s arrived.

The most exciting experimental U.S. tank was the T 95 which, in the 1950s, was under development, incorporating all manner of revolutionary devices. It was to have a gas-turbine engine, variable-level suspension and a 90 mm smooth-bore gun. The Americans, in fact, staked much on the smooth-bore gun, believing they could make it superior to high-velocity rifled guns. They failed at great cost which is why they were forced to adopt the successful British 105 mm gun.

M60 A2—a complex adaptation for the Shillelagh weapon system.

The first post-war British tank programme was based on what was known as the FV 200 series—a basic hull, suspension and automotive system which could be adapted to all sorts of purposes. Like the U.S. programme it largely fell apart under the pressure of events. The medium version was never completed since modified Centurions were much easier to acquire and, some thought, better than the experimental FV 201.

Centurions of 4th Royal Tank Regiment parade in Germany in 1960.

The most extensively developed of all British tanks became, in fact, the Centurion.

Mark 3 had the 83·4 mm gun;
Mark 4 was to have the 95 mm howitzer but was cancelled;
Mark 5 had the U.S. Browning ·30 machine-gun instead of the British Besa 7·92 mm;
Mark 7 had increased radius of action and better ammunition stowage;
Mark 8 was the same as 7 but with a resiliently mounted gun mantlet;
Marks 6, 9 and 10 were respectively, 5, 7 and 8 with the 105 mm gun fitted and with a thicker glacis plate;
Marks 11, 12 and 13 were respectively 6, 9 and 10 fitted with infra-red night-fighting equipment and the ·5 in ranging machine-gun.

There is an Israeli modified Centurion, with the French 105 mm gun, called "Ben Gurion".

The heaviest and biggest gun-tank ever put into production by the British was the Conqueror, based on the FV 200 series. It weighed 68 tons, mounted a 120 mm gun and was powered by a fuel-injection engine. It incorporated a range-finder, highly sophisticated fire-control equipment and an automatic device for ejecting spent cartridge-cases through the turret side: all broke down on every conceivable occasion. The tank was phased out of service in the mid-1960s, fortunately never having been asked to fire a round in anger.

The first new Russian production tank to appear after 1945 was the T 54—a vastly improved T 44 which still preserved the best features of all its Christie-type predecessors. The prototype appeared in 1947 and the first production models in 1949. The 100 mm gun was the same as in SU 100. Like the Americans and British the Russians indulged in a programme of staged evolution:

T 54A had a bore evacuator and night-vision equipment;
T 54B had an infra-red searchlight and a stabilised gun; Schnorkelling equipment was introduced;
T 55 in 1958 had a more powerful engine—an increase over T 54 to 580 from 520 hp;
T 62, in 1961, was longer, wider and lower, and mounted a new 115 mm smooth-bore gun firing fin-stabilised missiles as the Americans had wished to do.

The first Chinese-manufactured tank was the T 59. Until then they had to make do with Russian products. Now they have to make do with something worse, for the T 59 is a bad copy of the T 54 devoid of night-vision and gun-stabilising equipment and lacking a powered traverse for its turret. Those sent to the Pakistani Army did not do well in battle in 1971.

The last Russian heavy tank was their T 10, derived from the JS III, weighing 50 tons and armed with the 122 mm gun. It was phased out of service as the T 62s appeared.

The first French medium tank to be built since 1940 was the ARL 44 of 1944, an up-gunned version founded on the old Char B hull. Fifty were made and were in service at the same time as a battalion of captured German Panthers, plus current U.S. tanks, until something more modern could be designed. The next attempt was a 50-ton vehicle with a 100 mm gun called AMX 50. **The second version of AMX 50 was the most powerful French tank ever** with its 1,000 hp Maybach engine and 120 mm gun. It weighed 56 tons, was very sophisticated and expensive—and was duly scrapped in the mid-1950s. Only five were built, but three had the first oscillating turrets—of which more later—ever fitted to tanks.

The first French production medium tank since 1940 therefore, did not appear in service until 1963, following a period of French flirtation with German and Italian designers (who favoured a European tank of about 38 tons) and total rejection of Germans' advances because an upper weight limit of 30 tons seemed preferable in French judgement. The result was AMX 30 which already weighs nearly 35 tons. Nevertheless this is a well-designed if complex tank, distinguished by its 105 mm gun and special hollow-charge ammunition (see page 196). Its armour is rather thin, however, and therefore it will be vulnerable in a stand-up fight.

France's AMX 30.

The first German tank to appear since the German Army was revived in 1955 is Leopard, a 40-ton machine armed with the British 105 mm gun. The first models betrayed the difficulties of designers whose art had been interrupted by a decade's inactivity, but the latest versions of this tank prove it a fine fighting vehicle. Internal arrangements have been improved, night-fighting equipment added, while the 830 hp engine gives a good power-to-weight ratio and so high a cross-country speed that the suspension sometimes proves inadequate to the task of giving the crew a smooth ride. It has been sold to many countries including Belgium, Norway and Holland.

The first production tanks of Swiss origin, was their Pz 58. It was decided to build this tank in 1951 and the prototype version appeared in 1958—an interesting feature its 20 mm cannon mounted coaxially with the 90 mm gun. The vehicle was put into production in 1961 as Pz 61. One hundred and fifty were made, the later models dispensing with the 20 mm cannon. Now an improved model, Pz 68, is being made.

The first Japanese tank since 1945 appeared in 1957 after design had been started in 1955. This was the STA 4 or Type 61 which, externally, looks similar to the U.S. M 47 and has the same 90 mm gun. In fact this tank incorporates a number of original features and most of the components are of Japanese manufacture. The engine is by Mitsubishi and is a turbo-charged diesel. But most fascinating of all is the ingenious way the designers have deliberately reduced size by nearly 2 ft all round compared with M 47 to take full advantage of the small stature of the Japanese soldier.

Swedish Strv 103 (S tank).

The modern trend in artillery—Britain's 105 mm in Abbot.

Chieftain night firing.

The next Japanese tank, the STB promises to be even more original than its predecessors. The first prototype appeared in 1969 and showed that some of the features of the defunct U.S. T 95 had been utilised—variable suspension among them. The gun, however, was the British 105 mm with assistance in loading—indeed this is the only non-Japanese feature in the vehicle.

The most startlingly original armoured fighting vehicle ever put into production may well be the Swedish S Tank (Strv 103). In this machine the turret is eliminated by mounting the main armament (105 mm gun) along the centre line of the hull. Laying in azimuth is accomplished by means of the hydrostatic steering drive, assisted by a clutch and brake system for very sharp turns. The whole vehicle is elevated or depressed by altering the relative setting of the road-wheel arms by means of a hydro-pneumatic jacking system. The driver/gunner and commander sit one either side of the 105 mm, and both have combined driving and gun-laying controls. The gun, a longer-tubed version of the British design, is loaded automatically. The radio operator faces rearward and is capable of driving in an emergency. The power plant consists of a Rolls-Royce K 60 diesel for normal operation out of enemy contact, while a Boeing gas turbine acts through the normal transmission as an additional source of power for full fighting load. Flotation is possible using a screen. A gyro-stabilised sight for the commander is another of the many innovations in this interesting and expensive vehicle. The original proposals for the design were put forward in 1956, the first prototypes ran in 1961 and production vehicles were ready for service in 1967. The earlier 45-ton KRV which was to have mounted an automatically loaded, smooth-bore 150 mm gun was abandoned.

U.S.A.'s XM 803—rejected by Congress.

The latest attempt by the U.S.A. to produce a main battle-tank has been a crashing failure. The project which started development in 1963 as a combined U.S./West German venture was called MBT 70. The aim was to build a highly sophisticated machine armed with the Shillelagh 152 mm gun launcher and running on a variable-level suspension—a development of the earlier, failed T 95 project. The Germans pulled out in 1970 because the machine was too expensive ($250,000 each) and elaborate, and because they wanted a high-velocity gun and not the Shillelagh. The Americans persisted and renamed the vehicle XM 803, but at the end of 1971, Congress refused the money for further development and the project was dropped.

XM 803 was the first tank to have the driver in the main turret, conning the machine from a contra-rotating sub-turret of his own.

The most powerful engine ever put in a tank (so far) is the 1,500 hp Daimler-Benz twelve-cylinder multi-fuel engine developed by the Germans for MBT 70. XM 803, however, was intended to have their U.S. Continental 1,475 hp engine.

Indian Vyjayantas (Vickers 37 tonner) on parade, followed by Centurions.

The most intriguing tank in service with any army is the Vickers 37-ton tank which Vickers built for India. A manufacturing plant has been set up in Madras. Called "Vijayanta" (Freedom) by the Indians it has also been sold to the Kuwaitis. It uses the British 105 mm gun and has the British Chieftain L 60 engine and transmission along with a suspension based on one developed and then cancelled by the British War Office for a light tank series called FV 300. Like AMX 30 the armour is somewhat thin and therefore this vehicle will not be at its best in a stand-up fight.

The most powerful tank in service with any army is the British Chieftain with its well-sloped thick armour and its 120 mm gun. It came into service in 1966 and is equipped with a built-in searchlight, "wet" ammunition stowage, a multi-fuel engine (L 60), and a ranging machine-gun among a host of other ancillary devices. It can be fully sealed in order to work on a nuclear and biological battlefield, it is equipped for Schnorkel deep-wading and has been demonstrated with a remote-control device by which a man can drive it without entering the vehicle—the **first full-scale fighting vehicle to have this facility.**

The demise of XM 803 puts the U.S. Army in great difficulty. It must be ten years before they can produce their own successor to M 60, which is already obsolescent and almost up to the limit in development and highly complex in its A 2 version. Therefore, they must either accept this inferiority in any near-future conflict or buy from a foreign nation. The question has to be asked if they will buy Chieftain, or wait for the next European tank (perhaps an Anglo-German venture). They must also question the wisdom of their General Staff and Tank Design establishments which in twenty-five years has:

(1) Failed to build a sound original tank design.

(2) Failed to produce a viable weapon system.

(3) Wasted many millions of dollars in abortive research and development.

RECONNAISSANCE AND LIGHT FIGHTING VEHICLES

The most extraordinary reversal of opinion with light vehicles has just occurred between the British and the Americans. Until the early 1960s the British believed that all reconnaissance vehicles should move on wheels while the Americans believed mainly in tracks. Almost simultaneously, however, the British decided to make tracked recce vehicles while the Americans turned towards armoured cars.

The British light vehicles, post-1945 were:

(1) **Saladin six-wheeled armoured car** with its 76 mm gun and a crew of three.

(2) **Ferret scout car** with its single machine-gun.

Both were made able to swim and were air portable, though Saladin could not be parachute-dropped.

The latest British light vehicle is Scorpion (FV 101) which has a power to weight ratio of 25 hp/ton, track-to-ground pressure of about 5·2 lb/in². Therefore it can cross very soft ground. It also has the latest surveillance equipment, both radar and image-intensification types. **Scorpion is the first all-aluminium armoured tank.**

The first U.S. light tank to go into production after 1945 was the M 41 Walker Bulldog which sprang from the T 41 project. Armed with a 76 mm gun, this fast tank became what amounted to standard equipment in a great many armies which could not afford anything bigger. Yet it failed in its original object to be air portable because, at 25 tons, it was far too heavy.

A very expensive and far from successful successor to M 41 in the U.S. Army is M 551— General Sheridan. This vehicle was specially designed to be air portable and incorporated many aluminium components including the hull, the engine and the tracks. It mounts the Shillelagh gun/missile system and has been employed in Vietnam where it has earned a very bad reputation with its crews for numerous shortcomings.

The first armoured car to be developed out of official U.S. policy for over two decades is the highly original, eight-wheeled XM 808 Twister, started in 1964. It consists of a fighting compartment with an overhead cannon suspended on two independent bogies (an engine in each) and linked by pivot yokes to permit movement in all three planes.

Armoured cars of the future? Variations of XM 808, the Twister.

What appears almost as a flashback to the past is the latest eight-wheeled German armoured car, the Daimler-Benz-Achtrad, weighing 19 tons. It looks so like the original pre-1939 German eight-wheeled types, is armed merely with a 20 mm gun and has a speed of 60 mile/h. It is, however, an inherent swimmer which the older German models were not.

The Russians hedge their bets when it comes to reconnaissance by employing both wheeled and tracked vehicles. There is the wheeled BTR 40K (BRDM) which is an inherent swimmer and, by lowering four auxiliary wheels, can increase its cross-country traction. And there is the PT 76 light amphibious tank which, like BTR 40K, propels itself through the water by hydro-jets.

The first French armoured car since 1940 appeared in 1950 and was the Panhard EBR. It had many highly original features—an almost symmetrical layout so that drivers at each end can drive the vehicle as fast backwards as forwards; **the first example of auxiliary wheels** to improve cross-country mobility; a very flat engine (only 12·5 in high) mounted centrally under the turret and **the first use in service of the oscillating turret**.

Another remarkable French armoured car was the Panhard AML 245 of 1959. It weighs only 5 tons and is notable for the variety and power of armament it has been made to carry in different versions. Model C has a 90 mm gun, Model E a 60 mm mortar and there is a model with twin 20 mm guns. In several types four SS 11s (anti-tank guided weapons) can be fitted while development is proceeding on a special turret to carry two big SS 12s with a range of 6,500 m.

The most successful of all French post-1945 fighting vehicles has been the AMX 13 tank. The long 75 mm gun (the same as mounted in the German Panther) is mounted in an oscillating turret. It has been sold to twenty-three different countries and seen action in two Israeli and two Indo-Pakistan wars. The penalty for light weight and relative cheapness is vulnerability, and AMX 13 has very thin armour and is easily damaged by mines. In action its gun is no compensation for these deficiencies and so it can only be considered as a useful air-portable, reconnaissance vehicle with useful anti-tank capabilities. It has since been up-gunned with a 90 mm and a 105 mm smooth-bore gun and is to be seen carrying four SS 11 A.T.G.W., or six of the latest HOT A.T.G.W.

The first Chinese light tank is the T 62 which is known to be a scaled-down Russian-type T 54 armed with an 85 mm gun.

FIRE-SUPPORT FIGHTING VEHICLES

Among the most important changes which took place in tank design during the Second World War was the increase in the main battle-tank's capability to provide a wide variety of heavy fire support for itself. Dual-purpose guns could fire as many different kind of projectile as artillery—and usually with greater accuracy; the T 34 was probably **the first tank to be given facilities for firing its gun indirectly at the target** like artillery. Really the only advantage of artillery over tanks was their ability to fire sustained, indirect concentrations—an essential facility which it was undesirable the tanks should match (except in special circumstances) since it would have downgraded their special characteristics as a direct-fire weapon. Nevertheless, the post-war approach to fire-support vehicle design had to be one of specialisation, too, to ensure that artillery, anti-tank and guided-weapon vehicles could keep pace with the tank force and give speedy assistance over and above the normal tank fire capability.

The unrivalled exponents in the creation of self-propelled artillery are the Americans. They not only produced a good chassis but took the view that it was more important to land a few heavy projectiles on target than many light ones—not that the delivery of heavies was very small in number. The tendency to adapt chassis and automotive parts from current tank construction grew.

The first American S.P.s to appear after 1945—in 1953—were the M 44 and M 52 armed respectively with the 155 m and 105 mm howitzers. Thus they can deliver the sort of "plunging" fire which high-velocity tank guns cannot give at the closer ranges.

The first American S.P.s with fully rotating and enclosed turrets appeared in the early 1960s. They are the M 108 with 105 mm and the M 109 with 155 mm—the latter having a nuclear capability.

The heaviest U.S. S.P.s are the M 107 with a long-barrelled 175 mm gun and the M 110 with the 8 in howitzer. Both have sacrificed all-round traverse but each has a nuclear capability.

The S.P. gun with the highest sustained rate of fire is the Swedish BankKanon 1A (AKV 151) with its 155 mm gun. The fully automatic gun can fire fourteen rounds per minute, fed from two magazines of seven rounds each. Prepacked magazines can be fed in two minutes to the gun from waiting lorries—thus partly overcoming the habitual artillery problem of bulk ammunition supply. Basic automotive parts are from the S Tank. The crew compartment is fully enclosed with traverse 15 degrees either side of centre.

Right out of step with everybody else the Russians have almost ignored new special S.P. artillery. Instead they have clung to wartime models supplemented by towed guns, though they have introduced some new self-propelled anti-tank guns, specially designed to support airborne forces. The ASU 57 with the 57 mm gun, and ASU 85 with the 85 mm gun weigh 5 and 14 tons respectively and, therefore, are only lightly armoured.

Somewhat dependent on the U.S.A. are the British and many other nations for their S.P. artillery, though the former have produced the Abbot with the 105 mm gun/howitzer and the French their 105 mm AMX and 155 mm S.P. howitzer—the former with an enclosed fighting compartment, the latter fully open. Only Model B of the former has a fully rotating casemate.

The first German S.P. gun to appear since 1945 is the Jagdpanzer Kanone with the same 90 mm gun as used in the U.S. M 47 tanks. Thus it follows in the tradition of the old Sturmgeschütz, but without making use of a more powerful gun than in use with current tanks.

German Jagdpanzer Kanone dug-in.

The last important British production improvisation was the Charioteer—a Cromwell hull with a special turret mounting the 83·4 mm gun and built in 1952 when modern tanks were at a premium. It was not long in British service but can be found working in Lebanon, Finland, Austria and Jordan.

ARMOURED PERSONNEL CARRIERS
The greatest proliferation of armoured fighting vehicles since 1945 has taken place among armoured personnel carriers because it was at last appreciated that infantrymen needed something better than his combat jacket to protect him and that, if he could be made as mobile as tanks, his place on the battlefield was secure.

Every major military authority laid plans for A.P.C.s, but their shape varied greatly one from another while, in priority for production, they tended to lag behind tanks and S.P. guns. Despite the old tendency to convert existing tanks into A.P.C.s by removing their turrets, a number of new designs began to appear. Some were on wheeled chassis and some tracked, the latter in the majority because they alone could accompany tanks in all conditions. The main disparities therefore centred upon what each army thought its A.P.C.s should do in battle, thence what additional armament and armour it should be given, and finally the layout which would decide the manner of entrance and exit from the vehicle. **At the outset** there was a consensus of opinion that the A.P.C. should act as a taxi by carrying its passengers close to the battle, through hostile defensive shell-fire, but dismounting them at a distance from the objective to make the final assault on foot. That way the A.P.C.s needed only bullet-proof armour and a machine-gun for self-defence since it was not intended to get involved in close combat. Typical of first products along this line of thought were the following vehicles:

Country	Name	Suspension	Men	Weight (tons)	Swimmer
Britain	Saracen	Wheeled	12	10	No
U.S.A.	M 75	Tracked	12	19	No
Russia	BTR 40	Wheeled	10	5	No
France	Hotchkiss	Tracked	10	8	No

The first nation to reject the "taxi" idea was Germany when she opted for the HS 30, tracked A.P.C., arming most of them with a turreted 20 mm cannon and making possible for the entire infantry complement of six to lean over the side to observe and shoot.

The latest A.P.C.s reflect an awareness of the need for them to be combat vehicles in the strict sense. Even when the original design was intended for taxi use (as for instance with the U.S. M 113) the subsequent addition of sub-turrets with heavy machine-guns has gone part of the way to meeting the combat requirements. Examples are as follows:

Country	Name	Suspension	Men	Weight (tons)	Swimmer	Armament (mm)
Britain	FV 432	Tracked	12	14	Yes	30 (a few)
U.S.A.	XM 701	Tracked	12	22	Yes	20
Russia	BMP 76 PB	Tracked	11	10	Yes	76 and Sagger A.T.G.W.
France	AMX VTT	Tracked	13	14	No	12·7
Germany	Marder	Tracked	10	27	Yes	20
Sweden	Pbv 302	Tracked	12	14	Yes	20

The most usual manner of entrance and exit in A.P.C.s is either by way of backward-facing doors in vehicles with frontally located engines, or out of the top in vehicles with a rearward-mounted engine. Clearly the rearward-exit system gives best initial cover to the crew though there are disadvantages in everybody emerging in file from the same place (thus offering an easy target) compared with simultaneous dismounting through a number of exists in the top.

Russian Combat Team—
BMP 76 APCs and T 55s.

ANCILLARY VEHICLES

The early processes of adapting tank hulls to special uses continues unabated. **The most common post-1945 special designs** have been bridgelayers, the reason being that, in Europe, over 80 per cent of all gaps are less than 20 m wide, and therefore it is well worth while to carry tank bridges which can span all but the very large rivers quickly. Most modern bridgelayers are based on a scissors-type span with an effective length of 20–22 m. French AMX, British Chieftain, and U.S. M 48 and M 60 equipments are of this type. However the British Centurion version had a single span which was launched up and over. The Russian T 54 MTU winches its 13 m long single span forward along a launching beam, while the German Leopard has a development of this system that involves one section being moved forward along the beam and locked to the second before both are launched as a single entity. The Centurion ARK FV 4016 follows wartime practice by driving into the obstacle before launching its spans fore and aft.

Most MBTs have associated recovery vehicles. The Centurion Beach Armoured Recovery Vehicle FV 4018 is unique in its ability to rescue drowned vehicles on a beach-head or to nudge off stranded landing-ships. The Russian T 54 T and ISU T are used at Schnorkelling sites where, if the tactical situation permits, they precede the gun-tanks and stand ready to recover any that are unable to complete the crossing.

Special engineer A.F.V.s are now less common than in 1945. The Centurion AVRE FV 4003 mounts a brushwood fascine for filling minor obstacles, a 165 mm demolition charge projector and can tow a trailer with stores. The U.S. M 728 is based on the M 60 MBT and has similar characteristics. Minefields can be cleared by heavy rollers pushed ahead of the tracks of the Russian PT 54 and the BTU dozer kit can be attached to almost all T 54/55. Dozer blades may also be attached to a number of other MBTs. We are unlikely to see a revival of the British FV 203, however, which was intended to have a minelaying compartment with its crew of nine sappers just for this purpose.

PART THREE—TECHNOLOGY

The greatest attention in tank technology post-1945 centred upon weaponry. Long guns continued in vogue along with the problems connected with their manufacture. The commonest way of manufacturing barrels was by auto-frettage which first seems to have been suggested by a French artillery officer named L. Jacob in 1907.

The first gun manufactured by auto-frettage was French—a 140 mm piece that appeared in 1913.

Saladins at night firing.

Auto-frettage is the name given to a form of gun construction which, simply, consists of over-stressing the inner surface of a barrel beyond its elastic limit, but not the outer surface, so that when the stress is removed the outer surface returns to a condition of tension while the inner surface remains in compression. Thus the whole structure is in a state of permanent stress, which allows lighter barrels of great strength to be made from a single forging. The process has usually consisted of filling the barrel with oil under very high pressure, but a new method was developed in the United States in the mid-1960s, for their version of the British 105 mm tank gun, mounted on the M 60 tank. This new method consists of forcing a dolly along the bore, before final machining. Although the dolly has to be made to extremely close tolerances the process does remove the considerable industrial problems of maintaining the high pressure required for the hydraulic application; at the same time the process allows less metal to be used in the forging itself, which is attractive to the gun and vehicle designers.

Canister ammunition (sometimes called "grape" in the distant past and "case" in 1916) was re-introduced in the Second World War for use with U.S. 37 mm tank guns—labelled "For use against Japanese only!" Later it was made for the British 20-pdr mounted in Centurion, to counter the mass infantry attacks experienced in the Korean War. The round consists of a metal canister fitted with a large number of steel pellets which, when fired, spread out in a wide cone. Although the effective range is short, canister has proved to be an effective anti-personnel weapon.

High explosive squash head (H.E.S.H.) ammunition is an armour-defeating round first introduced for general service use in the 76 mm gun mounted in the Saladin armoured car; it is also used in the Malkara A.T.G.W., the 105 mm gun mounted in Centurion and the 120 mm guns mounted in Conqueror and Chieftain. A low-velocity, chemical energy round, H.E.S.H. performance, unlike that of solid shot, is independent of range provided a hit is obtained. When the round strikes armour plate the explosive filling "pancakes" on the armour and, when the slight-delay-action fuse detonates it, sends a shock wave through the plate which detaches a large and lethal scab at very high velocity from the underside. The only indication of a strike on the outside of a vehicle attacked by H.E.S.H. is often an indentation on the plate, while inside is utter devastation caused by the shattering effect of the high-velocity scab. H.E.S.H. can also be moderately effective as conventional high explosive against unarmoured targets.

Hollow-charge projectile performance is seriously degraded not only by spaced armour but also if the projectile is rotated in flight to obtain accuracy. This affects adversely the penetrating jet formed from the explosive-cone war-head. To enable such a projectile to be used effectively from a high-velocity tank gun, the French have developed a unique non-rotating projectile in which the hollow charge itself is mounted on ball-bearings within the projectile case. Thus, although the latter is spun conventionally by the barrel rifling, giving the projectile the required accuracy, the actual hollow charge spins very slowly and is able to perform effectively on striking the target. This projectile is in service with the 105 mm gun mounted on the French AMX 30 tank and was introduced in 1967.

Gun cleaning—Saladin and crew.

The general-purpose machine-gun (FN 7·62 mm MG), originally designed as a machine-gun for the infantry, was first used as part of a tank weapons system on Chieftain, where it replaced a United States machine-gun which had proved unsatisfactory. The weapon has had to be modified at the rear end in order to fit an A.F.V. mounting, but it has proved successful as secondary armament and, on Scorpion, as a ranging machine-gun also.

Visual range estimation is one of the chief sources of error affecting chance of hit in an anti-tank engagement. Various forms of optical range-finder have been fitted in armoured vehicles, particularly by the Germans in the Second World War. In British service the first tank to have an optical range-finder built into the design was Conqueror, having a coincidence instrument which came into service in the 1950s, while the United States M 47, also in the 1950s, was the first to be fitted with a stereoscopic range-finder.

The ranging machine-gun is a range-finding device introduced into Centurion Mark 9 in the early 1960s to economise on main armament ammunition by using subcalibre tracer rounds for conventional bracketing of the target. Although spotting rifles had appeared in earlier equipments, this was the first purpose-designed ranging machine-gun installation forming part of a tank weapons system. Based on a ·5 in Browning machine-gun firing controlled bursts of three rounds at a reduced rate of fire, the system gives a greatly increased chance of a first-round hit with the main armament round, and provides a saving in his sight. The gunner fires a number of bursts from his ranging machine-gun and then, from his observation of the strike of the bursts relative to the target, fires a main armament round using the appropriate part of the ballistic graticule to lay the gun. The great merit of this device over optical range-finders is that it automatically compensates for both wind effects and for any trunnion tilt which may be present —both significant factors when firing low-velocity ammunition. The ranging machine-gun as installed in Centurion and later in Chieftain is not intended as an offensive weapon, and is therefore in addition to and not instead of the normal coaxial machine-gun which forms the secondary armament of these vehicles.

The laser range-finder is a more recent addition to the field of tank-mounted range-finders. The elapsed time for a transmitted laser pulse to be reflected and returned from the target is used to calculate instantly the exact range from the observer, the figure being usually displayed on a digital "read-out". Probably the most accurate and quick method of range-finding yet devised, the laser range-finder is bound to have a significant effect not only on the chance of obtaining a first-round hit, but also on the speed of engagement. Although not yet in service, its general introduction as a component of tank fire-control systems can only be a matter of time.

Gun-laying in armoured fighting vehicles has traditionally been achieved by traversing the turret in which the gun is mounted for changes in azimuth angle and by rotating the gun about its trunnions for changes in elevation; both by means of handwheels or some form of powered system operating through more or less simple gear-trains. The post-war period has seen two significant departures from this concept, both resulting from a desire to achieve a lower vehicle silhouette. The first idea was tried out on AMX 50 and applied to the French EBR 75 Panhard armoured car, which came into service in the early 1950s, and then to AMX 13. The gun-elevation trunnions are, in effect, moved to the outside of the turret so that changes in elevation are achieved by rotating the entire top of the turret about the trunnions; this arrangement is known as an "oscillating turret" and allows the gun mounting to be rigidly fixed close to the turret roof to permit a comparatively simple arrangement for automatic loading. The second idea is that of the much more recent and revolutionary Swedish S Tank introduced in the late 1960s, in which the main armament is rigidly mounted in the hull of the tank, elevation being achieved by raising and lowering the hull on its suspension, and traverse by slewing the entire vehicle by means of sophisticated steering arrangements. This gun, too, has automatic loading, although the French were the first to apply this well-developed naval and anti-aircraft system to tank main armament.

Firing on the move with mechanical precision first became a practical proposition when a stabiliser in both elevation and azimuth was introduced in Centurion Mark 3 in 1949. Azimuth stabilisers had previously been in service notably in the United States Sherman tank and in some German vehicles; these early versions had not really justified themselves, whereas the Metrovick equipment in Centurion proved very successful in service. The arrangement consists of a closed-loop, electro-servo stabilisation system in which changes in vehicle heading and pitch attitude are sensed by restrained gyroscopes; elevation and traverse servos maintain the gun and turret on their original headings in response to correcting signals received via amplifier units and metadyne generators.

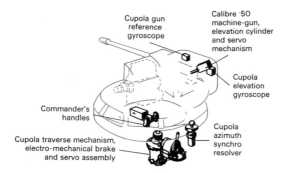

M60 A2 turret—full of black boxes.

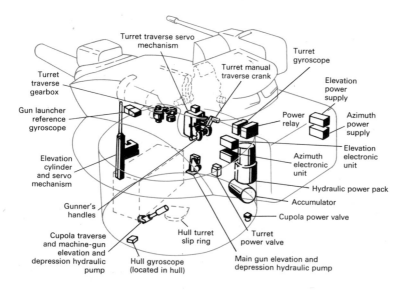

Target indication poses a major problem in the fire control of tank weapons. The tank commander, who normally selects the target, used to indicate it precisely by spoken words to the gunner, who had in his turn to lay and fire the gun. A major advance in this field took place in the 1950s, when the Reflector-cum-Periscope (R.C.P.) sight was introduced into later marks of Centurion. One episcope in the commander's cupola was replaced with a special periscopic sight in which a reflected graticule from a collimator linked to the gunner's sight was visible. This device enabled the commander, with his own elevating handwheel and overriding power traverse controller, to lay the gunner's sight accurately on to the target.

Automatic line-up of commander's sight, gunner's sight and gun followed the R.C.P. sight in an attempt to introduce what was known as a "fully integrated fire-control system". The British Conqueror tank, taken into service in the 1950s, was the first to include a facility whereby the commander, after laying his own sighting equipment accurately on to a target, had merely to press a button to align automatically the gunner's sight and the 120 mm gun on to the same target; an added facility was that the commander could also fire the gun himself if necessary. Furthermore, the commander, who sat in his own sub-turret, had completely independent operation from the main turret, so that while the gunner engaged one target the commander could be selecting another and ranging on to it with his optical range-finder. Although Conqueror was the first tank to incorporate such a sophisticated fire-control system, it must be admitted that the design had a number of unsatisfactory features and after a short time in service the equipment was modified to eliminate automatic line-up in azimuth, leaving the facility in elevation only.

Barrel bend was first noticed as a phenomenon by naval gunnery experts at the beginning of the twentieth century. The bending of the long barrels of high-velocity guns as they become hot during firing, a condition often accentuated by cold winds and rain, **became an important factor in tank gun accuracy in the 1950s**, when the gradual elimination of other errors made improved shooting possible. It has not been possible so far to eliminate completely the effects of barrel bend, but the introduction into British service of the thermal sleeve for tank guns has done much to maintain the correct bore-axis/gunner's-sight relationship. The equipment consists of a fabric strap-on sleeve which encloses all the exposed part of the barrel and effectively insulates it from the effects of rain, wind and solar radiation. First adopted for the 105 mm gun on Centurion, it also forms part of the standard equipment for the 120 mm gun on Chieftain.

A ballistic computer will form an essential component in any advanced fire-control system. Such a system, combined with a laser range-finder and known as "Cobelda", has been developed in Belgium for use on the German Leopard tank and is the first such arrangement to be seen on an armoured fighting vehicle, a pre-production equipment having been installed in 1969. The ruby laser determines the range and a number of sensors in the system provide information on other ballistic variables. This data is fed into the computer which then predicts the trajectory of the type of projectile which has been selected. The computer output is transferred to a simple graticule in the gunner's sight which, when laid on to the target, ensures that the gun is laid with the correct angles of elevation and azimuth; in addition the computer can give the correct lead angle for engaging a moving target. Operation is simple, the gunner being required to do no more than press an ammunition selector switch and fire the laser, in addition to operating the normal gun controls.

Smoke for concealment of tanks has usually been provided by grenades, main armament smoke ammunition or by smoke generators. The Soviet T 55, which first appeared in 1961, **is the first tank to be fitted with a device using the vehicle's own exhaust system** to generate smoke although the British Marks V, VII, VIII and Mediums B, C and D had a system of introducing sulphuric acid in 1918. The simple Russian idea allows unburnt vaporised diesel fuel to be pumped into the hot exhaust system, which thus emits a dense cloud of white smoke; an effective screen is produced, with the enormous advantage that it can be turned on and off at will.

M 551, General Sheridan, fires its Shillelagh missile.

Aluminium armour was first used on the United States M 113 armoured personnel carrier, originally introduced into service in 1960, and the hull of Sheridan: it has since formed the protection for some British armoured vehicles, notably Scorpion and Fox. While requiring greater thickness of metal for an equivalent degree of protection than that provided by steel armour, aluminium armour provides a significant saving of weight which is very attractive—particularly for light vehicles which may have to be air-transported.

Nuclear, biological and chemical warfare protection began to be incorporated in most modern armoured vehicles in the 1960s. In general protection depends on sealing the crew compartments and then pressurising the sealed vehicle to a level slightly above atmospheric. The air sucked in is cleaned by filters and is then normally ducted to the various crew positions; if the sealing breaks down for any reason provision is usually made for the crew's service respirators to be plugged into the clean-air system through special outlets in the ducting.

Gun fumes within the fighting compartment of an A.F.V. have always been a hazard and an irritant to the crew. With the introduction of high-velocity guns, with their characteristically long barrels, the tendency of gun fumes to flow back into tank turrets when the breech was opened, became more marked. One of the most effective devices to counter this problem, and the first to enter British Army service, was the fume extractor fitted to the barrel of the 20-pdr gun mounted in Centurion Mark 3; a similar design was adopted for the 105 mm gun and the 120 mm gun on Chieftain and in the tanks of other nations too. This simple device consists of a cylinder fitted round a short length of the barrel, covering a number of gas ports drilled in the barrel itself. As the projectile passes up the barrel, some of the gas from the propellant charge enters the cylinder through the ports. The gas thus trapped re-enters the bore after shot ejection and causes a flow of air from breech to muzzle, effectively discharging all gun fumes through the muzzle of the gun instead of back into the fighting compartment through the open breech.

Empty cartridge-case disposal has often influenced turret design, since enough room must be left behind the main gun to accommodate the empty case when it is ejected from the gun after firing; in addition a basket has to be provided on the turret floor, into which the case must fall. As tank guns have increased in size, so this problem has assumed greater significance. Conqueror incorporated a novel solution in the shape of a system which automatically ejected the empty 120 mm case right outside the turret. The empty case was extracted from the gun and fell on to a hoist on the turret floor, the action closing a switch and starting the hoist motor; the case was then lifted up a chute, and as it rose a door in the side of the turret opened and the case was pushed through on to the ground outside. However, the main step forward in this field came with Chieftain, whose 120 mm gun was the first quick-firing (Q.F.) gun (i.e. with sliding breech and semi-automatic action) to use bag charges instead of metal cartridge-cases; the propellant is contained in a bag which is all consumed when the charge is ignited, thus leaving no cartridge-case to be disposed of.

The reclining driver position on the Chieftain tank is a configuration which allows the overall height of the vehicle to be reduced, since the conventional arrangement must allow headroom for the driver to sit upright when closed down.

In Chieftain the driver reclines on his back to drive closed down and adopts the conventional upright position only when driving "head out".

Night-fighting tended to be neglected in British Army service after 1945 until the late 1950s, when the effort being put into night-fighting techniques by the U.S.S.R. began to be appreciated in the West. The first significant step forward in British Army service came with Chieftain; the vehicle is equipped with a powerful infra-red lamp which, coupled with infra-red night sights, gives this tank an extremely effective night-fighting capability. A further advance has come with the development of the "image intensifier" night sight, a device which makes use of the natural illumination to be found even at night to give clear vision without the aid of a vulnerable searchlight.

Additional fuel supplies carried on the outside of tanks makes the vehicle very vulnerable to attack, although the need to increase radius of action is always pressing. One unique British solution, introduced in Centurion in the 1950s, was the Monotrailer. This consisted of a one-wheel armoured trailer containing 200 gal of fuel, towed behind the tank. The castor action of the one wheel meant that the tank's freedom of action was not too severely limited— though the device was never popular with tank crews—and explosive bolts were provided so that the trailer could be jettisoned instantly in an emergency or when going into action.

Fitters working on transmission of a Chieftain. The engine has been removed.

Germany's fast Leopard with its British 105 mm gun.

M 109 with its 155 mm gun—a fine example of modern American self-propelled artillery.

Fox—a light British armoured car with its 30 mm automatic cannon.

The power pack for the Chieftain tank, comprising two-stroke, compression-ignition main and generator engines is the first to have a multi-fuel capability; the ability to run on several different types of fuel without significant variation in power output is clearly important in a war situation, where supplies of particular fuels may be scarce. The auxiliary engine has the unusual capability of being able to start the main engine by cranking it hydraulically and can warm up the main engine coolant in cold conditions. In addition the power pack can be fairly easily removed from the vehicle as a unit, complete with radiators, fans, etc.

Tracked vehicles for reconnaissance have never been popular in British Army service because, it has been claimed, tracks limit vehicle speed and are too noisy. The new Scorpion Light Tank, however, is the first tank where design has been able to overcome these objections. The vehicle's speed of 50 mile/h on roads and absence of track noise (the tank is considerably quieter than many wheeled vehicles) has been achieved by a new design of track which incorporates extensive rubber bushing and the use of large rubber pads.

T 62s crossing a river with Schnorkel tubes erected.

The crossing of water obstacles by means of Schnorkelling devices was the subject of experiments within the U.S.S.R. as early as the 1930s. However, it was not until after the Second World War that standard equipment came into service in the Soviet Army, which can be said to be the first to have its tanks factory-equipped on a large scale with Schnorkelling equipment. In peacetime training a heavy conning-tower is fitted to the tank turret for water-crossing, and this can be used as an escape-hatch for the crew in the event of an emergency, while in war a narrower tube, carried on the vehicle and erected by the crew themselves, is used. Control is effected by radio, with an observer on the bank watching the Schnorkel tube of a submerged tank and giving the driver appropriate radioed directions to keep him on course.

Amphibious tanks (provided by Vickers) were also early on the scene in Russia and the Soviet PT 76 amphibious tank introduced in 1952 is the first to employ hydro-jets as a means of water-propulsion. Water, sucked in through ports on the underside of the tank, is pressurised by pumps driven by the main engine and expelled at the rear. Steering is effected by adjustment of "clam shell" covers over the rear ports. The vehicle is highly manœuvrable when afloat and is capable of some 6 knots in the water.

Navigation of armoured vehicles in devastated areas or desert terrain has been made a great deal easier by the introduction in the mid-1960s of the Land Navigation System. **This is the first vehicle navigating system** to be used in service and is the only one providing automatic dead reckoning which, when deriving directional information from the earth's magnetic field, operates entirely without gyros. The system can also accept inputs from a gyro-compass in a more elaborate installation on, for example, a main battle-tank, where large masses of magnetic material move relative to the vehicle hull. The equipment not only provides a continuously up-dated six-figure grid reference of the vehicle position, relative to the military grid superimposed on all service maps, but also indicates the vehicle's compass heading.

The first operational British/Australian ATGW—Malkara is fired from a Hornet.

The anti-tank guided weapon (A.T.G.W.) has found a place in recent years amongst anti-armour weapons as the need to achieve a first-round hit at long range in an anti-armour engagement has assumed ever greater importance.

The first practical A.T.G.W. system to be seen in service was the French SS 10 wire-guided missile—originally as in most other A.T.G.W. systems intended for use in the dismounted role, but later adapted for a vehicle mount. As SS 11 mounted on the AMX 13 tank it was in fact the first tank-mounted missile system to appear in service.

FV 438 firing a Swingfire ATGW.

The first A.T.G.W. system specifically designed for and in service on an armoured vehicle was Malkara, Australian-manufactured to a British requirement, which has seen service mounted on a 1-ton armoured truck and called "Hornet". The missile was large and heavy and carried a 60-lb H.E.S.H. warhead, but as a first-generation system has been effective enough. The British Aircraft Corporation's Swingfire followed in the late 1960s, a much smaller missile with increased range and with an equally effective, though much smaller warhead. Originally conceived as a ground-mounted weapon, Swingfire nevertheless first appeared in a variant of the FV 432 armoured personnel carrier called FV 438. The vehicle is large enough to enable the crew not only to fire the missile from under armour, but also to reload the launcher tubes from within the vehicle. A wheeled armoured vehicle mounting Swingfire, a variant of the Ferret scout car known as FV 712, is also in service and the system is to be mounted on a version of the new light tracked vehicle family, the A.T.G.W. variant being known as "Striker".

The first combined gun and A.T.G.W. system to appear is the United States Shillelagh system, mounted on the Sheridan light tank; in this system the missile is launched from a breech-loading 152 mm gun which also fires conventional ammunition. Unlike some earlier European systems in which the missile trailed a wire behind it, down which guidance signals were passed from the controller, Shillelagh uses automatic infra-red data links, so that all the controller has to do is to establish the line of sight to the target by laying his sight graticule on to it; the guidance system then automatically brings the missile on to that sight line, which it follows to the target.

SECTION VII
Appendices

Appendix 1

TANK NOMENCLATURE

Right from their inception armoured fighting vehicles were in need of a name—hence the christening of the "Tank" to describe the first operational machine of all. Each tank-producing nation has since adopted its own system of tank nomenclature and varied it as time has gone by. The following is an outline of the systems used at various times by the five principal tank-making countries. But there are many anomalies: the subject is a quicksand with exceptions to disprove every rule.

Britain began in 1915 with "Wilson" or "Centipede" but later became known as "Big Willie", then "Mother" and finally "Heavy Tank Mark I".

When the new "Medium" and various "Support" tanks were introduced in 1917 names became:

Heavy Tank Mark V; Medium Tank Mark A plus a name—"Whippet", for example; Gun Carrier Mark I; and Supply Tank.

After the war a similar system was continued (except that the letter system for marks was replaced by Roman numerals) even though the weight parameters for each category were subject to fluctuations of the moment. Light tanks were introduced, of course, by about 1929. From about 1924 onwards each new type was given an "A" prefix—the "Independent" in fact being A 1. In addition experimental versions of an "A" type would take the additional letter E; there were three A 6s, for instance—A 6 E1, A 6 E2 and A 6 E3 though these vehicles were commonly known as "sixteen-tonners".

In late 1934 a rationalised system was laid down by the General Staff dividing all tanks into three groups—lights, cruisers and heavies while retaining the "A" prefix for developing models.

In late 1941, however, partly at the instance of Winston Churchill, names were adopted—thus A 12, Infantry Tank Mark II which had been officially adapted in 1937 from Infantry Tank Mark I (A 11), became also known as Matilda, and A 15, Cruiser Mark VI, became the Crusader which itself blossomed into various Marks—Crusader II, etc.

In 1945 the "A" prefix for developing models was superseded by the letters FV followed by a number, until the vehicle came into service, and in 1951 the classifying of tanks by weight gave way to a continuation of the "C" series of names. Thus Comet and Centurion, which were pre-1951, were followed by Conqueror, Charioteer and Chieftain among others.

Post-war reconnaissance vehicles have adopted the "S" series of names with armoured cars such as Saladin and light tanks like Scorpion.

France. The first French tanks were regarded as artillery vehicles and known originally as "*artillerie d'assaut*" and later as "*char d'assaut*". Normally each French name was prefixed by that of its maker and then the year of its derivation. Hence Char d'Assaut St. Chamond (M 16), but at the same time they specified heavy tanks which took the special title of Char de Rupture C.

When first the Infantry had total control of tanks the old system prevailed, but when the Cavalry tried to enter the armour business and discovered that, by regulation, they were not permitted to have tanks they merely adopted a new name for fighting tanks. Thus while all Infantry-owned tanks continued to be known as *"chars"* (plus a weight classification of Légèr, Moyens, Bataille or Lourds) taking the maker's name first letter, followed by the year's number (Char Légèr Renault of 1935 thus became the light R 35), the Cavalry adopted in 1931 an even more complicated *"auto-mitrailleuse"* nomenclature:

(1) *Auto-mitrailleuse de Découverte*, or AMD, was a distant reconnaissance armoured car.

(2) *Auto-mitrailleuse de Reconnaissance*, or AMR, was a light tank.

(3) *Auto-mitrailleuse de Combat*, or AMC, was a medium gun tank.

But in 1935 was added to Cavalry classification the Char de Cavalerie of which the new Chars Légers H 35 became one, yet was still known as H 35.

Since 1945 an entirely new system has been adopted to define vehicles other than *chars*:

(1) *Auto-mitrailleuse Légère*, AML, a light reconnaissance vehicle.

(2) *Engin Blindée de Reconnaissance*, EBR, an armoured reconnaissance vehicle or armoured car.

(3) *Engin Legérè de Combat*, ELC, a light battle vehicle.

(4) *Engin de Transport de Troupes*, ETT, an armoured personnel carrier.

Chars continued to be known as such, but now took the manufacturer's letters as prefix with a figure representing the weight class of the vehicle. Hence AMX 30 is the product of Atelier de Construction d'Issy-les-Moulineaux, in the 30-ton class, though, in fact, it weighs more than 30 tons.

Germany. The first German tank of 1917 was named after the Government department—A7V—which sponsored it. Thereafter the Germans named their tanks as PanzerKampfwagen (PzKpfw or PzKw) adding letters and numerals. Their first medium tank thus became PzKpfw L K.I.

During the post-Versailles years, when Germany was forbidden tanks, a few clandestine types were built, their existence disguised by reference to them as different types of tractor. Only after rearmament had been openly announced in 1934 did the formal series of PzKpfw marks come into recognised use while each vehicle regardless of class received a Sonderkraftfahrzeug (SdKfz) number. Thus was to come PzKpfw I to VI with the modifications to each Mark of the type notified by the addition of a letter. Hence PzKpfw IIIJ. Support vehicles were treated slightly differently in some cases and as follows:

(1) Self-propelled anti-tank guns—Jagdpanzer IV (SdKfz No.).

(2) Armoured cars—Panzerspahwagen (SdKfz No.).

(3) Assault guns—Sturmgeschütz III (SdKfz No.).

(4) Armoured infantry carrier—Schützenpanzerwagen (SdKfz No.).

From 1942 onward the practice of naming vehicles became normal with PzKpfw VI (SdKfz 181) becoming known as Tiger I and so on.

It should be noted that experimental tracked vehicles were often given a VK (Vollkettenkraftfahrzeug) number which was dropped once the type was accepted for production.

When Germany again turned to building an army in 1953, she had to make do at first with other people's armoured vehicles. She mostly kept the old nomenclature, but simplified the battle-tank to Kampfpanzer. Existing names were accepted and the practice of adding names to fighting vehicles of German manufacture continued.

When Russia set up her own tank construction industry in the 1920s she at once adopted a system of T numbers for all her tanks, denoting modification by the addition of a letter—T 26B, for instance. This rule was soon broken in the early 1930s, however, by the need to differentiate between the various speed and weight classifications. The introduction of the fast Christie-type cruisers brought about the BT series—the letter standing for Bystrokhodnii Tank, or fast tank. The habit of naming the heavy, prestige-type tanks after personalities began in 1937 when the biggest Russian tank so far was entitled Sergeij Mironovitsch Kirov (SMK)—the beginning of a personality cult which ended with the Stalin series and Stalin himself. Today the Russian system retains much of its original character while the other categories of vehicles are differentiated by a letter system:

(1) PT—Light tank.

(2) BRDM—Armoured car.

(3) BTR—Armoured personnel carrier.

(4) SU—Self-propelled gun.

(5) ASU—Airborne self-propelled gun.

After the First World War America persevered with a haphazard nomenclature culled from the miscellany of acquired foreign tanks. In the 1920s came rationalisation. Only experimental types were produced and these took T numbers, modified by E numbers e.g. T 1 E2. But, as with the French Government, regulations forbade the Cavalry to possess tanks of its own, and so cavalry A.F.V.s had to be named by subterfuge. They were called Combat Cars with the addition of a number. But already it had been deemed necessary to differentiate between light, medium and heavy tanks taking an M number when in production. So a rather complex but progressive system evolved. For example, T 5 Light became Cavalry Combat Car M 1 and was the same as Infantry Tank Light M 1. Later, when the Armored Corps was formed and the Infantry monopoly broken, Combat Car would be dropped. Thereafter, for example, Medium T 5 E2 could be named Medium M 3 in 1940–41. The addition of extra letters and numbers to indicate new marks was finally adopted and so the original Medium M 4 finished up in one version as Tank Medium M 4 A3 E8.

For some time the Americans resisted the temptation to name their tanks, though the British always gave the names of American generals to those American tanks they took into service during the Second World War. Thus M 4 in its original version became General Sherman, the M 4 A4 version receiving the nomenclature Sherman Mark V.

Since the Second World War the Americans have maintained the T and M system while drifting into the habit of giving names to some of their tanks. But in the 1960s the T was substituted by XM for experimental models. Thus XM 551 became M 551 (General Sheridan).

Appendix 2

CAMOUFLAGE

There are few subjects more likely to excite the pundits and model makers—particularly the latter—than that of A.F.V. camouflage and colour schemes. As likely as not the reason for so much disagreement over the subtleties of shading is the fact that original examples of First and Second World War paints are practically extinct. Nearly every museum exhibit has so often been repainted that any comparison with the past is impossible, while those who served with the tanks at the time are getting old and have forgotten. So the first rule in any debate about A.F.V. camouflage of the past is to remember that it is almost impossible to separate right from wrong—and the more so since, even when official colour schemes can be quoted, there was never any guarantee that the manufacturer kept to specification, that the paint was not adulterated by quartermasters "in the interests of accounting" or that units and individual crews did not introduce their own preferences with the final application.

Nevertheless there have been many official attempts within every army to impose a standardised system, bearing in mind that the over-riding aim was to distract the enemy—to break up the vehicle's outline rather than paint it, chameleon-like, to resemble the surrounding countryside. For example the first British tanks to go into action in 1916 often adopted dazzle-painting somewhat similar to that being used by ships at sea.

First World War. British tanks generally wore olive-green paint, sometimes speckled by yellow, such as artillery had always used. The French did much the same though they also sometimes used grey. Information about the Germans is sparse but it seems likely that they adopted *feldgrau*.

Second World War. Europe. British tanks were painted either in olive-green or a muddy brown. Attempts at disruptive painting were rare and in any case would have been largely negative due to the crews' habit of carrying piles of kit on the outside of their tanks—as a commensurate fire risk. White paint was occasionally used in snow conditions, but this was not universal. French tanks went in for a combination of green, grey, yellow and brown mixed into a genuine disruptive pattern. They also took quite a lot of care to reduce shine—something which so often distinguished British tanks. The Germans, early on, used a bluey grey but reverted to a basic yellow-brown, a battleship grey or sage-green which they could embellish with any colours that happened to be available and which suited the local conditions. It is worth noting that they issued spray-guns to their tanks so that changes could be easily and quickly made by the crews. In winter, of course, they used white, sometimes speckling it with other colours. The Russians also followed German practice, though without so much elaboration in that they hardly ever went in for disruptive patterns. American practice was very similar to that of the British.

Desert (Middle East). Both sides used a light sandy yellow though the Germans frequently superimposed it with greens and blacks—a practice only rarely employed by the British and Americans.

Jungle (Far East). The Allies mostly employed a dark olive-green, occasionally adding an irregular yellow pattern. The Japanese were more ambitious, devising a blotchy pattern of greens, blacks and yellows of which the latter was sometimes the predominant colour.

A British Armoured Regiment (17th/21st Lancers) on show—
  Two front rows : Scout cars, Command vehicles and Chieftains.
  Three squadrons of Chieftains.
  Rear row : Stalwart swimming supply vehicles, recovery vehicles, bridgelayer and supply trucks.
  Overhead : Sioux helicopter.

Appendix 3

PRINCIPAL ARMOURED FIGHTING VEHICLE CAMPAIGNS AND BATTLES

Title	Date	Major contestants	A.F.V.s engaged (approx.)
FIRST WORLD WAR	1914–18	Allies—Britain, France, Belgium, Russia, Serbia, Italy and U.S.A.—versus Germany, Austria-Hungary and Turkey	Miscellaneous armoured cars from start. No tanks until September 1916
Channel ports	Sept–Nov 1914	Britain and France versus Germany	A few improvised Allied armoured cars
Somme	Sept–Nov 1916	Britain versus Germany	50 Mark I British tanks
Nivelle offensives	Apr–May 1917	Britain and France versus Germany	60 British and 150 French tanks
Flanders	June–Nov 1917	Britain versus Germany	300 British tanks
Malmaison	Sept 1917	France versus Germany	92 French tanks
Cambrai	Nov–Dec 1917	Britain versus Germany	476 British tanks
German Western offensive	Mar–July 1918	Germany versus Allies	20 German tanks. 1,000-plus Allied tanks and armoured cars
Allied final offensive	Aug–Nov 1918	Allies versus Germany	
Amiens	Aug 1918	Britain and France versus Germany	600 British and French tanks plus armoured cars
Albert	Aug 1918	Britain versus Germany	300 British tanks
St. Mihiel	Sept 1918	France and U.S.A. versus Germany	185 French tanks. 174 American tanks
Meuse-Argonne	Sept–Oct 1918	France and U.S.A. versus Germany	750 French tanks. 140 American tanks
Hindenburg Line and beyond	Sept–Oct 1918	Britain and U.S.A. versus Germany	80 British tanks. 20 American tanks
INTERWAR ACTIONS **Russian Revolution**	1917–20	Reds versus Whites and Anglo-French assistance	86 British tanks and 100 French tanks on the White side until surrendered to the Reds. Many armoured cars on both sides

continued

The latest production tank—Britain's agile Scorpion, one of a family of new fighting vehicles.

The standard U.S. battle tank—M60 A1—product of many modifications.

Left to right—German Pz II, Lynx,
Pz III, Tiger II.

The greatest collection of fighting vehicles
in the world—Tank Museum,
Bovington Camp, Dorset, England.

Guns of all ages and nations.

Left to right—Sherman I, Sherman
Firefly, Cromwell. In foreground
Matilda CDL.

Title	Date	Major contestants	A.F.V.s engaged (approx.)
Interwar Actions continued			
Gran Chaco War	1932–35	Bolivia versus Paraguay	20 British-type tanks and carriers
Abyssinian War	1935–36	Italy versus Abyssinia	298 Italian light tanks (carriers)
Spanish Civil War	1936–39	Nationalists, Germans and Italians versus Republicans and Russians	100 German light tanks 120 Italian light tanks and armoured cars 700 Russian tanks Many local improvisations
Manchurian Incident	Aug 1939	Japan versus Russia	180 Japanese tanks 498 Russian tanks
SECOND WORLD WAR	1939–45	German-Italian-Japanese Axis versus almost the entire world	Armoured cars in virtually all campaigns and no longer specially mentioned herein
Poland	Sept 1939	Germany versus Poland	3,195 German tanks 190 Polish tanks
Finland	Nov 1939–Mar 1940	Russia versus Finland	1,500 Russian tanks
Norway	Apr–June 1940	Germany versus Norway, Britain and France	50 German tanks
Low Countries and France	May–June 1940	Germany versus Belgium, Holland, France and Britain	3,379 German tanks 3,500 French tanks 620 British tanks, mostly light 50 others
Cyrenaica "Compass"	June 1940–Feb 1941	Britain versus Italy	275 British tanks 380 Italian tanks and carriers
Balkans	Apr–May 1941	German-Italian Axis versus Yugoslavia, Greece and Britain	1,000 Axis tanks 200 Allied tanks
Cyrenaica	Apr–May 1941	German-Italian Axis versus Britain	50 Axis tanks but increasing to 130 120 British tanks
Cyrenaica "Battleaxe"	June 1941	Britain versus German-Italian Axis	200 British tanks 170 German tanks
Russia "Barbarossa"	June–Dec 1941	Germany versus Russia	3,200 German tanks 20,000 Russian tanks
Cyrenaica "Crusader"	Nov–Dec 1941	Britain versus German-Italian Axis	756 British tanks plus 50 per cent reserve 249 German tanks 150 Italian tanks
Russia Winter counter-offensive	Dec 1941–Feb 1942	Russia versus Germany	2,000 Russian tanks 1,450 German tanks
Far East Philippines	Dec 1941–Apr 1942	Japan versus U.S.A.	200 Japanese tanks (est.) 50 American tanks

Title	Date	Major contestants	A.F.V.s engaged (approx.)
Second World War *Far East continued*			
Burma	Dec 1941– Mar 1942	Japan versus Britain	70 Japanese tanks (est.) 120 British tanks
Cyrenaica German counter-offensive	Jan 1942	German-Italian Axis versus Britain	84 German tanks 89 Italian tanks 150 British tanks
Russia Baravenko	Jan and May 1942	Russia versus Germany	5,000 Russian tanks 3,000 German tanks
Cyrenaica/Egypt "Theseus"	May–June 1942	German-Italian Axis versus Britain	332 German tanks 228 Italian tanks 849 British tanks
Russia Caucasus/Stalingrad	June–Nov 1942	Germany versus Russia	3,000 German tanks 1,250 Russian tanks
Egypt 1st El Alamein	July–Aug 1942	Britain versus German-Italian Axis	150 British tanks and rising fast 55 German tanks } rising slowly 30 Italian tanks
Alam Halfa	Aug–Sept 1942	German-Italian Axis versus Britain	200 German tanks 240 Italian tanks 935 British tanks
2nd El Alamein	Oct–Nov 1942	Britain versus German-Italian Axis	1,441 British tanks 210 German tanks 280 Italian tanks
Russia Stalingrad	Dec 1942– Jan 1943	Russia versus Germany	894 Russian tanks 675 German tanks
Kharkov	Feb–Mar 1943	Germany versus Russia	350 German tanks 50 Russian tanks
North Africa Battle for Tunis	Nov–Dec 1942	Britain, U.S.A., France versus German-Italian Axis	80 British/U.S.A. tanks 40 German tanks
Kasserine	Feb 1943	German-Italian Axis versus others	150 German tanks 20 Italian tanks 350 American tanks 100 British tanks
Final offensive	Mar–May 1943	Allies versus German-Italian Axis	2,200 Allied tanks 130 Axis tanks
Russia Kursk ("Citadel") and Russian counter-offensive	July–Sept 1943	Germany versus Russia	2,700 German tanks then into decline 3,300 Russian tanks rising
Sicily	July–Aug 1943	Allies versus German-Italian Axis	600 Allied tanks 200 Axis tanks

Title	Date	Major contestants	A.F.V.s engaged (approx.)

Second World War continued

Italy
Advance to Cassino | Sept–Nov 1943 | Allies versus Germany | 800 Allied tanks
250 German tanks

Russia
Dneiper | Aug–Dec 1943 | Russia versus Germany | 2,400 Russian tanks
2,100 German tanks

Smolensk | Aug–Oct 1943 | Russia versus Germany | 1,400 Russian tanks
500 German tanks

Ukraine | Dec 1943–
Jan 1944 | Russia versus Germany | 2,000 Russian tanks
2,200 German tanks

Italy
Rome | May–July 1944 | Allies versus Germany | 1,400 Allied tanks
250 German tanks

Western Europe
Invasion | June 1944 | Allies versus Germany | 5,300 Allied tanks
1,500 German tanks } Available tho' not all committed

"Goodwood" | July 1944 | Britain versus Germany | 1,350 British tanks
300 German tanks

"Cobra" | July 1944 | U.S.A. versus Germany | 1,500 American tanks and increasing
110 German tanks

Eastern Europe
Invasion of Poland | July–Aug 1944 | Russia versus Germany | 6,000 Russian tanks
1,800 German tanks

Southern Europe
Invasion of France | Aug–Sept 1944 | Allies versus Germany | 700 Allied tanks
100 German tanks

Gothic Line | Aug–Sept 1944 | Allies versus Germany | 1,200 Allied tanks
200 German tanks

Western Europe
Ardennes | Dec 1944–
Jan 1945 | Germany versus Allies | 970 German tanks
800 American tanks, increasing fast to about 2,000 American and British

Eastern Europe
Drive to the Oder | Jan 1945 | Russia versus Germany | 4,100 Russian tanks
1,150 German tanks

Far East
Burma | Dec 1944–
Aug 1945 | Britain versus Japan | 250 British tanks
80 Japanese tanks

Western Europe
Drive to the Rhine | Feb–Mar 1945 | Allies versus Germany | 5,000 Allied tanks
500 German tanks

Far East
Manchuria | Aug 1945 | Russia versus Japan | 5,500 Russian tanks
1,000 Japanese tanks

Title	Date	Major contestants	A.F.V.s engaged (approx.)
POSTWAR ACTIONS			
Korea			
Advance to Pusan	Jan–Aug 1950	N. Korea versus United Nations	240 North Korean tanks decreasing to zero 20 American tanks increasing to about 1,000
Middle East			
Sinai	Oct–Nov 1956	Israel versus Egypt	400 Israeli tanks 500 Egyptian tanks
India			
Punjab	Aug 1965	Pakistan versus India	Numbers uncertain, but about 400 each side
Middle East			
Sinai, Jordan and Syria	June 1967	Israel versus Egypt, Jordan and Syria	1,000 Israeli tanks 1,300 Egyptian tanks 500 Syrian tanks 250 Jordanian tanks

Appendix 4

IMPORTANT ARMOURED FIGHTING VEHICLES WHICH ENTERED SERVICE

Type	Length (ft in)	Width (ft in)	Armour max. (mm)	Weight (tons)	Power Plant (hp)	Max Speed (mile/h)	Main armament	Crew
1916–18								
Britain								
Heavy Mark I (male)	32 6	13 9	10	28	105	3·7	2 × 57 mm	8
Heavy Mark IV (male)	26 5	12 10	12	28	105	3·7	2 × 57 mm	8
Heavy Mark V (male)	26 5	12 10	12	29	150	4·6	2 × 57 mm	8
Heavy Mark V (male)	32 5	12 10	12	33	150	4·6	2 × 57 mm	8
Medium Mark A (Whippet)	20 0	8 7	12	14	2 × 45	8·3	4 mg	3
Medium Mark C (Hornet)	26 0	8 4	12	20	150	7·9	4 mg	4
France								
Medium Schneider M 16	20 0	7 0	24	13·5	60	4·2	1 × 75 mm	6
St. Chamond M 16	26 6	8 11	17	23	90	5	1 × 75 mm	8
Light Renault FT	16 6	5 10	22	6·5	39	5	1 × 37 mm or 1 mg	2
Germany								
A7V	24 6	10 2	30	32	100	5	1 × 57 mm	16
1919–39								
Britain								
Vickers Medium I	17 6	9 1	6·25	11·7	90	15	1 × 47 mm	5
Cruiser Mark I	19 3	8 4	14	12	150	25	1 × 40 mm	6
Infantry Mark I	15 11	7 6	60	11	70	8	1 mg	2
Light Mark VI B	13 0	6 9	14	5·5	89	35	2 mg	3
Cruiser Mark IV	19 9	8 4	30	15	340	30	1 × 40 mm	4
France								
D 1A	16 0	7 3	30	12	150	12	1 × 37 mm	3
Somua S 35	17 8	7 1	55	20	190	25	1 × 47 mm	3
Renault R 35	13 4	6 2	45	9·8	82	12·5	1 × 37 mm	2
B 1 *bis*	21 9	8 3	60	32	300	17·5	1 × 75 mm 1 × 47 mm	4
Hotchkiss H 35	14 1	6 0	34	11·4	75	17·5	1 × 37 mm	2
Italy								
CV 3/33	9 11	4 6	14	3·35	43	26	2 mg	2
M 11/39	15 6	7 2	30	11	105	20	1 × 37 mm	3

Type	Length (ft in)	Width (ft in)	Armour max. (mm)	Weight (tons)	Power Plant (hp)	Max Speed (mile/h)	Main armament	Crew
1919–39 continued								
Russia								
T 26B	16 3	8 0	15	9·4	91	17·5	1 × 45 mm	3
BT 2	19 2	7 2	13	10·2	343	38	1 × 37 mm	3
T 35	32 4	10 8	30	45	500	18	1 × 76·2 mm 2 × 45 mm	10
BT 7	18 10	7 8	22	13·8	450	33	1 × 45 mm	3
Germany								
PzKpfw IA	13 2	6 10	13	5·4	60	25	2 mg	2
PzKpfw IIC	15 10	7 1	30	8·8	140	16	1 × 20 mm	3
PzKpfw IIID	18 0	9 8	30	19·3	320	25	1 × 37 mm	5
PzKpfw IVA	18 8	9 4	20	17·3	250	18·5	1 × 75 mm	5
PzKpfw 38t (Czech)	13 6	6 8	25	9·7	125	26	1 × 37 mm	4
Japan								
Type 89A	16 8	7 2	17	13	118	15	1 × 57 mm	4
T95 Kyu-go	10 1	6 8	14	7·4	110	28	1 × 37 mm	3
T97 Chi Ha	16 7	6 8	25	14	170	24	1 × 57 mm	4
U.S.A.								
M 1 Combat Car	13 7	7 0	15	9·7	250	50	2 mg	4
1940–45								
Britain								
Infantry Mark II (Matilda)	18 5	8 3	78	26·5	2 × 87	15	1 × 40 mm	4
Infantry Mark III (Valentine I)	17 11	8 9	65	17	135	15	1 × 40 mm	3
Infantry Mark IV (Churchill I)	24 5	10 8	102	38·5	350	17	1 × 76 mm 1 × 40 mm	5
Light Mark VII (Tetrarch)	14 1	7 7	10	7·5	165	40	1 × 40 mm	3
Cruiser Mark VI (Crusader I)	19 8	8 8	40	19	340	26	1 × 40 mm	5
Cruiser Mark VII (Cromwell IV)	20 10	9 7	76	27·5	600	38	1 × 75 mm	5
Churchill VII	24 5	11 4	152	40	350	12	1 × 75 mm	5
Comet	21 6	10 0	101	32·5	600	29	1 × 77 mm	5
Italy								
M 13/40	16 2	7 3	40	14	105	19	1 × 47 mm	4

Type	Length (ft in)	Width (ft in)	Armour max. (mm)	Weight (tons)	Power Plant (hp)	Max Speed (mile/h)	Main armament	Crew
1940–45 continued								
Russia								
Heavy KV1A	22 5	11 0	90	43·5	600	21	1 × 76·2 mm	5
Medium T 34/76A	19 9	10 0	45	26·3	500	33	1 × 76·2 mm	4
Light T 70	14 4	8 0	45	9·2	2 × 70	27	1 × 45 mm	2
T 34/85	20 3	9 10	75	32	500	31	1 × 85 mm	4
JS II	22 6	10 2	160	46	600	22	1 × 122 mm	4
T 44	20 3	10 6	90	32	520	32	1 × 85 mm	4
JS III	22 2	10 8	230	46	600	25	1 × 122 mm	4
Germany								
PzKpfw III J	17 9	9 7	50	22	320	28	1 × 50 mm	5
PzKpfw IVG	19 4	9 7	50	23·6	300	25	1 × 75 mm	5
PzKpfw Panther D	22 11	11 5	80	43	650	28	1 × 75 mm	5
PzKpfw Tiger I	22 8	12 5	100	55	700	23	1 × 88 mm	5
PzKpfw Tiger II	24 2	12 6	150	68	700	23	1 × 88 mm	5
Japan								
T 97 Chi-nu	16 8	6 8	50	18·8	240	24	1 × 75 mm	5
U.S.A.								
M 3 Light (Stuart 1)	14 9	7 7	43	12·3	250	35	1 × 37 mm	4
M 3 Medium (Grant)	18 6	8 10	50	27	340	26	1 × 75 mm 1 × 37 mm	6
M 4 Medium (Sherman I)	19 7	8 9	76	30	353	25	1 × 75 mm	5
M 24 Light (Chaffee)	19 4	9 10	38	18	2 × 110	35	1 × 75 mm	4
M 4 A3 E8 Medium	20 7	8 9	100	33	450	25	1 × 76 mm	5
M 26 (Pershing)	21 4	11 8	102	41	500	30	1 × 90 mm	5
After 1945								
Britain								
Centurion 3	24 9	11 1	152	49	650	21	1 × 83·4 mm	4
Conqueror	25 9	12 11	200	65	810	21	1 × 120 mm	4
Vickers MBT	29 10	10 5	30	37	650	35	1 × 105 mm	4
Chieftain	25 1	11 6	—	51	650	26	1 × 120 mm	4
Scorpion	14 5	7 2	—	7·2	195	50	1 × 76 mm	3
France								
AMX 13	16 0	8 3	40	14·5	270	37	1 × 75 mm	3
AMX 30	20 11	10 3	—	34	720	40	1 × 105 mm	4

Type	Length (ft in)	Width (ft in)	Armour max. (mm)	Weight (tons)	Power Plant (hp)	Max Speed (mile/h)	Main armament	Crew
After 1945 continued								
Russia								
PT 76	22 8	10 4	30	14	240	27	1 × 76 mm	3
T 54B	21 10	10 8	170	36	520	30	1 × 100 mm	4
T 10	23 11	11 2	216	50	700	30	1 × 122 mm	4
T 62	22 6	11 2	140	37	580	30	1 × 115 mm	4
Germany								
Leopard	22 0	10 7	—	39	830	44	1 × 105 mm	4
U.S.A.								
M 47 Medium (Patton)	23 8	11 9	110	44	810	30	1 × 90 mm	5
M 48 Medium (Patton)	23 1	12 4	178	45	820	32	1 × 90 mm	4
M 103 Heavy	24 4	12 6	178	57	810	23	1 × 120 mm	5
M 41 Light	19 1	10 10	31	25	500	40	1 × 76·2 mm	4
M 60 A1 Medium	22 8	11 11	110	48	750	30	1 × 105 mm	4
M 551 Sheridan	20 8	9 2	—	15	300	43	1 × 152 mm	4
M 60 A 2	24 0	11 11	—	45	750	32	1 × 152 mm	4
Sweden								
Strv 103 (S)	24 11	10 11	—	38	1 × 240 1 × 300	31	1 × 105 mm	3
Japan								
Medium T 63	20 8	9 8	64	32	600	28	1 × 90 mm	4
Switzerland								
PzKpfw 61	21 11	10 0	—	36	630	31	1 × 105 mm	4

Appendix 5

DATA OF A.F.V. MAIN ARMAMENTS WHICH ENTERED SERVICE

Gun	Calibre (mm)	Length calibres	Muzzle velocity (ft/sec)	Type of projectile	Mounted in
1916–18					
Britain					
6-pdr	57	40	—	H.E., shot, case	Mark I and some Mark IIs
6-pdr	57	23	1,350	H.E., shot, case	Mark II–V*
France					
75 mm raccourci	75	16	656	H.E.	Schneider C.A.
75 mm M 1897	75	36	1,788	H.E.	St. Chamond
37 mm M 1918	37	21	1,273	H.E.	Renault FT, R 35, FCM, H 35, NC 27
Germany					
Sokol	57	23	1,200	H.E.	A7V, LK II
U.S.A.					
M 1916	37	21	1,204	H.E.	M 1917
1919–39					
Britain					
3-pdr	47	32	1,750	H.E.	Vickers Mediums
2-pdr	40	52	2,600	Shot	Infantry and cruisers 1938–42, Tetrarch I, Ram I, Sentinel I, Daimler I, A.E.C. 4X4, Coventry,
				H.E., smoke	Vickers Medium, A 9
3·7 in mortar	94	15	490	H.E., smoke	A 10
3 in howitzer	76	23	600	H.E., smoke	Cruisers V, VI; Infantry II, III, IV; Tetrarch
France					
Howitzer SA 35	75	17·1	725	H.E.	B 1
M 1935	47	34	2,200	Shot, H.E.	B 1, S 35, D 2
	25		2,953	Shot	Panhard 178, AMR, AMC
M 1938	37	33	2,300	Shot, H.E.	H 39, R 40, H 40

Gun	Calibre (mm)	Length calibres	Muzzle velocity (ft/sec)	Type of projectile	Mounted in
1919–39 continued					
Germany					
KwK 30	20	71	2,625	Shot, H.E.	Pz II, Sdkfz 232
KwK	37	45	2,445	Shot, H.E.	Pz III, 38t
KwK	50	42	2,247	Shot, H.E.	Pz III
Pak 38	50	60	2,700	Shot, H.E.	Pz III
KwK	75	24	1,263	Shot, H.E., smoke, case	Pz IV, Pz III, SdKfz 233, Stu III
Italy					
37/40	37	40	1,200	Shot, H.E.	M 11/39
47/32	47	32	2,067	Shot, H.E.	M 13/40
1939–39					
Russia					
M 30	37	35	1,960	Shot	BTs, BA 10, T 26B, T 32
M 20	45	46	2,490	Shot, H.E.	BT 7, T 26B, BA 10, T 35, T 70
	76·2	16·5	1,050	Shot, H.E.	T 28, T 35
M 38	76·2	24	1,300	Shot, H.E.	T 28, BT 7
U.S.A.					
M 6	37	53	2,900	Shot, H.E., canister	M 3 Lights, M 3 and M 6 Mediums, Locust, Greyhound, Staghound
M 2	75	31	1,850	Shot, H.E., smoke	M 3 and M 6 Mediums
Japan					
90	57	18·5	1,150	Shot, H.E.	T 89, 92, 94, 97
1	47		2,700	Shot, H.E.	T 97
94	37	37	1,900	Shot	T 95
1940–45					
Britain					
6-pdr	57	45	2,675	Shot	Crusader III
6-pdr	57	52	2,950	Shot	Churchill III, IV; A.E.C. IV; Cavalier; Centaur; Cromwell I; Ram II; Valentine VIII–X
75	75	40	2,050	Shot, H.E., smoke	Cromwell, A.E.C. III, Staghound III, Churchill VII
17-pdr	76·2	58·4	2,950	Shot, H.E., smoke	Sherman Firefly, Challenger, M 10, Archer, Centurion 1, Avenger
77	76·2	50	2,750	Shot, H.E., smoke	Comet
95 howitzer	95	20	1,050	H.E., H.E.A.T., Smoke	Centaur; Cromwell IV, VI; Churchill V, VIII; Alecto

Gun	Calibre (mm)	Length calibres	Muzzle velocity (ft/sec)	Type of projectile	Mounted in
1940–45 continued					
Germany					
KwK 40	75	43	2,428	Shot, H.E., smoke, H.E.A.T.	Pz IV, Stu IV
KwK 40	75	48	2,461	Shot, H.E., smoke, H.E.A.T.	Pz IV, Pz Jag 38, Puma
KwK 42	75	70	3,068	Shot, H.E.	Panther, Pz Jag IV
KwK 36	88	56	2,657	Shot, H.E., H.E.A.T.	Tiger I
KwK 43	88	71	3,340	Shot, H.E., H.E.A.T.	Tiger II, Jagdpanther, Elephant, Rhinoceros
Pak 44	128	55	3,020	Shot, H.E.	Jagdtiger, hybrids
Italy					
75	75	18	1,562	Shot, H.E.	Semovente 42, P 40
Russia					
M 38/39	76·2	30·5	2,007	Shot, H.E.	T 34
M 40	76·2	41·5	2,172	Shot, H.E.	T 34, KV I, SU 76
M 44	85	51·5	2,599	Shot, H.E.	T 34, KV 85, ASU 85
M 43	122	45	2,562	Shot, H.E.	SU 122, Stalin, T 10
	100	54	2,953	Shot, H.E.	T 54, T 55, SU 100
M 38/40	152	—	1,900	H.E.	JSU 152
U.S.A.					
M 3	75	40	2,050	Shot, H.E., smoke	M 3, M 4 Mediums
M 5	76	50	2,600	Shot, H.E., smoke	M 6 Heavy, M 10, Sherman 4
M 6	75	40	2,030	Shot, H.E., smoke	M 24 Light
M 1 A2	76	55	3,400	Shot, H.E., smoke	M 4 A3 E8 Medium, M 18
M 3 A2	90	53	2,800	Shot, H.E.	M 26, M 36, M 46 Mediums
T 5 E1	105	—	3,000	Shot, H.E.	M 6 Heavy, T 28 Heavy
After 1945					
Britain					
20-pdr	83·4	68	4,800	Shot, H.E., smoke, canister	Centurion 3, Charioteer
105 L7	105	51	4,850	Shot, H.E., smoke, canister	Centurion and the tanks of N.A.T.O. Vickers MBT
76	76	28	1,780	H.E., H.E.S.H., smoke, canister	Saladin, Scorpion
120	120	54	4,450	Shot, H.E., H.E.S.H., smoke	Chieftain
Rarden	30		3,600	Shot, H.E.	Fox

Gun	Calibre (mm)	Length calibres	Muzzle velocity (ft/sec)	Type of projectile	Mounted in
After 1945 continued					
France					
	75	61·5	3,281	Shot, H.E.	AMX 13, EBR
	105	56	3,280	H.E.A.T., H.E., smoke	AMX 30
Germany					
Pz K	90	40	—	Shot, H.E.	Jagdpanzer Kanone
Russia					
	115	54		H.E.	T 62
U.S.A.					
M 41	90	48	3,200	Shot, H.E.	M 48, T 32 Heavy
T 123	120		3,500	Shot, G.E., smoke	M 103 Heavy
Sweden					
	105	62		Shot, H.E., smoke	Strv 103 (S)

Appendix 6

ANTI-TANK GUIDED WEAPON DATA

Nation	Name	Min./max. range (m)	Speed (m/sec)	Wt (lb)	Guidance system	Warhead
Britain	Malkara	450/3,200	100	200	Wire link	H.E.S.H.
	Vigilant	200/1,375	136	34	Wire link	H.E.A.T.
	Swingfire	150/4,000	185	56	Wire link	H.E.A.T.
France	SS 10	300/1,600	80	33	Wire link	H.E.A.T.
	SS 11	500/3,000	150	67	Wire link	H.E.A.T.
	SS 12	700/6,500	150	150	Wire link	H.E.A.T.
	ENTAC	400/2,000	85	26	Wire link	H.E.A.T.
	HOT	75/4,000	260	55	Wire link	H.E.A.T.
	ACRA	75/3,500+	620	50	Infra-red link	H.E.A.T.
Germany	Cobra	550/1,800	85	22	Wire link	H.E.A.T.
U.S.A.	T.O.W.	25/2,000	278	40	Wire link	H.E.A.T.
	Shillelagh	50/3,000	300	55	Infra-red link	H.E.A.T.
Russia	Sagger	400/3,000	150	25	Wire link	H.E.A.T.
	Snapper	500/2,300	89	48	Wire link	H.E.A.T.
	Swatter	400/2,500	150	60	Wire link	H.E.A.T.
Sweden	Bantam	400/2,100	79	13	Wire link	H.E.A.T.

Appendix 7

TANK STRENGTHS OF THE NATIONS—1972

Let it be honestly stated that the following tables of strengths are only rough estimates based upon information released by the nations concerned, estimates which can well serve as security cover to disguise actual strength or weakness. Frequently—particularly in the case of the major powers—it is impossible to reach any positive figure of their immense strength; invariably stocks of reserve machines are unknown; all too often it is possible only to give the number of divisions, brigades or just battalions thought to be available. Sometimes strengths are in flux even as the list is being prepared—when nations go to war and sustain losses or increase their strength by purchases from neighbours and allies or by capture from the enemy. Only for what it is worth, therefore, the list below is included in this book, the compilation rather more a feat than a matter of definitive fact.

Nation	Tanks	or	Tank divs	Bdes	Bns	Remarks
Australia	140				2	
Belgium	640			2		
Britain	900				12	
Bulgaria	1,930			5		
Canada	60					
China			5			Imponderable
Czechoslovakia	3,500		4			
Denmark	200					
Finland	100			1		Armd bde at half strength
France	1,000		5			
Germany (East)	2,425		2			
Germany (West)	3,300			12		
Greece	470		1			
Hungary	1,700		2	5		
India	1,450		1	2		Before war of 1971
Iran	960		3			
Iraq	900		2			
Israel	1,075			4		
Italy	1,100		2			
Japan	700		1			
Jordan	290		1	1		
Korea (North)	750		2			
Korea (South)				2		
Libya	121				4	
Mongolia	140				2	
Netherlands	750			2		
Pakistan	1,070		2	1		Before war of 1971
Poland	3,580		5			

Nation	Tanks	or	Tank divs	Bdes	Bns	Remarks
Tank strengths of the Nations 1972 continued						
Rumania	1,700		2			
Russia			51	102		Innumerable
South Africa	240					
Spain			1	2		
Sweden					7	
Switzerland	850		1			
Syria	780		1	2		
Thailand					3	
Turkey			1	4	4	
U.S.A.			3	5		Innumerable
Vietnam (North)	410				2	
Vietnam (South)	400				6	
Yugoslavia	900			14		

Appendix 8

BUILDING A TANK

The requirement for a new tank usually appears as the result of battlefield, war games and trials experience linked to knowledge of current technical developments rather than inspired insight by an individual inventor. It is probably stated in general terms, discussed among interested military, political and industrial parties and finally appears as a Preliminary Design from an official Military Vehicles Design or Engineering Department.

Discussion will cover a wide range of complex subjects of which the following are the most important taken from a list that is almost inexhaustible.

Analysis of the threat to the vehicle from:
- Ballistic missiles—both chemical and kinetic energy.
- Guided missiles.
- Mines.
- Gas and biological weapons.
- Nuclear, flame, blast and radiological weapons.
- Fire—from external and internal sources.

Analysis of the vehicle's hitting power from an evaluation of known and future weapons and their effects on armour, men and other material; and information on enemy targets—present and future, the strength of their protection leading to the selection of the most appropriate armament.

Analysis of mobility:
- Strategic—transportation between and within theatres of war within the existing and expected limitations of sea, land and air facilities.
- Tactical—movement to and across the battlefield with regard to speed, cross-country capability, obstacle crossing and swimming or wading, range of action, reliability and economy.

Analysis of production and maintenance problems:
- Materials—availability and costs.
- Production facilities—those in existence and those which might have to be created.
- Storage.
- Spares backing.

Feasibility. To save time and costs every attempt is made to demand a vehicle which falls within existing technical knowledge, but sometimes it is found necessary to ask for an improvement that may be impossible to provide at once. Its feasibility has then to be proved—a study undertaken to meet a target set by the General Staff. From this study not only feasibility itself but also some idea of the time and cost factors are obtained, in connection with the research and development which will have to be undertaken.

Building a Tank continued

General Staff Requirement. (G.S.R.) This is the official document issued to the Design and Engineering Establishment (in the U.S.A. it is called a Quantitive Military Requirement—Q.M.R.). It is accompanied by authority for the Establishment to proceed with the design and the production of working development projects which often take the shape and form of what, eventually, comes into service. Usually a number of prototypes are produced to hasten development.

Trials. These are continuously undertaken by the Design and Engineering Establishment as the project progresses. Soldiers join in with what are known as User or Troop trials. The results are collated and changes incorporated in the plan for the final design. It is not unknown for trials to enforce a change in the General Staff Requirement either because something proves impractical or because some unlooked-for advantage suddenly becomes feasible.

Pre-production models. Because the mechanics of mass production often demand redesign of many original components it is common practice to build a pre-production model of any complex design and to test it before the production line is put into full operation. In any case it is invariably true that modifications are constantly in the pipe-line so that no one tank of the first batch is the same as the next.

Production is not the last stage, for it is at once followed by an influx of fresh modifications as experience with service units indicates weaknesses which may have withstood handling by experienced trials teams but which are not in the least proof against the ravages of normal crewmen.

Major modifications. In peacetime a tank remains in service for about twenty years. In wartime it will be much shorter because battlefield demands will accelerate change. A well-founded basic design should be capable of significant improvements with greater power plant, thicker armour and larger armament, and be strong enough to sustain increases in weight. It is preferable if modifications can be made without reworking in the factory, but this is not always possible.

Sources and Bibliography

This bibliography is selective in that it mentions only those books which are of fundamental importance for obtaining a clear idea of tank development in all fields. There are many tank books which merely transmit the contents of their predecessors, only a few which contain the results of deep original research. Of them all there are some which are both out of print and practically unobtainable. The list below is intended to act as a guide to reading, but the only true way of nearing the heart of the matter is by carrying out research among the official records (when they are made available) and in museums and libraries. The most fruitful sources outside the various libraries of national archives such as are to be found, particularly, in London, Paris, Freiburg, Washington and (subject no doubt to the strictest control) Moscow, are:

The Royal Armoured Corps Tank Museum, Bovington Camp, Dorset, England.
The Imperial War Museum, London.
The Tank Museum, Aberdeen, N.J., U.S.A.
The Patton Museum, Fort Knox, Va., U.S.A.

possibly in that order of merit. There are many more smaller collections but none so profuse in material and actual hardware.

Anon. *Illustrated records of the development of AFVs of different nations.* R.A.C. Tank Museum, England.

Anon. *Tank data 1 and 2.* U.S. Army Ordnance, Aberdeen Museum, U.S.A.

Anon. *The military balance 1971/72.* International Institute for Strategic Studies, London.

Anon. *50 years on tracks.* Holt Caterpillar Traction Co.

Anon. *The story of 79th Armoured Division.* Privately.

Anon. *History of U.S. Armor.* Patton Museum Society.

Andronikov, N. and Mostovenko, W. *Die Roten Panzer.* Lehmann's Verlag, Munich.

Barker A. J. *The civilising mission.* Cassell, London.

Blumenson, M. *The Patton Papers I, 1885–1940.* Houghton Mifflin, New York.

Brereton, J. *Russian tanks 1915–1965.* Feist, London.

Cooper, B. *The ironclads of Cambrai.* Souvenir, London.

Crisp, R. *Brazen chariots.* Muller, London.

Crow, N. (ed.). *AFVs of World War I.* Profile Publications, Leatherhead.

Crow, N. (ed.). *British AFVs 1919–1940.* Profile Publications, Leatherhead.

Crow, N. (ed.). *British and Commonwealth AFVs 1940–1946.* Profile Publications, Leatherhead.

Crow, N. (ed.). *American AFVs of World War II 1930–1950.* Profile Publications, Leatherhead.

de Gaulle, C. *Vers L'armée de Métier.* Berger-Levrault, Paris.

de la Gorce. *The French Army.* Weidenfeld and Nicolson.

Disney, P. A. *Tactical problems for armor units.* M.S.P.C., Harrisburg, U.S.A.

Dutil, L. *Les Chars d'assaut.* Berger-Levrault, Paris.

Eimannsberger, L. von. *La Guerre des Chars.* Berger-Levrault, Paris.

Erickson, J. *The Soviet High Command.* Macmillan, London.

Fuller, J. F. C. *Memoirs of an unconventional soldier.* Nicolson and Watson, London.

Fuller, J. F. C. *Lectures on FSR II.* Sifton Praed, London.

Fuller, J. F. C. *Lectures on FSR III.* Sifton Praed, London

Fuller, J. F. C. *Machine Warfare.* Hutchinson, London.

Foss, C. *Armoured fighting vehicles of the world.* Ian Allan, London.

Gillie, M. *Forging the thunderbolt.* M.S.P.C., Harrisburg, U.S.A.

Garforth, R. *Soviet military doctrine.* Free Press, Glencoe, U.S.A.

Guderian, H. *Panzer leader.* Joseph, London.

Guderian, H. *Achtung! Panzer!* U.D.V., Stuttgart.

Horne, A. *To lose a battle.* Macmillan, London.

Icks, J. *Tanks and armoured vehicles.* Duell, Sloan and Pierce, New York.

Icks, R. J. *Famous tank battles.* Doubleday, New York.

Joly, C. *Take these men.* Constable, London.

Jones, R., Rarey, G. and Icks, J. *The fighting tanks (1916–1933).* W. E. Inc, U.S.A.

Kennedy, R. *The German campaign in Poland, 1939.* Dept. of Army, Washington.

Liddell Hart, B. H. *The other side of the hill.* Faber, London.

Liddell Hart, B. H. *The Tanks.* Cassell, London.

Liddell Hart, B. H. *The Rommel papers.* Collins, London.

Mackintosh, M. *Juggernaut.* Secker and Warburg, London.

Macksey, K. *Armoured Crusader.* Hutchinson, London.

Macksey, K. *Tank—a history of AFVs* (with J. Batchelor). Macdonald, London.

Macksey, K. *Tank warfare—a history of tanks in battle.* Hart-Davis, London.

Magnuski, J. *Wozy Bojowe 1914–1964.* W.M.O.N., Warsaw.

Manstein, E. von. *Lost victories.* Methuen, London.

Marshall, S. L. A. *Armies on wheels.* Faber, London.

Martel, G. le Q. *In the wake of the tank.* Sifton Praed, London.

Martel, G. le Q. *An outspoken soldier.* Sifton Praed, London.

Mellenthin, J. von. *Panzer battles.* Cassell, London.

Milsom, J. *Russian tanks 1900–1970.* Arms and Armor.

Nehring, W. *Die Geschichte de deutschen Panzerwaffe 1916 bis 1945.* Propylaen, Berlin.

Nenninger, T. *The development of American armour, 1917–1940.* Unpublished.

Newman. *One hundred years of good company.* Ruston and Hornsby Ltd.

O'Ballance, E. *Korea 1950–1953.* Faber, London

Ogorkiewicz, R. *Armour.* Stevens, London.

Ogorkiewicz, R. *Design and development of armoured vehicles.* Macdonald, London.

Pafi, B. and others. *Corrazati Italiani 1939–1945.* D'Anna, London.

Pitt, B. (ed.). *Purnell's history of the Second World War.* Purnell, London.

Pugh, S. (ed.) (later Crow, N.). *Armour in profile.* Profile Publications, Leatherhead.

Seaton, A. *The Russo-German War, 1941–1945.* Barker, London.

Senff, H. *Die Entwicklung der Panzerwaffe im deutschen Heer zwischen den beiden.* Verlag Mittler.

Senff, H. *Weltkrieg.* Verlag Mittler.

Senger und Etterlin, F. M. von. *German tanks of World War II.* Arms and Armour Press, London.

Seymour, W. *An account of our stewardship.* Vauxhall Motors Ltd.

Shepherd, E. W. *Tanks in the next war.* Bles, London.

Singer. *A history of technology.* Clarendon, Oxford.

Stern, A. *Log book of a pioneer.* Hodder and Stoughton, London.

Swinton, E. *'Eyewitness'.* Hodder and Stoughton, London.

Teveth, S. *Tanks of Tammuz.* Weidenfeld and Nicolson, London.

Wiener, H. *Truppendienst Taschenbuch.* Verlag Carl Uebereuter, Vienna.

Wiener, H. *Die Armeern der Warschaur Pakt-Staaten.* Verlag Carl Uebereuter, Vienna.

Wiener, H. *Die Armeen der NATO-Staaten.* Verlag Carl Uebereuter, Vienna.

Wiener, H. *Die Armeen der neutralen und blockfreien Staaten Europas.* Verlag Carl Uebereuter, Vienna.

Williams-Ellis, C. and A. *The Tank Corps.* Country Life, London.

Wilmot, C. *The struggle for Europe.* Collins, London.

Index

725.98

BRIDGES OF BRITAIN

BRIDGES OF BRITAIN

Eric de Maré

B. T. Batsford Ltd   London

© Eric de Maré 1975
First published 1954
New and revised edition published 1975
Reprinted 1987
ISBN 0 7134 2925 9

Filmset by Tradespools Ltd, Frome, Somerset
Printed and bound in Great Britain by
Butler & Tanner Ltd, Frome, Somerset
for the Publishers B. T. Batsford Ltd
4 Fitzhardinge St, London W1H 0AH

Contents

1 *Right*, the most beautiful stone arch in Britain: a wood-engraving of William Edwards' Pont-y-Pridd of 1750, with its pierced haunches.

2 *Next page*, the central tower of the Forth Railway Bridge of 1890.

The endpapers show an engraving of Old London Bridge by John Norden. Unless otherwise stated, all photographs are by the author.

1 Introduction

Long out of print and now a book-collector's item, my *Bridges of Britain* was published by Batsford in 1954. Since then a remarkable period of bridge building has occurred here with the laying of new roads. Also since then public interest in the look of things has grown (no doubt stimulated by television) – not least in the buildings and artifacts of the past that are studied under the new discipline of Industrial Archaeology. Hence this revised volume in which the original text has been shortened, fresh words and pictures have been added, and a traveller's glossary provided of the most interesting bridges of all periods to be seen in England, Scotland and Wales.

Any work which helps people to become more aware of their environment must be of some value, and that makes another apology for this book. It is offered as informative entertainment to the layman so that when he moves around the country he will not pass the many bridges he crosses in blind and blasé boredom but, by realising what they mean in terms of social history, human endeavour, and formal beauty, he will stop to contemplate them for a moment and so find pleasure.

Few bridges are ugly. The reason is that a bridge has one uncompromising function – a limitation that makes for purity of form, a purity that can reach beyond practical prosiness to the poetry of structure, whether as an intimate Elizabethan sonnet rich in texture or a grand modern epic of astounding span. If all good design seeks to express the poetry of structure by working beautifully, can its decoration have a place? Decoration must, of course, always be related to structure and enhance its expression by articulation, but in general the bridge designer has rarely called on the sculptor to embellish his creations in that way; the scale of a bridge is often too large to allow decoration to tell and the whole must be effective at a distance. Form, texture, and sometimes colour provide the effect. Most mediaeval bridges are undecorated in themselves, even if the small chapels with which they were often endowed possessed contemporary ecclesiastical stone carving in windows, doors and pinnacles. Renaissance bridges are the most highly decorated we have, their embellishment well integrated with structure in balustrades, carved keystones and cutwaters. (English Bridge at Shrewsbury, for example, would be impoverished by the loss of the vigorous dolphins above the cutwaters, while cast iron of a later period offers some good examples, as on plates 73–5). The eighteenth century produced many small bridges of character to enhance the noblemen's picturesque parks, and there playful decoration was fully justified. Almost no modern bridges are decorated, even when the architect has been called in for obscure reasons to help the engineer, but sometimes across a motorway paint has been applied to a steel span with gay effect.

At their best, bridges can be seen as symbols of architectural purity in which firm construction, function, and pleasing form are combined. As Palladio wrote three centuries ago, 'Bridges ought to have the self-same qualifications as we judge necessary to all other buildings, that they should be commodious, beautiful, and lasting'.

Bridges are symbols in other ways, and that is perhaps why they move us. They touch us at an unconscious level, representing human control of the environment, the handshake, security, mutual aid, resolution of psychic tensions, a monument to tribal

cohesion, a gathering place 'where thousands meet but none can stay'. They represent direction, purpose, and serene stability. Finally they represent time and its passing because bridges make history, not least in their ecological effects on whole regions. As John Buchan wrote:

'The Bridge, even more I think than the Road, is a symbol of man's conquest of nature . . . From the most primitive times it has been a dominant fact in the life of each community. A bridge ruled the lines of traffic. There might be a dozen roads of travel but they all drew to a point at the river crossings. Cities grew up around them, and castles were built to command them. Battles were fought for their possession, and schemes of strategy were based upon them. With them are linked many of the great feats of arms, from Horatius at Rome to Napoleon at Lodi. History – social, economic, and military – clusters more thickly about bridges than about towns and citadels'.

It is not surprising therefore that myths have developed around the activity of bridge building since early times. The gods are always on the watch in their vengeful way and experience has taught that many have malevolent natures which are never more readily stirred than by the human presumption of building bridges to make life easier. 'Every bridge demands a life' is an ancient superstition that is felt even among the workers who construct, often in some peril, the great steel and concrete spans of today. In the old days the river spirits, seeing themselves likely to be deprived of their regular toll of drowning folk when a new bridge was erected at a ford, fought to prevent the comple-

Decoration of bridges
3 *Left,* carved keystone and balustrade on
John Gwynn's Magdalen Bridge, Oxford, of
1779.
4 *Above,* one of the dolphin cut-waters on
English Bridge, Shrewsbury, 1774, also by
Gwynn.

tion of the bridge and to secure as many lives as possible during its construction. To appease them, human sacrifices were deliberately made during building operations. Thus floods, storms, and accidents might be prevented and the vindictive spleen of the gods allayed. Such blood ceremonies are worldwide. An example is recorded in Sir Mark Sykes's *Dar-Ul-Islam* in a legend he heard at Zakho:

> 'Many years ago workmen under their master were set to build the bridge; three times the bridge fell and the workmen said, "The bridge needs a life". And the master saw a beautiful girl, accompanied by a bitch and her puppies, and he said, "We will give the first that comes by", but the dog and her little ones held back, so the girl was built alive into the bridge, and only her hand with a gold bracelet upon it was left outside'.

Folklore all over the world connects bridge-building with the sacrificial rite. In old China, for instance, an animal was often built into a pier during construction. The old superstition persists, for when the first edition of this book was published Mr W. P. Warner, engineer, wrote: 'I thought the following, which happened as recently as 1939, might be of interest to you. I was supervising the construction of a lifting-span bridge across a river in Assam; an Indian woman brought a live month-old baby to me and asked me to bury it in the concrete foundations, in order that the bridge would be safe for all time. My Indian workmen were most enthusiastic about it, and my flat refusal was not at all well received'.

In the Christian era the monotheistic Devil displaced the numerous evil ones and all over Europe bridges still bear the name of the Prince, who does not insist on the life of a human being; that of a dog will do. He was indeed at one time happy enough to erect a complete bridge overnight in fair exchange for a life. In the Middle Ages, when bridge building had become a holy activity, bridges were blessed in ceremony and sancti-

Structural development
5 *Left*, Post Bridge, Dartmoor, a clapper bridge perhaps 2000 years old of monolithic slabs of granite each about fifteen feet long.
6 *Above right*, the steel Humber Suspension, under construction in 1975, will have a single span of 4626 feet, the longest in the world.

fied by religious emblems; then every bridge bore its cross, if not its chantry or chapel. Thus the Devil could be kept at bay and the traveller proceed safely on his way.

Our country offers no ancient bridges that can compete in size with the great ones of the Continent. We have no Roman viaducts like that at Segovia or the Pont du Gard near Nîmes which awed even the garrulous Rousseau into silence and filled Charles Kingsley with a simple fear. Of mediaeval structures we have nothing to equal France's Pont des Consuls at Montauban, her towered Pont Valentré at Cahors, or her twelfth-century Pont d'Avignon that gave Bénézet his sainthood. Nor have we competed in later years with such dramatic *tours de force* as Aldequela's eighteenth-century viaduct at Ronda in southern Spain. Yet for over a century, from the erection of Iron Bridge across the Severn in 1779 to that of the Forth Railway Bridge in 1889, Britain led the world in bridge design. Then the initiative passed for a time to America and the Continent, notably in the superb concrete bridges of the Swiss Robert Maillart and the Frenchman Eugène Freyssinet, but now we can match in wiry grandeur the suspensions of New York and San Francisco with our estuarial spans of steel across the Firth of Forth and the Severn. A new bridge at present (1975) under construction across the Humber will, indeed, produce the widest suspension span in the world (6), a bridge 1000 feet wider in size than the new suspension linking Europe with the Middle East across the Bosphorus, which, in fact, was designed by a British firm of engineers. Recently our new motorways have generated a number of splendid concrete spans that compare in nobility with any on the Continent or in Scandinavia.

11

In general however, our bridges are like the national temperament, that is, shy of overstatement. The landscape rarely calls for drama except across the estuaries. The watery countryside mostly needs a host of small bridges and even our most important river, the Thames, nowhere demands the colossal. Like the landscape our bridges are of great variety, and therein lies their special interest. We possess a remarkable heritage, and many a bridge five centuries old and more still continues its useful function, gallantly bearing the weight and fury of modern traffic. We have the doubtful honour, too, of having inaugurated the Industrial Revolution which made modern technology possible in bridge building as in other activities. With that revolution we produced the first iron bridge in the world (58) and the first few of the great civil engineers. Today the country possesses some 200,000 road bridges, which is about one bridge to every mile of roadway, and, until recently at least, the railway system required some 60,000 bridges, mostly built in the Victorian age, an age that produced a greater number of bridges than had existed in Britain before.

Probably the first structures human beings erected were bridges because, as they wandered, easy access across a river or ravine was more important than housing. Back in the misty forests of prehistory the only bridges that existed were those that nature had built, such as the Rainbow Arch in Utah and the Pont d'Arc in France. Arches like these, as well as overhanging stratifications of stone, gave men their first inspiration to build the corbelled arch – not the true arch of voussoirs but a series of overlapping cantilevers. Two other kinds of natural bridge also provided ideas: the fallen tree across a chasm and the looped vine on which to swing across a stream. So four of the basic types of bridge which span the centuries were in natural existence before artificial bridges were attempted: the Beam, the Suspension, the Cantilever, and the Arch – at least the corbelled arch, for the true arch is a human invention. Up in the North, still barren from the Ice Age, rocks and stones were abundant from the grinding of the glaciers, and there streams could often be crossed from stone to stone where these had tumbled. This gave men another notion: the placing of boulders to form stepping stones where they were needed. (The Latin *pons*, a bridge, may derive from *ponere*, to place). A development would have been the piling of stones into piers across which monoliths could be placed to form a so-called clapper bridge. Such were the first multi-span bridges.

From the simple trunk thrown across a stream eventually developed that sophisticated bridge Robert Stephenson built in the middle of the nineteenth century to carry railway trains through two enormous rectangular iron tubes across the Menai Straits – a pure, if eccentric, beam type (76–78). So also, in effect, is the great trussed railway bridge, known as the Royal Albert (79), that Brunel designed to cross the Tamar at Saltash.

Of cantilever constructions, the Forth Railway Bridge (83) is the most notable example of modern times, with its great double, balanced cantilevers supporting short suspended beam spans between them. The first modern cantilever of iron, however, was erected in 1867 across the River Main at Hassfurt in Germany with a centre span of 425 feet, its designer being Heinrich Gerber. Many fine cantilevers can be seen in the new reinforced concrete spans which often look deceptively like low arches.

The suspension type no doubt first occurred in southerly lands, where having learned to plait and weave, men fashioned ropes made from liana plants and bamboo which they tied to tree trunks on either side of a river in order to swing across hand over hand. There followed a more useful structure of two strands crossed by woven mats to

Stone and iron
7 *Left*, Bakewell Bridge, Derbyshire, a particularly complete and regular mediaeval example of pointed stone arches.
8 *Right*, Britannia Railway Bridge across the Menai Straits of 1850 by Robert Stephenson. Its iron tubes make this a beam bridge.

form a pathway with handrails on each side. (Marco Polo described the making of bamboo bridge cables 300 paces long). The final development was the flat roadway hanging from the curved catenaries, the kind we build now of steel cables but one which was built with different materials far away and long ago by primitive societies in the Himalayas.

A Chinese record of the 7th century A.D. mentions the use of iron chains for suspension bridges built in the Indus valley, but the first suspension in Europe was a bridge of iron chains at Market Harborough; it is mentioned in an Act of 1721 while a map of the town published in 1776 marks the Chain Bridge across the Welland there. A chain suspension bridge only two feet wide, called Winch Bridge, was erected across the Tees near High Force in 1741; this spanned 59 feet. In these early types the floor was laid directly on to the chains. The suspension having a suspended and level roadway was conceived by the American James Finley in 1801, his first patent bridge of this kind being built in 1816. The following year John and Thomas Smith erected a chain suspension across the Tweed at Dryburgh in Roxburghshire and they claimed that it was the first of its sort in Britain; here the chains were made of rods ten feet long with welded eyes and coupling links, forming a span of 261 feet. It cost £500.

The main credit for the development of the iron suspension must go to Captain Brown, RN (1776–1852), later Sir Samuel Brown, who designed the famous Chain Pier at Brighton, completed in 1823 (100). Brown invented an improved way of making links for iron cables which led to the introduction of chain cables in the Navy. He next invented that type of flat iron link used in early suspension bridges which he patented in 1817 and

14

which allowed suspensions to be of much larger span than before. However, without Cort's method of producing wrought iron, first used in 1784, the suspension could not have developed as it did. In 1820 Brown built the first large suspension in the country, wide enough to take carriages: Union Bridge spanning the Tweed near Berwick (123). Six years later the first mail coach from London to Holyhead passed over the new Menai Bridge, Thomas Telford's masterwork with a central span of 579 feet, the largest suspension bridge yet erected (68, 125). The next development was the application of steel cables in place of chains by the Roeblings in the USA.

A rare combination of cantilever and suspension, sometimes called the cable cantilever, is exemplified by Ordish's Albert Bridge, Chelsea, completed in 1873 (55), and in the modern case of the George Street Bridge, Newport (92). This type seems to have been invented by the Frenchman Poyet and the first example was Captain Napier's King's Meadow Bridge of 1817 which crossed the Tweed below Peebles with a span of 110 feet.

The arched bridge works in the opposite way to the suspension – that is not by tension but by compression. (A beam is in compression in its upper part and in tension below). The discovery of the true arch is attributed to the Sumerians who used sun-baked bricks placed side by side in a ring of radiating voussoirs or tapering wedges. So structure was brought alive, seeming to be always at work in that the weight above the crown is perpetually transferred down through each voussoir to the springings and abutments – an invention of immense importance made around the year 4000 B.C. (From the Babylonians has come the visionary legend of the great single span of brickwork jumping 660 feet across the Euphrates to link two palaces). The arch itself with the joints all pointing to a centre does all the work and if a level road is built above it the spaces on each side between road and arch, called spandrels, can be either solid or open.

The semi-circular Roman arch has limitations because the wider it is the higher

Cantilever and Catenary
9 *Left,* contemporary sketch to show how the Forth Railway Bridge works with balanced cantilevers supporting short beams.

10 *Below,* a project for a suspension chain bridge with road supported above the catenary instead of being hung below it, of a type which does not need two towers. (From Weale's *Bridges,* 1843).

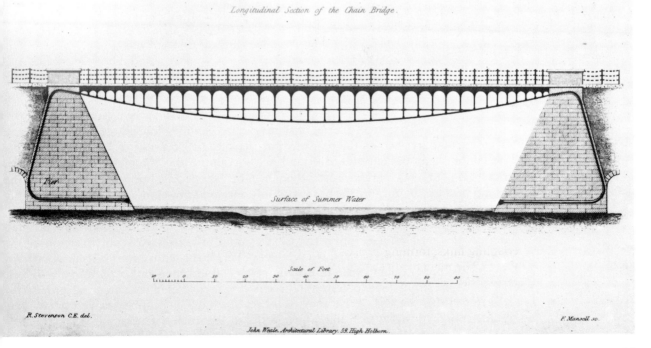

Longitudinal Section of the Chain Bridge.

Pier

Surface of Summer Water

Scale of Feet

R. Stevenson C.E. del.

F. Mansell sc.

John Weale, Architectural Library, 59, High Holborn.

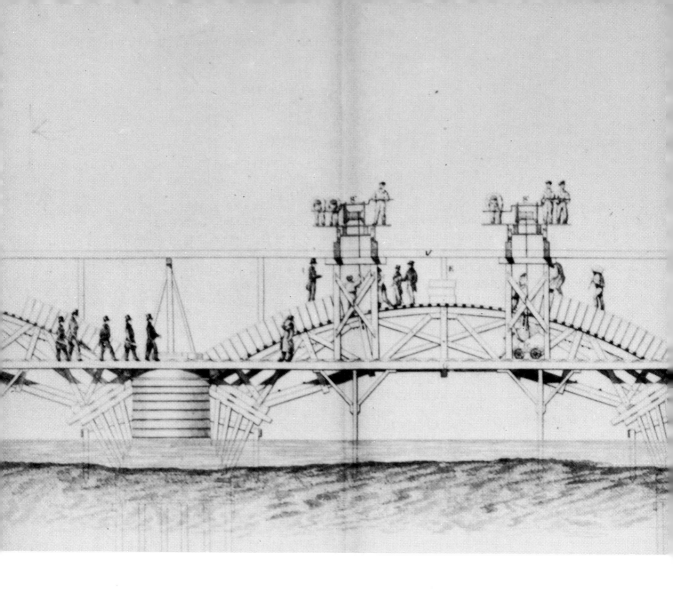

it must be. Small arches in a series of spans can make a long low bridge but with a single semi-circular arch of size the roadway may have to be sloped at each end with ramps; hence the hump-backed bridge of the English countryside. The great French engineer, Perronet (1708–94), who has been called the father of modern bridge building, solved the hump problem by turning the arc into a low, elegant semi-ellipse, a system that greatly increases the pressures of the splaying forces on the abutments at either end of the bridge; in between, of course, each ellipse will press against its neighbour in mutual aid. Perronet, indeed, designed bridges with a rise to span ratio of 1:10. Grosvenor Bridge over the Dee at Chester, opened in 1834, is a product of Perronet's innovations in its possession of the largest pure masonry span in Britain, being 200 feet long with a rise of only 40 feet.

Some steel bridges of today may seem to be arched as in the bowstring girder type, but in fact they are tied so that they really act like huge skeletal beams with the weights going straight down at each end. The new one at Runcorn is an example (89).

Two eccentric types of bridge are the pontoon and the lifting, or movable. The

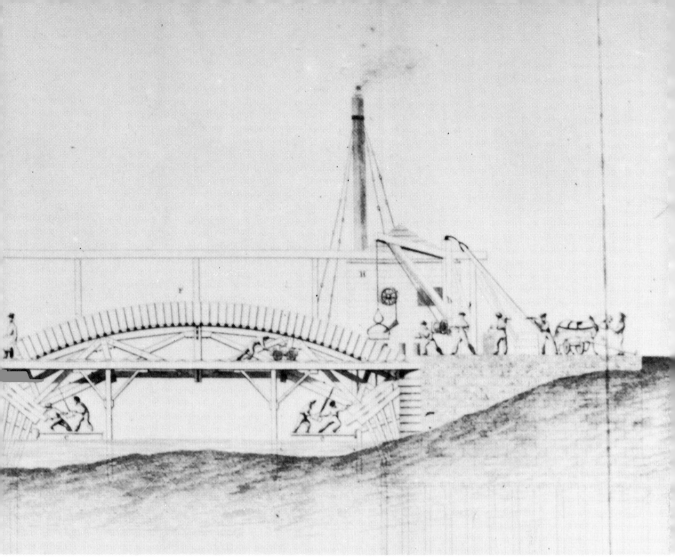

11 Detail from an engraving showing the
building in 1832 of Hutcheson Bridge,
Glasgow, of elliptical stone arches, designed by
Robert Stevenson (not to be confused with
Stephenson) who also designed the chain
bridge shown on the previous page. (From
Weale's *Bridges*).

pontoon would be a beam bridge using floating boats instead of piers resting on the river
bed. Cyrus commanded the laying of the first pontoon bridge on record, while his father's
counsellor, Darius, organised the erection of the fabulous bridge of boats, 1000 yards
long, by which an army of over half a million men (or so they say) was able to advance, and
subsequently retreat, across the Bosphorus. According to legend, Xerxes, son of Darius,
built an even more remarkable military bridge, a double row of 360 anchored ships
spanned by planks and earth. Today armies still build pontoon bridges and these tend to
be of plywood floats spanned by planks.

   An important type of movable bridge is the bascule (evolved from the drawbridge
of the moated mediaeval castle), in which one span can be lifted to allow the passage of
tall ships. Old London Bridge had such a bascule between two of its piers. The canals of
the early industrial era possess many bridges which can be lifted by pulling on a chain.
At Barton, where the first of the important canals, that of the Duke of Bridgewater,
crosses the River Irwell, the huge nineteenth-century iron bridge which replaced Brindley's

aqueduct of stone when the Manchester Ship Canal was dug, can be swung on a pivot still full of water to allow ships to pass (62). At Newcastle is another iron example that pivots. The most important movable bridge in Britain, however, is Tower Bridge where two bascules can be lifted to allow ships to enter the Pool of London; at first the power was hydraulic but lately it has become electric. A special type which has a moving part is the transporter where a carriage to take people and vehicles is suspended from a beam at a high level to allow shipping to pass below at any time, as in the Middlesbrough example (121) or the elegant white elephant at Newport (17).

The oldest existing bridge in the world belongs to the Aegean culture which preceded the Greek. It is a small slab structure of stone of single span across the Meles River in Smyrna, not more than 40 feet long. Homer used it, and St Paul too, nearly nine centuries later. The Greeks built very few bridges and these were mainly similar small slab structures; they hardly needed many bridges for they travelled mostly by sea.

Next to our own, the Roman civilization was the greatest bridge-building epoch in history, and the one from which the European tradition developed – directly, if crudely, in the Middle Ages, and at a remove in the return to classical forms in Renaissance years. The Romans took over the true arch from the Etruscans, using stone, marble, brick and mass concrete; they used timber too and built a bridge of timber across the Thames when they founded *Londinium*. In Britain no doubt the Romans used timber for most of their bridging, for the material was abundant all around; so little remains in our country of Roman bridges except a small rustic arch here and there or a broken causeway glittering beneath the water where once the ordered legions came and went. But many Roman examples still stand on the Continent to impress us with their virility, a notable one being that built for the Emperor Trajan at Alacantra in Spain with a centre arch of 78 feet span.

Like the builders of the Middle Ages the Romans also regarded bridge construction as something of a religious activity. Those who built the ancient *Pons Sublicius,* the first to span the Tiber, are believed to have belonged to a religious body called *Collegium Pontifices,* headed by the *Pontifex Maximus,* Greatest Builder of Bridges. This body developed social power and came to control all those roads and bridges which were essential to the coherence of the empire; so powerful did it become in the end that the Roman Emperors (and later the Popes) assumed the title of *Pontifex Maximus.*

When the Roman Empire fell many of the old skills were lost. Yet some were retained, not least by the Benedictine monasteries which helped more than most to evolve a new culture from the confusion. Among the skills preserved was the making of artificial stones from clay when stone was scarce, so that in Scandinavia today bricks are still called Monk Stones.

As Church organization established some order after the Dark Ages, a building boom began throughout Europe in roads and bridges as well as in cathedrals, churches and monasteries. Religious bridge building fraternities were formed and then the stimulus of the Crusades brought new and glamorous ideas like the pointed arch to create the evolving splendour of Gothic vaulting by replacing the heavy and restrictive round arch and square bay of the Norman or Romanesque style. In spite of the uncertainties of travel a surprising amount of movement had developed by the thirteenth century; roads of a sort were built and many of the old straight Roman roads, if patchy and decrepit, remained in use. This stimulated the erection of a multitude of crude but solid bridges throughout Europe. The War Bridge with its defensive tower and the Chapel Bridge were

Wide arches
12 *Left,* Grosvenor Bridge, Chester, of 1823, designed by Thomas Harrison, has the widest masonry arch in Britain at 200 feet.

13 *Below,* a contemporary engraving of Brunel's viaduct at Maidenhead carrying the Great Western Railway across the Thames with the two widest pure brick arches in Britain.

the significant types along the mediaeval roads, two of the most famous being St Bénézet's at Avignon and Peter of Colechurch's at London, both erected in the twelfth century with chapels rising at their centres.

Compared with the splendid feats of stone engineering in church building, the mediaeval bridges are surprisingly ponderous, relying for stability on brute mass and built so that if one arch failed the neighbouring arches would remain standing on their own. Nevertheless they charm us with their bold, unpretentious austerity, their rich patina and their casual asymmetry. They show two innovations: the building of road recesses which often continue the angular cutwaters up to parapet level where pedestrians could retreat from passing carts and quadrupeds, and the ribbed arch which could save a third of the tooled masonry work and could reduce dead weight and thrusts on piers. The ribbed arch consists of parallel ribs spanned by stone slabs which in their turn support rough masonry up to road level. Twizel Bridge in Northumberland with its graceful single arch is an outstanding example of ribbed construction (24).

The old mediaeval bridge of London requires a special mention now because for centuries it gave life to the City; London was in effect the parasite of the bridge. Without the wooden structure the Romans built at the same place London would, in fact, not have come into being. And in its mediaeval form with its houses, shops, its fair chapel, its gateways, its drawbridge, its great starlings like small pointed islands that protected the piers from buffeting and scouring, its thudding waterwheels, its roaring waters and its ceaseless bustle, it was a wonderful, noisy structure – the key to the City and the pride and emblem of the nation. By its means London was linked not only to the fertile farms of the southern counties but to the whole of the Continent. For over six centuries London had no other crossing and to its citizens it was their greatest vested interest.

This was the first great stone bridge to be erected in these islands. Begun in 1176

Rising bridges
14 *Left,* a drawbridge at Whitchurch across the Welsh section of the Shropshire Union Canal.

15 *Above*, Tower Bridge, London, last bridge before the sea, completed in 1894 with two rising bascules that allow ships to enter the Pool.

on piles of elm wood spanned by oak planks, it replaced the earlier structure of elm. It took 33 years to complete under the direction of Peter, priest and chaplain of St Mary's of Colechurch in the Poultry. It had 20 spans, the seventh being a wooden drawbridge and the rest irregular pointed arches. (Those who want to know its complete history must turn to Gordon Home's enthralling *Old London Bridge*). Owing to its broad piers and starlings it was as much a weir as a bridge, and as a dam that slowed down the ebbing water (with a 5-foot drop as the river ebbed) it created those famous Frost Fairs on frozen water that occurred above-bridge during cold winters through the centuries.

London Bridge was at its finest in Tudor days when Nonesuch House was built on it, a kind of timber-framed block of luxury flats inhabited by noblemen – 'a beautiful and chargeable peece of worke' according to Stow. At that time Norden made engravings of the bridge and described it as 'adorned with sumptuous buildings and statlie and beautiful houses on either side, inhabited by wealthy citizens and furnished with all manner of trades comparable in itself to a little Citie, whose buildings are so artificially contrived,

Transporters

16 *Above*, a rope and timber job from a book of 1590.

17 *Right*, Newport Transporter Bridge built of steel in 1906. This type allows ships to pass below at any time without the need to raise a roadway.

and so finely combined, as it seemeth more than an ordinary streete, for it is as one continuall vaute or roofe, except certain voyde places reserved from buildings, for the retire of passengers from the danger of carres, carts and droves of cattell, usually passing that way'.

In 1757 all the houses were removed and the two central arches were widened into one Great Arch, all according to the designs of George Dance, the City Surveyor. But its end was near and in 1824 Rennie's new London Bridge was begun just to the west of the old structure (19). This was opened in 1831 and three years later no vestige remained of the fabulous old bridge which had served London for so long.

The Renaissance refined the arch and brought advances in building techniques, notably in mechanical plant and in caissons for foundation laying as a development by prefabrication of the old timber cofferdams. The most beautiful of Renaissance bridges was the Santa Trinita in Florence by Michelangelo and Ammanati which was destroyed in the Second World War but has been rebuilt in facsimile. The most famous of Renaissance bridges on the Continent is Da Ponte's Rialto Bridge that spans 88 feet across the Grand Canal at Venice; like Pontevecchio, Florence, High Bridge, Lincoln, and Pulteney Bridge, Bath, (47) it is one of the few housed bridges left in the world.

By the eighteenth century, knowledge had become so systemized that the civil engineer with his specialized skill took the place of the architect in designing bridges; old Westminster Bridge, London's second crossing, was designed by a Swiss engineer called Labelye in the middle of the eighteenth century (20, 48). The best works of that century were

those of Jean Perronet, whose finest work was the Neuilly Bridge near Paris with its long, low, leaping arches (demolished 1938). As already noted, Perronet developed the segmental masonry arch to a high refinement and was able to reduce the thrusts on piers by making each arch push against its neighbour so that the whole structure could become lighter and continuous.

The Renaissance developed the truss largely because timbers long enough to span 60 feet or more were becoming increasingly hard to obtain. The truss uses the principle of triangulation, the triangle being the only figure in geometry whose shape cannot be distorted unless one of its parts is changed in length. The truss became of growing use for temporary centering when masonry arches were built, but the great days of the permanent wooden truss began when the brothers Grubenmann, Swiss village carpenters of the eighteenth century, erected their superb timber structures; they continued in the nineteenth century when the American pioneers spanned the rivers with timbers cut from the primeval forests (often roofing their spans against the snow). The greatest span achieved with timber trusses in the USA was the roofed Colossus over the Schuylkill at Fairmont, Pennsylvania; built in 1812 to the design of an architect, Louis Wernwag, it achieved a single span of 340 feet, only 50 feet less than the timber span the Grubenmanns had built at Wettingen in 1758.

The truss was later developed in iron when the early railers were busy both here and in the States, the first application being Sir John M'Neile's bridge on the Dublin–Drogheda railway with a span of about 40 feet. The most splendid development of the iron truss, however, came with the building of Crumlin Viaduct across the Ebbw Vale in 1857 (lately demolished) which applied the Warren triangular lattice girder (82).

To conclude this sketchy world survey we must point to the development of navigational aids in the seventeenth century as the true start of the Industrial Revolution: to the full application of the steam engine by Watt, particularly in pumping to allow deeper mining than even Newcomen's early pumps could accomplish; to the digging of the English canals which, by linking iron with coal, made the Revolution possible; to the improvement of roads after the Turnpike Acts; to the arrival of the railways; to Bessemer's method of steel production, and finally to the rediscovery of concrete and its unprecedented combination with steel to form reinforced concrete.

Up to the end of the nineteenth century most ferrous structures were of cast or wrought iron and, even though Bessemer had patented his steel-making process in 1856, steel was not generally used for bridges until the end of the century, the Forth Railway Bridge of 1889 (83) being an early example (if one excepts the eccentric case of the suspension span of steel chains crossing the Danube at Vienna designed by Von Mites and built as far back as 1828 before Bessemer's invention had been conceived).

Steel brought a revolution, for it is stronger, less brittle, than iron and it is almost perfectly isotropic, that is to say it will react under stresses uniformly in every direction so that computations in its use can be exact. A great aid to steel production towards the end of the nineteenth century was Martin and Seimens open-hearth process. High tensile steel is the latest development and this has engendered such slim suspensions as the

18 *Left*, engraving of London's old mediaeval bridge as it was in 1745 shortly before the houses were demolished. This remained the City's only crossing for over five centuries.

19 *Below*, the opening of Rennie's new London Bridge in 1831, engraved from a painting by Stanfield. It has been rebuilt in Arizona.

20 *Above*, an aquatint of Labelye's Westminster Bridge of 1750 with its fifteen stone arches. This was London's second crossing.

21 *Right*, by way of structural contrast and a result of two centuries of technical developments, this elegant footbridge of post-tensioned concrete across the A2 at Swanscombe, Kent, has a three-hinged arch with cantilevered side spans; it was designed by J. A. Bergg (Photograph: Colin Westwood).

Severn Bridge. Greater strength and rigid, continuous structure in steel has also come with the welded joint whereby the old, weakening rivets and bolts can be discarded. As well as metal fatigue, corrosion has raised some difficulties in the use of steel, for steel rusts far more quickly than iron; the Forth Railway Bridge, for instance, must be continually painted – work that takes three years to complete and then starts all over again.

The Romans used mass concrete made with natural hydraulic binders, and this material has been rediscovered fairly recently – initially in the Portland cement used by Smeaton in his Eddystone lighthouse. In 1824 Joseph Aspdin, a Yorkshire bricklayer, invented an artificial cement which is the basis of modern concrete, and in 1877 the first bridge of mass concrete was built with three arches across the River Axe at Seaton in Devonshire to a design by a civil engineer named Philip Branna. But concrete did not come into its own until married to steel. The originator of reinforced concrete seems to have been W. B. Wilkinson, a plasterer, who in 1865 erected a fire-resisting cottage in that composite fabric. From that small start of just over a century ago reinforced concrete has become the most important building material in the world today, not least in bridging.

When steel and concrete are combined, the concrete takes the compression, for it is weak in tension, while steel rods incorporated in the lower part of a beam, for example, take the tension, thus greatly lightening structure. With improved steels this combination of materials has been much advanced by stretching the rods or wires within the concrete with jacks by pre-stressing or post-tensioning. This has lightened structure even further and to a point of great elegance. The invention must be credited to Eugène Freyssinet of

France. It acts in the way a row of books can be lifted and held by pressing the hands hard against the lower half to prevent the books from slipping down. The Medway Bridge near Rochester, carrying the M2 motorway with a central span of 500 feet, was a landmark in the development of prestressed concrete (96).

Concrete was of particular value in the momentous bridge building decades of the 'fifties and 'sixties in Britain that resulted from the new road developments, particularly of motorways. Then some 3000 new bridges were erected in Britain both in reinforced concrete and steel, including those splendid achievements of the Forth and Severn. The older roads need about one bridge per mile, but motorways require about two and a half per mile – one reason for the great number of new bridges.

Four thousand years ago men were building useful bridges. To span 20 feet was then a triumph. The Golden Gate Bridge, San Francisco, opened in 1937, has a suspension span of 4200 feet. Amman's Verrazano Narrows suspension across the mouth of New York Harbour opened in 1964 with the widest span in the world at 4260 feet, while the new Humber will reach 4626 feet. Now engineers agree that a suspension span of 10,000 feet could be built. The wider the span of a bridge, the fewer and narrower its supports, and the lighter its construction (since a bridge must carry not only traffic but its own weight as well), the more efficient it must be. In one civilizing activity at least we have advanced with giant strides.

Tower on the Welsh Bridge
Shrewsbury

2 Mediaeval

Almost nothing remains of bridges in Britain built before the Middle Ages except a few clapper, or cromlech, bridges, which, as a type, are prehistoric, and a few Roman relics like the bridge abutments of stone at Chollerford, Northumberland. In the early Middle Ages fords were more common than bridges at river crossings, as the large number of place-names ending with the suffix -ford indicate, and it is just at those points where rivers possessed bridges or dependable fords that towns grew up. Rivers, with their fords and bridges, have formed our whole road system and a glance at a map will show that almost every old town in the land is situated on or near a river – Malvern and Shaftesbury being rare exceptions.

Two points on any river become important in history, for at those points towns have developed: first, the point nearest the mouth where a bridge could be built and an inland port established; secondly, the lowest point on the river which was always possible to ford even in the worst weather. In the case of the Thames, London was the first and Wallingford the second. (When William the Conquerer took London he went all the way to Wallingford to cross the Thames and then eastward along the north of the river).

The mediaeval builders were well supplied with fairly heavy plant such as water-driven hammers for making wrought iron, water-driven pumps, hoisting engines, tackles, and rams on shear-legs. Main foundations consisted of timber piles shod with iron on which boards were laid (hardwood sunk in mud does not rot). Stone, set in lime mortar, was mostly ashlar which came either from local quarries or was carried from a distance by water, even from abroad.

Not only the monasteries, but also town corporations, landowners and religious guilds undertook the building of bridges; the King himself was directly concerned and no bridge of stone could be erected without his consent. Finance came, in the main, from private bequests, including episcopal indulgences, and maintenance was often covered by tolls. Bridges were frequently 'farre in decay for lakke of tymely reparacion', and frequent catastrophes may be a reason why mediaeval bridges, built at a period that produced such beautiful, aetherial and intricate workmanship in stone elsewhere, were so often rough, heavy, and ready structures; to lavish fine craftsmanship upon them would have been discouraging, so that bridges were perforce utility structures only – if we except the attendant chapels and chantries.

Every mediaeval bridge had its cross, but of bridge crosses now only a stump remains here and there to mark the passing of the Roundheads. Some bridges were further dedicated by a chapel attended by one or more Bridge Priests. Only three with chapels remain: at Wakefield (27) and Rotherham (28), both in Yorkshire, and at St Ives in Huntingdonshire (26). Of these Wakefield is the least debased and, as its Decorated work shows, it belongs to the fourteenth century.

Of war bridges two good examples survive: Warkworth in Northumberland and Monnow Bridge at Monmouth (29), both of which retain their defensive towers. Stirling Bridge, Scotland – at one time the key to the Highlands and of great strategic importance – remains a fine structure but has lost its gateway (30).

Scotland retains a fair number of mediaeval bridges, perhaps because the demands of modern traffic have been less pressing there than elsewhere in Britain. Wales has its well known bridge across the Dee at Llangollen, part of which has survived from 1131. Two bridges of the southwest deserve special mention on account of their lengths: Wadebridge in Cornwall with 15 arches and Bideford in Devon with 24. The strangest and most haunted of all Gothic bridges is that at Crowland in Lincolnshire (31). Called Trinity Bridge, or Three-Ways-to-Nowhere, it may have been erected by the local abbey as a symbol of the Trinity rising above the flat and watery landscape.

The thoroughfares the bridges served included many a straight old Roman road, and all roads were busy enough with men, horses, and the heavy, lumbering, two-wheeled carts of the peasants. Now and then a horse litter would pass, or a lordly four-wheeled carriage, awkward but luxurious, gilded, carved, brightly painted, and protected by a hooped awning of fine tapestries. A prelate would ride by, a peripatetic London magistrate on his way to the county court, a bishop with his train, a merchant or farmer on his way to market, a wandering minstrel, a journeyman mason or carpenter, a herbalist quack, a group of jugglers, a running messenger or a knight at arms with his retinue. A tied serf in his leather jerkin would stop his tilling for a moment on some rustic strip to stare in wonder as the King rode by followed by a splendid throng and a host of lesser parasites – not so rare a sight as might be imagined, for the Court travelled incessantly on state affairs from town to town, from manor to manor, accompanied by cartloads of rolled documents. With all this movement bridge building was important in mediaeval times.

22 *Page 28*, Defence tower of the old mediaeval Welsh Bridge at Shrewsbury from a romantic etching of 1820. The bridge no longer exists.

23 *Below*, mediaeval transport in the form of a carriage of the fourteenth century depicted in the Luttrell Psalter.
24 *Right*, the 90-feet arch of Twizel Bridge, Northumberland, longest mediaeval span in England, with its economical ribbed construction.

Ribbed arches
25 *Above*, Ludford Bridge, Ludlow.
26 *Right*, the chapel bridge of St Ives,
Huntingdonshire.

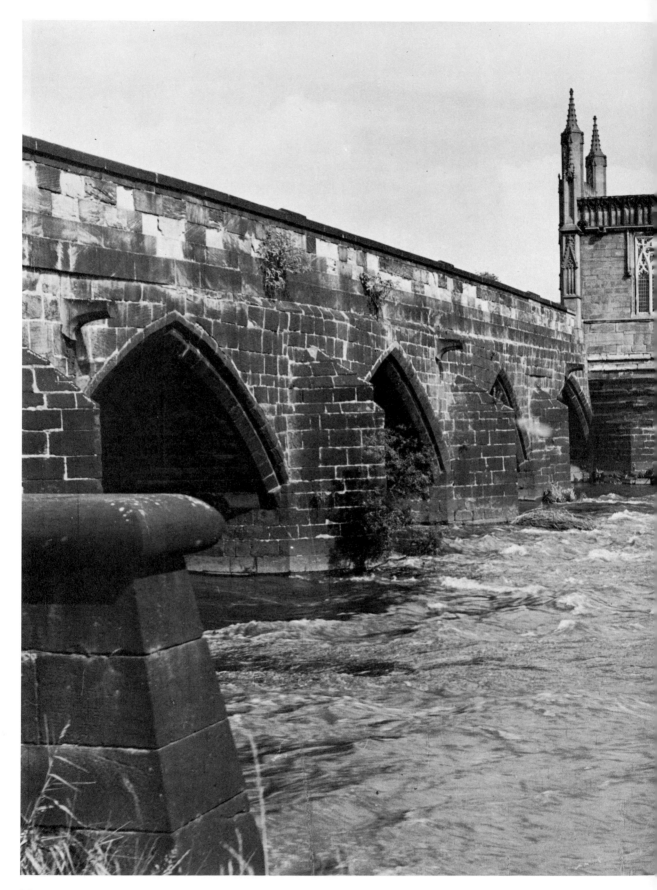

Chapel bridges
27 *Left*, Wakefield Bridge, Yorkshire, with its Decorated fourteenth-century chapel.
28 *Below*, the chapel of 1483 at Rotherham Bridge, Yorkshire, with its pinnacles and castellations.

War bridges
29 *Above*, Monnow Bridge, Monmouth, built
in 1272 with a tower but widened at a later
date.
30 *Right*, Stirling Bridge of about 1400 was the
key to the Highlands and once possessed a
tower.

Pointed arches

31 *Above*, the curious Trinity Bridge,
Crowland, Lincolnshire, or Three-Ways-to-
Nowhere, with its three pointed arches and
three approaches, probably belongs to the
fourteenth century; now dry, it once stood
above the confluence of three streams and may
have borne a large cross; the carved figure
probably came from Crowland Abbey.
32 *Right*, Radcot Bridge on the upper Thames,
also of the fourteenth century and now the
oldest on the river.

3 Post-Reformation

As the unifying power of the Mother Church declined and nationalism in its modern form was born, the defensive tower and the chapel ceased to concern the bridge builder, partly because his work was now secular and partly because the war bridge had become obsolete with the discovery of gunpowder. Renaissance trends eventually brought immense developments but they were delayed for two centuries. In Britain the years between the mid-sixteenth and mid-eighteenth centuries were not great bridging years, although with the growth of trade many small structures for pack-horse trains were erected, the longest surviving one being Essex Bridge, crossing the Trent with fourteen arches at Great Haywood in Staffordshire.

The eighteenth century was more active, mainly in the latter part when the canals were begun and after the General Turnpike Act of 1773 came – with the help of men like Metcalf and Macadam, and later Smeaton and Telford – to improve roads that had everywhere decayed into an appalling condition of potholes and mud, and to bring before long the brief, picturesque epoch of the stage coach before the railways arrived.

The foundation and upkeep of bridges by religious bodies were necessarily abandoned at the Dissolution, and in 1530 an Act was passed that placed the same responsibility on counties for the maintenance of bridges as was borne by parishes for the upkeep of highways, though small bridges were often maintained by parishes. When bridges were rendered unsafe by storm or flood, private individuals could repair the damage on their own initiative and later claim their expenses in court.

It is impossible to draw a firm line in time between the eighteenth-century works of the architect and the nineteenth-century works of the engineer – between this chapter and the next. The adapted Roman mode of Palladio and his followers with its classical grammar was often the work of the new professional man the Renaissance had produced, the educated architect. His was scholarly work, precise, dignified, carefully proportioned, and far less weighty than the Gothic works of the master masons, but in technique it showed at first few revolutionary advances on mediaeval structure. After the architect came the early engineer, often a craftsman, to develop bridge construction with new methods and materials. Telford was a mason and Smeaton trained himself as a craftsman.

Two bridges of strong baroque character still stand: Vanbrugh's uncompleted Grand Bridge across the lake on the axis approach to Blenheim Palace in Oxfordshire, so bold and extravagant that the Duchess of Marlborough declared in high dudgeon that it 'passed all men's understanding' (41) and General Wade's fine military bridge with its four obelisks at Aberfeldy, one of many built at the same time to open up the Highlands (37).

To the eighteenth century belongs the beautiful arch by William Edwards at Pont-y-Pridd with its span of 140 feet and its haunches pierced with tunnels to lighten the structure and allow the passage of flood water. This principle has reached its latest development in the open spandrels of modern concrete bridges (95). The great arch of 149 feet span built at Ceret in the fourteenth century has the earliest surviving open spandrels.

Important eighteenth-century bridges are those designed by the architect John Gwynn: Magdalen at Oxford (3, 33), English at Shrewsbury (4), Worcester, and Atcham (50). Others include Robert Adam's housed Pulteney Bridge at Bath (47), Labelye's Westminster (demolished 1851 and the first case in Britain where caissons were used for the foundations) (20, 48), Mylne's noble Blackfriars with its nine elliptical arches (third across London's river, demolished in the 1860s) (49), Smeaton's bridges at Perth, Coldstream (38), and Banff, and, on the upper Thames, Taylor's Maidenhead, Paine's Richmond and Chertsey, Hayward's Henley, and two elegant toll bridges above Oxford at Swinford and Lechlade whose designers are unknown. All these were built of stone in classical style.

Some notable Georgian bridges stand in the parks of the aristocracy: the elaborate, roofed Palladian one at Wilton designed by the Architect Earl, ninth Lord Pembroke (44), Robert Adam's swaggy, balustered one of three arches with its weir at Kedleston Hall, Derbyshire (45), James Paine's classical one with niches and statues at Chatsworth, Derbyshire, John Soane's simple, single span at Tyringham, Buckinghamshire (42), and the curious little Hindoo folly, with a divine and frondy grot beneath it, by Cockerell and Repton, at Sezincote, Gloucestershire (43).

The Cambridge Backs display a delightful range of small post-Reformation bridges, the two oldest being of the seventeenth century and the most sophisticated and highly decorated examples of the period in the country: Clare (52) and St John's. The latter, built about 1698, has been attributed to Wren but is more likely to have been designed by his assistant Hawksmoor. Trinity, designed by James Essex, was built in 1766 in an elegant way with parapets ending in horizontal curls (53–4). All have three segmental arches. A pleasing eighteenth-century bridge is Queen's (51), one of several Mathematical Bridges of timber which Essex erected in and around Cambridge.

The two finest bridges of the eighteenth century, already mentioned, are the second and third that London acquired: Labelye's Westminster with its 15 diminishing semi-circular arches of Portland stone and the darker Purbeck (20, 48), and Robert Mylne's Blackfriars (49) which applied the economical elliptical French arch in its nine spans of which the centre one was 100 feet wide. Later, Mylne was among those who submitted ideas for a new London Bridge, but finally John Rennie's design was accepted and carried out (19); and with Rennie we come to the Great Age and the next chapter.

33 *Page 40*, Magdalen Bridge, Oxford, designed by Gwynn and completed in 1779. The tower of Magdalen College is in the background.

34 *Left*, a wood engraving of a packhorse convoy, an important means of transport before the Industrial Revolution.

35 *Above*, Stopham Bridge, crossing the Arun in Sussex, was built in Tudor times; its central arch was built high, possibly at a later date, to permit the passage of boats.

36 A stone packhorse bridge of 1822 crossing the Nidd near Burnt Yates in the West Riding.

37 One of the few baroque bridges in Britain
is that at Aberfeldy which crosses the Tay in
Perthshire; it is one of General Wade's 40
eighteenth-century military bridges built to
open up the Highlands.

Pierced bridges. Tunnels through the spandrels or haunches both lighten weight on foundations and allow passage of flood-water.

38 *Below*, Smeaton's Coldstream Bridge of 1766 crossing the Tweed on the Scottish border.

39 *Right*, Pant-y-Goytre Bridge over the Usk, Monmouthshire, built about 1821 by John Upton of Gloucester.

Park bridges
40 *Left*, the Grand Bridge at Blenheim built for the first Duke of Marlborough in 1711, a piece of uncompleted baroque theatricality by Sir John Vanbrugh designed to contain rooms below the road and an arcade above it.
41 *Top left*, a contemporary engraving of the design as intended.
42 *Top right*, John Soane's single-arch at Tyringham Park, Buckinghamshire.
43 *Right*, the little bridge, with fern filled grot below, inspired by the Elephant Caves of India, at Sezincote House, Gloucestershire, designed by Samuel Cockerell about 1805.

44 The elaborate roofed Palladian bridge at
Wilton Park, Wiltshire, built in 1737 by the
ninth Lord Pembroke. Copies with variations
stand both at Stow and Prior Park, Bath.
(Photograph: Reece Winstone)

Adam bridges
45 *Left*, Robert Adam's bridge with weir at Kedleston Park, Derbyshire.
46 *Below*, Aray Bridge, Inverary, with pierced spandrel.
47 *Right*, the housed Pulteney Bridge, Bath, of 1769. (Photograph: Leighton Gibbins)

54

Georgian road bridges
48 *Top left,* an arch of Labelye's Westminster
Bridge completed in 1750, from a painting by
Samuel Scott, the English Canaletto. The
bridge stood for only a century.
49 *Below left,* an engraving of Robert Mylne's
Blackfriars Bridge under construction in 1766.

50 *Below,* Atcham Bridge, Shropshire, John
Gwynn's most beautiful structure completed in
1776 as one of the three he built across the
Severn.

At the Cambridge Backs
51 The timber Mathematical Bridge at Queen's
College erected in 1749 to the design of James
Essex. Reconstructed in 1902; sometimes called
Newton's Bridge; also attributed to one called
Etheridge.

52 Clare Bridge of about 1640, the oldest and
perhaps the most beautiful along the Backs,
designed by Thomas Grumbold. (Photograph:
J. Allan Cash)

At the Cambridge Backs
Trinity Bridge of 1760 by James Essex.
53 *Above*, the abutment detail.
54 *Right*, general view of the three elliptical
arches. (Photograph: J. Allan Cash)

4 Industrial Revolution

The marriage of coal and iron conceived the Great Age of British bridge building. It extended from the erection of Ironmaster Abraham Darby's Iron Bridge of 1779 in Coalbrookdale (58–9), the cradle of the Industrial Revolution, to that of the Forth Railway Bridge in 1889 (83–4). The way to heaven now lay not through feudal hangover, land ownership, cultivated leisure for the few, and picturesque landscape, but through hard work, industrial stock, church or chapel attendance, and the dark, Satanic mills of the Manchester Men. The Industrial Revolution began in a practical sense with the opening in 1761 of 'Heav'n-taught' Brindley's canal to link the Duke of Bridgewater's mountain of coal at Worseley with Manchester and Liverpool, thus inaugurating the brief Canal Era. That era produced a few major aqueducts (60, 61) and a host of minor bridges (63–6), almost all of which own a simple beauty arising from their subtle, undecorated curves and arches, their ageing patina of brick and stone, and their unselfconscious functionalism.

With the building of the first public line between Stockton and Darlington, opened in 1825, railways began to oust canals as the main form of heavy transport. (An interesting little bridge on the line, completed in 1824, which combines cast and wrought iron can be seen at the York Railway Museum). Iron brought the steam pump, the steam pump and the canals brought more coal, more coal brought more iron, more iron brought more railways and, with them, the greatest bridging activity this country had yet known. Coal, iron, and steam also stimulated heroic developments in bridge construction; they engendered new aids to building such as heavy mechanical pile drivers, pneumatic caissons for foundations, and steam traction for hauling and raising heavy parts. Technical advances became imperative in railway development, for railways required wide spans of great tensile strength that could bear heavy live loads. Curiously the railways solved their own problem of acquiring adequate supplies of iron ore in that the excavations of tunnels and cuttings revealed unsuspected new ironstone beds, eventually disclosing the great bed which runs in a crescent from the Tees to Weymouth.

The four great engineering names of the age are John Rennie, Thomas Telford, George Stephenson, his son Robert, and Isambard Kingdom Brunel. Rennie (1761–1821) and Telford (1757–1834) were contemporaries whose lives spanned the Canal Era; both were Scotsmen of humble origin who applied their remarkable gifts in an age that offered opportunity to men of vigour and intelligence. Both built road bridges and both built in stone and in iron, but Telford was also responsible for many canals and their crossings and was the more prolific of the two, not least in the use of iron, while Rennie carried the masonry arch to its final development, his most famous bridges being the three he built across the Thames in London: Waterloo in granite (the noblest bridge in the world, according to Canova), Southwark of cast iron and granite, and the new London, also of granite (19). His first important bridge, however, was the one across the Tweed at Kelso, completed in 1803.

Telford's masonry bridges never reached the standard of design or interest of his graceful iron ones. His Buildwas Bridge of 1796 was the third bridge of iron in Britain, the earlier two being Iron Bridge (58) and then Tom (Rights-of-Man) Paine's Wearmouth

Bridge at Sunderland, long since defunct. Among Telford's important masonry feats are Dean Bridge, Edinburgh (124), Mouse Water Bridge, Lanark, and Chirk Aqueduct. His two masterworks, however, contain much iron: the stupendous Pont Cysylltau Aqueduct on the Welsh section of the Shropshire Union Canal (61), and the suspension road bridge across the Menai Straits with its central span of 579 feet (67–8). He built many smaller structures, and, as County Surveyor of Shropshire for most of his working life, he erected no less than 42 bridges in the county, five in iron.

The success of Menai led to other suspensions, notably those at Marlow and Hammersmith (replaced in 1887 by Bazalgette's surviving suspension) by William Tierney Clark (1783–1852), who with his brother Adam built the famous chain bridge over the Danube between Buda and Pest, and that of Brunel (1806–1859) across the gorge at Clifton near Bristol (69). Brunel was also responsible for many bridges on his Great Western Railway, notably the extraordinary affair of fish-bellied girders with their great oval tubes crossing the Tamar at Saltash in Cornwall (79), and the three bridges of red engineering brickwork carrying his line three times across the Thames at Maidenhead (13), Moulsford and Basildon. Brunel also built the iron viaduct (opened in 1851 and demolished in 1958) that took the South Wales Railway across the Wye at Chepstow with a main span largely composed of a tube 309 feet long; no beauty but structurally interesting.

George Stephenson (1781–1848), son of a colliery fireman, who became the pioneering railway engineer, built a number of splendid viaducts, including the Sankey of brick faced with stone, on his Liverpool and Manchester line – a line on which he also erected several smaller structures with cast-iron girders. His son Robert (1819–1859) produced the Royal Border Viaduct of masonry at Berwick, called the Last Act of the Union, the High Level Bridge, Newcastle (87–8), carrying road and rail on two levels by means of six skeleton lintols of iron, cast and wrought, each 125 feet wide, and his tubular iron railway bridges, the Britannia and the Conway (76–8), on the Chester–Holyhead line – the first examples of the flat beam in modern bridge construction. Opened in 1850, the Britannia contained the longest railway span in the world until Roebling completed his Niagara Suspension five years later.

Two great railway bridges must finally be noted: Liddell, Gordon and Kennard's Crumlin Viaduct of iron, partly wrought, across the Ebbw Vale, using the Warren Triangular Girder, which was opened in 1857 and sadly demolished a few years ago (82), and then Baker and Fowler's dinosaur, the Forth Railway, opened in 1890 (83–4). Such great viaducts, awesome in their pride, are the best landscape legacies of the Railway Age.

55 *Page 60*, A tower of the iron Albert Bridge, Chelsea, of 1873 by R. M. Ordish; half suspension, half cantilever, known as the stayed type.

56 *Left*, Stephenson's Rocket, from a Victorian wood engraving, symbolizes transport in the age of steam and iron. The Industrial Revolution brought many structural developments, not least in the laying of foundations such as, *right*, 57, this pneumatic iron caisson of the 1860s. A. iron ballast; B. water ballast; C. lifting chains; D. air lock; E. winch ropes inside columns.

58, 59 Iron Bridge across the Severn in Coalbrookdale, built in 1779 as the first bridge of iron in the world. It was shipped down river in sections from Abraham Darby's iron works and was erected in three months. Total span is 100 feet 6 inches.

60 Cotton-king Oldknow's Marple Aqueduct,
Cheshire, carrying the Peak Forest Canal,
depicted in an aquatint of 1803.

61 Pont Cysylltau Aqueduct carrying the Welsh
Section of the Shropshire Union Canal across
the Dee. Designed by Thomas Telford and
completed in 1805 with an iron trough
supported on tall stone columns.

62 The Barton Swing Aqueduct carries the
Bridgewater Canal across the Manchester Ship
Canal; it is swung open still filled with 1500
tons of water.

Canal bridges of iron, brick, stone and timber.
63 *Left*, a precast type at Braunston on the Grand Union.
64 *Below left*, at Great Haywood where the Staffordshire and Worcestershire Canal joins the Trent and Mersey.
65 *Right*, a wooden swing bridge on the Gloucester and Berkeley Ship Canal.
66 *Below*, a simple stone bridge on the Macclesfield Canal.

Telford's Suspension Bridge across the Menai
Straits between North Wales and Anglesey,
opened in 1826, has a span of 579 feet. It was
partly reconstructed in 1940 to take modern
traffic. See also page 133.
67 *Below*, a close-up of the chains.
68 *Right*, the arched approach on the Anglesey
side.

Suspension spans
69 *Top*, Brunel's Clifton Bridge crosses the
Avon Gorge with a span of 702 feet; begun in
1836, it was not completed until 1864.

70 *Above*, Telford's iron Conway Bridge
completed in 1826 with inept towers intended to
harmonize with the architecture of Conway
Castle. On the left of the bridge is Stephenson's
tubular railway bridge.

71 A charming small footbridge of steel built
across the Dee at Cambus-o'-May,
Aberdeenshire, in 1905; the approach to a
suspension bridge, however small, provides a
monumental effect by virtue of the framing of
one tower by the other.

72 Thomas Page's Chelsea Suspension Bridge
in a print of 1852, showing Wren's Chelsea
Hospital beyond. The bridge was opened in
1858 but was replaced by the present suspension in 1934.

Iron decoration
73 *Top Left*, wrought iron centre of Chepstow Bridge across the Wye, opened in 1816.
74 *Below*, spandrel detail of the cast-iron arch of Telford's Waterloo Bridge at Bettws-y-Coed, built in 1815, the year of the Battle of Waterloo.
75 *Right*, Surrey end of Blackfriars Railway Bridge of 1864.

79

Robert Stephenson's two tubular bridges of
iron.
76 *Left*, the end of Britannia Bridge of 1850
across the Menai Straits with its flanking lions.
77 *Below left*, the Conway Bridge of 1849
(from a contemporary print).

78 A tube of the Britannia under construction
(from a contemporary print).

79 Brunel's strange
fish-bellied girder
railway bridge of 1859
across the Tamar,
known as Saltash, or
Royal Albert, Bridge.

80 The noble
Victorian brick
viaduct at Balcombe
carrying the London–
Brighton line across
the Ouse Valley.

Viaducts
81 *Above*, a pair in hard stone at Chapel-en-le-
Frith, Derbyshire.
82 *Right*, Crumlin in the Ebbw Vale, opened
in 1857 and demolished in the 1960s. It was
important in its early use of the Warren
triangular girder.

83, 84 Baker and Fowler's Forth Railway
Bridge of 1890. An early steel bridge, it was
hand-tailored on the spot and consists of three
balanced cantilevers joined by short beams.
The tubes are 12 feet in diameter, and the total
length, with approaches, is over one and a half
miles.

5 Modern

As iron represented the Railway Age so steel and concrete represent the age of the petrol engine. The arch of Iron Bridge (1779) has a span of 100 feet 6 inches. The great steel bow, hinged and trussed, of Bayonne Bridge over the Kill van Kull, New York (1931) has a span of 1652 feet, so beating Sydney Harbour Bridge (opened a few months later) by exactly two feet. Our own Tyne Bridge, Newcastle (1930) with its trussed and tied arch, or bowstring girder, is only 531 feet, but even that is impressive (87, 115). More so is the Runcorn–Widnes Bridge (1961) by Mott, Hay and Anderson, with its span of 1082 feet, which has replaced the old Widnes Transporter across the Mersey (89). An elegant and smaller bowstring with a simple, slender tied arch by the same engineers is the new Scotswood crossing the Tyne with a span of 140 feet, which in 1968 replaced the old suspension of 1831. Such bowstring types are strong and particularly suitable for heavy modern road traffic.

An interesting development is the stayed girder type which is a kind of hybrid of cantilever and suspension. Here the deck is not suspended from a parabola with hangers but from cables sloping down from towers to deck. Since the deck here takes large compression forces, such bridges are unsuitable for spans over 1500 feet. A precedent, as we have seen, is the beloved Albert Bridge, Chelsea, completed in 1873 by the engineer Ordish (55). Two modern examples are the Wye Viaduct and George Street Bridge, Newport, both by Mott, Hay and Anderson (91–2). The Wye Viaduct, which is virtually a continuation of the Severn Suspension, has a stiffened box girder stayed by steel cables stretching down from two slender pillars supported by steel trestles. A larger version of the type is that at Newport with a main span across the Usk of 500 feet, achieved by four tall towers of hollow reinforced concrete and a number of steel wires passing over rollers within the tops of the towers and supporting a deck of boxes made of cellular steelwork.

The two new British bridges which have surprised the world are the great ethereal suspensions of the Forth (93) and the Severn (85, 90, 108), by the engineers Mott, Hay and Anderson in association with Freeman, Fox and Partners. The Forth, which replaced the ferry in 1964, consists of two towers of high tensile steel rising 512 feet and supporting catenary cables of 11,618 galvanized high tensile steel wires wrapped with binder wire and painted. Two Warren truss girders run the full length of the bridge under the deck along the central span of 3300 feet. 30,000 tons of steel were used here as against the 50,000 required for its narrower neighbour, the Forth Railway Bridge. 250 men were employed in its construction as against 4500 for the railway structure, although it must be remembered that in the latter case all steelwork was tailor-made on the site, and that the engineers were taking no chances after the Tay Bridge disaster and so somewhat overbuilt their work.

The Severn Bridge, carrying the London–South Wales motorway that reduces the journey between South-West England and South Wales by 50 miles, was completed in 1966 with a main span 60 feet shorter than that of the Forth. The deck support consists of a shallow box of welded steelwork instead of girders, while the suspenders of wire cable are not vertical but run in a series of triangles. A third large new suspension, but one of far less visual attraction than either the Forth or the Severn, is that crossing the Tamar close to Brunel's Royal Albert Viaduct at Saltash, opened in 1961.

New bridges of reinforced concrete, large and small, have been built in the last two decades in great numbers all over the country. A small example but one of importance is the delightful Garret Hostel footbridge of 1960 at Cambridge designed by the late Anthony Morgan. Spanning 80 feet, it is the first bridge of post-tensioned concrete to have been erected in Britain (109).

Two important concrete bridges now cross London's river: Waterloo (98) and the new New London (99). Waterloo, completed in 1945 by Rendell, Palmer and Tritton, is a beam bridge of five spans looking like an arch type; it is the most graceful London's river possesses. New London, completed in 1973 by Harold King, City Engineer, with Mott, Hay and Anderson, to replace Rennie's granite structure (now re-erected in Arizona) is not visually thrilling but interesting and practical, being composed of four prestressed concrete box beams in precast segments strung together with cables like a string of beads and forming three flat 'arches' that are in fact cantilevers with a central suspended beam, the central span totalling 340 feet.

Of large new concrete bridges of character on the motorways must be mentioned the long one taking the M2 across the Medway at Rochester (96), the arched spans with open spandrels of the Taf Fechan (95) and the Nant Hir on the Heads of the Valleys Road, South Wales, Bridstow Bridge on the Ross Motorway, and the strutted Wentbridge Viaduct on the A1 near Doncaster (97), to say little of the several elevated roads such as the Hammersmith Flyover and the Chiswick–Langley section of the M4. There is also a fine arched, open spandrel example over the Lune to carry the Lancaster bypass. A particularly beautiful concrete bridge is the Clifton crossing the Trent at Nottingham, which like New London Bridge has two cantilevers and a suspended span.

The upper Thames has two important crossings: Runnymede, carrying the Staines bypass with steel arches encased in Portland stone, and Thames Bridge below Maidenhead carrying the M4 on a welded steel span faced with bricks.

As materials grow stronger, structures grow lighter and spans wider. Yet even today, for all their precise calculations and skills, engineers are not infallible; they make mistakes and disasters sometimes occur. A bridge may still demand one life or more, as in the spectacular failure by oscillation of the Tacoma Narrows Bridge in 1940 when a little dog perished.

85 *Page 90*, the Severn Suspension Bridge has a central span of 3240 feet. It was completed in 1966 and shortens the journey between England and Wales by 50 miles.
86 *Left*, a Rolls-Royce Silver Ghost symbolizes the petrol age.

87 *Right*, the Tyne Bridge, Newcastle, a tied arch bridge of 531 feet span opened in 1930. Beyond is a swing bridge of 1876, and beyond that again Stephenson's double-decker High Level Bridge of 1849 which takes road and rail.
88 *Above*, a hinge of the Tyne Bridge.

89 Mott, Hay and Anderson's Runcorn–Widnes tied arch, or bowstring, bridge of 1961 with a span of 1082 feet. This type is strong in order to cope with heavy road traffic. (Photograph: John Cleare)

New road bridges
90 *Left*, the Severn Suspension under construction showing the raising of a prefabricated section of the steel box deck into place. (Photograph: British Steel Corporation)

Above, two examples of the stayed girder, or cable cantilever, type.
91 *Top*, the Wye Viaduct which virtually continues the Severn Bridge on the Monmouthshire side.
92 *Bottom*, George Street Bridge, Newport. (Photographs: William Tribe)

93 The Forth Road Bridge of 1964 has a span of 3300 feet. The cables of high tensile steel wires support two truss girders.

Reinforced concrete
94 Arup's eccentric Kingsgate footbridge of
1965 across the Wear at Durham University;
the band was built on the bank and swivelled
into position on to its tapering-finger supports.
(Photograph: de Burgh Galwey)

95 Rendel, Palmer and Tritton's Taf Fechan
Bridge, Heads of the Valleys Road, Wales, of
1960 with arch span of 227 feet. (Photograph:
W. E. Middleston)

Reinforced Concrete
96 *Above,* Freeman, Fox's elegant Medway
Bridge of 1963 carrying the M2 near Maidstone, Kent; its prestressed cantilevered
central span is 500 feet, longest of its kind in
the world. (Photograph: Leonard Hill)
97 *Below left,* Maynard Lovell's Wentbridge
Viaduct carrying the A1 near Doncaster; it
required 90 miles of steel tube scaffolding to
erect. (Photograph: Maurice Broomfield)
98 *Below,* Waterloo Bridge, London, completed 1942, is not an arched bridge but a beam
bridge, widest span being 250 feet; facing is of
Portland stone.

99 Harold King's New
London Bridge of
1972 which replaced
Rennie's stone bridge
of 1831. The three
spans are of
prestressed concrete
box beams forming
cantilevers with central
suspended beams.
The main span is
340 feet wide.

100 Captain Brown's Chain Pier of 1823 at
Brighton after its destruction by the hurricane
of 1833 (depicted in an engraving of 1842). It
was rebuilt but was finally destroyed in the
storm of 1896.

6 Failures and Fantasies

The pressure of flood water was the main cause of failure in mediaeval times but as piers grew slimmer and spans wider this hazard was lessened. Suspension types have suffered most, mainly on account of oscillation and undulation caused by wind. The disaster of Tacoma Narrows Bridge (Galloping Gertie), which occurred in 1940 only four months after the bridge had been opened, was the most dramatic, and an object lesson to modern engineers throughout the world. Even Telford had some trouble at Menai, and an English disaster occurred on Captain Brown's Chain Pier of 1823 at Brighton, which collapsed in a hurricane in 1833 (facing page) and finally in the great gale of 1896. The only cure for oscillation is to stiffen the deck.

The 1870s and '80s saw a series of failures of iron railway bridges; on the American railroads iron-truss bridges were failing at the rate of 25 a year. Rescue came from two sources: the rapid evolution of metallurgy and of structural engineering as exact sciences, and the use of steel. Britain's worst disaster in iron occurred at the Tay Bridge near Dundee which collapsed less than two years after completion. At over two miles this was the longest railway bridge in the world. Everyone was proud of it, even William McGonagall, Dundee's braggart son and the world's worst poet, who wrote an ode to the bridge. The first stanza, he later admitted, 'will possibly be as much as you can stand':

> *The Tay Bridge is a beautiful span,*
> *And the river Tay runs through it;*
> *A wonderful work by the hands of man,*
> *Many strangers come for to view it.*

Its designer, Thomas Bouch, received the accolade, and then on a Sunday evening, three days after Christmas 1879, a strong gale blew against its 84 spans as a mail train was steaming across it. Thirteen spans collapsed and the train plunged, carriage after carriage, into the icy water with its 80 passengers, none of whom survived. A Board of Trade enquiry found that 'the bridge had been badly designed, badly constructed, and badly maintained'. Four months later, his spirit broken, Sir Thomas Bouch expired.

The subject of bridges that failed in the sense that they were never built would fill another volume, but a few curious, sometimes beautiful, and often grandiose projects must be mentioned in concluding this survey. In 1793 a certain William Bridges designed a splendid affair of masonry, almost a folly, to cross the Avon Gorge at Clifton (104). It had a tall central arch 220 feet high and 180 feet wide to allow tall ships to sail below. Each of the five storeys in its abutments was 40 feet high and contained granaries, a corn exchange, wharfs, storage for coal, a market, a museum and library, a marine school, besides various offices, stables, warehouses and 20 dwellings. Above the arch was a chapel, a tollhouse, a belfry, and, at the very apex, a lighthouse, while in the spandrels two windmills revolved.

A number of schemes for the Clifton Bridge across the Avon Gorge were prepared for a competition, including a Gothic affair by Telford in his old age: in the end even the winning design by Brunel was not executed in its first form (69). Telford also designed a suspension in 1814 to cross the Mersey at Runcorn with a single leap of 1000 feet which appears in an engraving at the end of the *Atlas* of his works; from the look of its gentle catenary it hardly seems viable.

Telford's finest project was his design of 1800 for a new London Bridge, having a single span of 600 feet of iron filigree forming a low arch (105). It was universally admired but apparently problems of approach rendered it impractical and Rennie's duller design was chosen. George Dance the Younger, architect of Newgate Gaol, was associated with Telford in his work as Clerk of City Works, and he produced a proud and imposing lay-out for the development of the Port of London as a whole, which contained a pair of arched bridges with bascules at their centres through which ships could pass (106). Between the two bridges on either bank lay two open places, the Monument dominating the north side and a new obelisk to commemorate the recent naval victories, the south. This monumental scheme has been preserved for posterity in an aquatint of 1800 by William Daniell.

Many small bridges were built to decorate the parks of the landed gentry but others never reached further than the engraver's plate or the architect's drawing. Robert Adam produced one in 1768 for Bowood Park, Wiltshire (103), as 'ruinous and in imitation of the Aqueducts of the Ancients'. Another is Sir John Soane's formal and serene Roman piece for Chillington Park, Staffordshire, of three semi-circular arches and a central temple (102). One of the earlier park bridges was the Grand Bridge of 1711 at Blenheim designed by Vanbrugh for the first Duke of Marlborough (41). It may be mentioned here again because it was never completed according to the architect's theatrical desires with a tall arcade and four towers 80 feet high. We can now see only the lower part of the ponderous structure and only the upper part of that, for its rooms, including a small theatre, have long since been half-submerged in an aquatic gloom by the lake created by Capability Brown.

A number of modern projects have been designed, most of them without hope of realization but merely for some purpose of commercial publicity. The Glass Age Development Committee, for example, has given us a lively scheme for a Thames road bridge in London, called the Crystal Span (107), bearing a seven-storey building enclosed in an air-conditioned glass envelope within which is included an hotel, art gallery, shopping arcade, open-air theatre and roof gardens – an enormous housed bridge like the Old London. And then there are several projects for a Channel bridge, one 25 miles long and composed of two decks slung between 24 suspension spans 250 feet above the sea – a forceful symbol of European unity. A Thames bridge which may, sooner or later, be achieved, is that across the proposed Thames Barrage at Woolwich.

We can continue to scheme and dream for the art of bridging will continue until the human span is crossed.

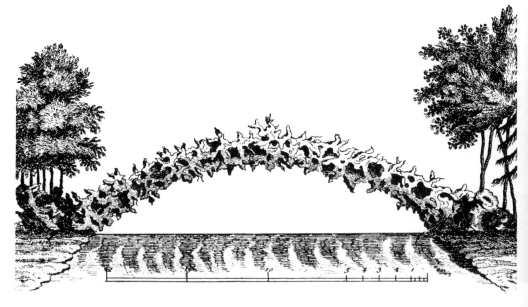

Elevation

102 Sir John Soane's dignified design for a bridge at Chillington House, Staffordshire.

Projects
101 *Below left*, a rococo footbridge from Over's *Ornamental Architecture*, 1758.

103 *Below*, a project by Robert Adam of 1786 for Bowood Park, Wiltshire, 'ruinous and in imitation of the Aqueducts of the Ancients'.

A Plan and Elevation for a Bridge over the River Avon at the Rocks of S... Bristol Hot W...

Ground Plan and Ro...

MU. LIB.

MARINE

MANUF.T

MANUF.T

ENGINE

INSCRIP: ANG: CON ST...

STONE W.F

N.o 1

W. BRIDGES, Invent.t et Delin.t

Demensions. The Great Arch 220 f.t high 180 f.t wide. Base 400 f.t Long 140 f.t wide. Ro...

Contents. N.o 1. A Light House. 2. A Toll House. 3. A Chapel, called S.t Vincent's. 4. 5. 6. Publick Gran...
& a Stone Wharf & Water Mill. 9. 10 Manufactories for Cotton. Wool. &c. 11. A Marine School. 12. A M...
16. Twenty Houses in the Scite of the Bridge. 17. Various Recesses for Out Offices, Stabling &c. 18. Clock T...

110

from *Sion Row Clifton*, to *Leigh Down*, near

20

COMˢ
ENGINE
14
St VINCENT
3
16'
PUB.GRA
4
17
PUB.GRA
5
16
15
17
CORN EX
6
16
17
COAL.WH
7
16
16
P.D. BRISTOL. Janʸ 1793.

00 f. Long 50 f. wide, Each Story 40 f. high, Gallery 6 f. wide.
Exchange for foreign train. 7. Coal Wharf & General Market.
ry, & Subscription Room. 13,14. Engine Rooms. 15, Vertical Windmills.
ase. 19. Watch House & Bellfry. 20 Road and Ground Plan.

104 William Bridges'
masonry fantasy for
the Avon Gorge,
Bristol, of 1793, with
central arch of 180
feet span – almost a
small town.

London projects
105 Telford's design for a single iron span of
600ft to replace Old London Bridge; the high
approaches necessary prevented its adoption.
106 *Right*, George Dance's layout for a new
Port of London with its pair of bascule bridges
(depicted in an aquatint of 1800 by William
Daniell); on the left is the Monument and on
the right a new obelisk to commemorate the
naval victories.

107 A modern fantasy called the Crystal Span offered by the Glass Age Development Committee to cross the Thames where Vauxhall Bridge now stands. Its seven stories, enclosed in a glass envelope, would include an hotel, art gallery, shopping arcade, open-air theatre and roof gardens. It is a clumsy affair without gaiety but interesting as a development of the ancient housed bridges such as Old London Bridge. (Photograph: *The Times*)

108 *Page 116*, the new Severn Suspension Bridge seen in dramatic silhouette. (Photograph: British Steel Corporation)

Gazetteer

This selective list of existing bridges, old and new, in England, Scotland and Wales, should be marked 'E. & O.E.'. The author would welcome letters from readers who discover any serious errors or omissions in case of a reprint.

Counties are arranged alphabetically and bridges appear in historical order except in the two cases of the Thames, both in London and on the upper river, where they are listed in geographical order going upstream.

The figures at the ends of entries refer to numbers of plates.

England

BEDFORDSHIRE

Bedford Bridge. 1813.
Of Bedford stone in five segmental arches of classical design. Carries the A6 between Luton and Kettering across the Ouse. JOHN WING of Bedford.

CAMBRIDGE: The Backs

Clare Bridge. c.1640.
The oldest along the Backs. Three segmental arches of stone with decorated balustrades, which may be the first of their classical sort in the country. A delight. THOMAS GRUMBOLD (52).

St John's Bridge. c.1698.
Similar in style to Clare but more elaborately decorated. Three segmental arches with rusticated voussoirs, balustraded parapets and panels carved in bas-reliefs. Attributed to Wren but probably by his assistant NICHOLAS HAWKSMOOR.

Trinity Bridge. 1760.
Three segmental arches of stone with solid parapets ending satisfactorily with horizontal curls. JAMES ESSEX (53–4).

Queens College Bridge. 1749.
A Mathematical Bridge of timber trusses forming a single span. Based on truss designs of Palladio. JAMES ESSEX (51).

King's College Bridge. 1818.
Single low segmental span of stone with delicate mouldings. Simple and pleasing. WILLIAM WILKINSON.

New Bridge. 1826.
Single arch roofed and fenestrated in Gothic style. THOMAS RICKMAN and HENRY HUTCHINSON. (Rickman was an early Gothic revivalist who gave us the terms Early English, Decorated and Perpendicular, categorizing developments of Gothic style.)

Garrett Hostel Bridge. 1960.
Single 80ft span in prestressed concrete to replace cast-iron bridge of 1837. Elegant and pleasing case of early prestressed bridge with bronze railings and stone abutments. GUY AND TIMOTHY MORGAN (109).

109 Right, Garrett Hostel Footbridge, Cambridge. Photograph: Edward Leigh, FIBP, FRPS)

117

CHESHIRE

Dee Bridge, Chester.
Late 13th century. Mostly red sandstone with seven pointed arches of varying spans and broad cutwaters. Defoe: 'A noble stone bridge over the River Dee, very high and strong built'.

Marple Aqueduct. 1802.
Solid masonry with pierced spandrels carrying Cotton-king Samuel Oldknow's Peak Forest Canal across river (60).

Grosvenor Bridge, Chester. 1834.
Single segmental arch, 200ft span, widest stone arch in the world until General Meigs completed Cabin John Bridge, Washington DC, in 1864 with a single span of 218ft. Handsome piece with classical trappings and a pair of Roman arches over footpaths at each end. Mainly Peckforton stone with some Scottish granite and some Chester red stone. Complete arch is in fact 230ft, for it continues beyond jambs of abutments. THOMAS HARRISON, born Richmond, Yorks, who also designed Chester Castle in Doric style as a prison and a number of other bridges; also country houses. (Grosvenor Bridge begun 1827 when he was nearly 80) (12).

Congleton Viaduct.
Typical long round-arched viaduct of the early railways striding powerfully across open countryside.

Stockport Viaduct.
Another typical viaduct of early railways, dramatic in scale in immutable landscape of grimy brickwork. Electrical excrescences now mar its skyline (110).

Manchester Elevated Road. 1960s.
Viaduct of 32 spans mostly of 105ft, composed of twin parallel prestressed concrete decks resting on tapering columns.

Runcorn–Widnes Bridge. 1961.
Replaced Widnes Transporter Bridge across Mersey. Two-pinned, bowstring, lattice-work steel arch with deck at high level. Main span 1082ft with side spans each 250ft. End cantilevers. One of MOTT, HAY AND ANDERSON's fine feats (89).

Hollow–Wood Farm Footbridge. 1963.
Main span 115ft of post-tensioned concrete box beam with steps at each end. Remarkable for its slimness. Crosses M6 motorway on its North Cheshire section.

Interchange Bridges, Birmingham– Preston Motorway, Cheshire section. 1963.
Carry interchange roundabouts. *In situ* post-tensioned box beams in two-span arrangements with row of central columns.

CORNWALL

Wadebridge.
15th century. Of local stone 400ft long with 15 (originally 17) pointed arches of 18ft 6in spans. Widened 1847 with segmental arches so reducing the projections of the cutwaters and spoiling the original design. With Bideford, Devon, it is one of the two longest bridges of the southwest. Carries the A39 between Camelford and St Columb.

110 Stockport Viaduct, Cheshire.

Gunnislake Bridge. c.1530.
Of white granite with six slightly pointed arches
of varying spans, longest at 21ft. A beauty with
bold cutwaters rising to refuges. Carries A390
between Liskeard and Tavistock on Devon
border. (Similar bridges across Tamar are Grey-
stone, between Tavistock and Launceston, and
Horse Bridge, Stoke Climsland).

**Royal Albert Railway Viaduct, Saltash.
1859.**
Of two great iron fish-bellied girders with elliptical tubes as top members, approached by a
series of iron beams resting on tall granite piers
(79). A Victorian grotesque, next to Clifton Suspension, BRUNEL's most famous structure. Close
to it also crossing the Tamar is the modern suspension road bridge, called Tamar.

Tamar Bridge, Saltash. 1961.
Central span of 1100ft. Towers of reinforced
concrete, main cables being of wire ropes, and
deck of reinforced concrete slab supported on
steel stringers. Close to Brunel's Royal Albert.

CUMBERLAND

Lanercost Bridge. 1724.
Two bold segmental arches of 67ft spans and
broad cutwater rising to a retreat. Takes road
between Brampton and Lanercost Abbey across
Irthing. Nearby are relics of an ancient bridge.
possibly Roman (111).

DERBYSHIRE

Bakewell Bridge.
Mediaeval. Stone with five unusually regular
pointed and ribbed arches with triangular cutwaters rising to refuges. Widened in 19th century. Carries road to Baslow across Wye (7).

Edensor Bridge, Chatsworth Park. 1683.
Graceful single, ribbed masonry arch of 66ft
span flanked by two projections rising to refuges.
Centre of parapet pointed. Carries A623 between
Rowsley and Baslow across Derwent.

Sheepwash Bridge, Ashford.
Possibly 17th century. Three low segmental
arches. Rough stonework with curious curving
parapet wall at one end forming a sheepwash.
Fits snugly into delightful landscape. On road
to Sheldon (112).

Chatsworth Park Bridge. 1762.
Classical stone design of three arches and projections with niches at each end and statues above
the two cutwaters. JAMES PAINE for Duke of
Devonshire.

Kedelston Hall Bridge. c.1770.
Park bridge of three segmental arches with
niched piers decorated at parapet level with
swags and other refined details of period.
ROBERT ADAM, who designed the Hall (45).

*111 Lanercost Bridge,
Cumberland.*

112 Sheepwash Bridge, Ashford, Derbyshire.

St Mary's Bridge, Derby. 1788.
Three semi-circular arches of stone making civilized design. At town end 14th-century chapel of former mediaeval bridge.

Railway Viaducts, Chapel-en-le-Frith.
Mid-19th century. Pair of impressive converging viaducts with high arches of stone (81).

DEVONSHIRE

Post Bridge, Dartmoor.
Unknown date, could be 2000 years old. Most famous of clapper bridges. Spans River Dart near Princeton-Mortonhampstead road. Derives name from granite posts set up in district to guide wayfarers to bridge in snow or darkness. Four great granite slabs about 15ft wide resting on two piers and two abutments of rough granite rocks, the whole being held together by sheer weight (5). (Two smaller slab bridges of granite on Dartmoor are that over the Wallabrook and the rugged Teignhead Bridge, south of Fernworthy.)

Bideford Bridge. 1315.
Crosses Torridge with 24 Gothic arches of stone, not one arch being same size as another. The whole 677ft long. Widened 1815 and again in 1923 (with concrete corbels). Possessed a chapel at one time and as a toll bridge provided handsome profits which the feofees gave to education, charity and some good dinners.

Holne Bridge.
15th century. Rough granite bridge of four arches, widest being 34ft. A pleasing Ancient Monument. Takes A384 between Ashburton and Princeton across Dart.

DORSET

Sturminster Newton Bridge.
Mediaeval. Fine bridge over the Stour, of six pointed arches across river and to the north a stone causeway with ten semi-circular arches built 1828. Has been widened over the cutwaters.

Crawford Bridge.
Mediaeval, rebuilt in 16th century. Nine segmental stone arches across Stour and three brick flood arches. Four bold triangular cutwaters and refuges on upstream side.

113 Elvet Bridge, Durham.

114 Barnard Castle Bridge, Durham.

COUNTY DURHAM

Elvet Bridge, Durham. 1225.
Ten pointed and ribbed arches of stone across River Wear. Was once housed like London Bridge and had a chapel at each end and a defence tower. Widened with round arches 1805 (113).

Barnard Castle Bridge.
Probably 15th century. Two masonry arches with skew arch at one end across Tees (114).

Prebends Bridge, Durham. 1772.
Three segmental arches. Recently restored.

High Level Bridge, Newcastle. 1849.
ROBERT STEPHENSON's double-decker taking railway on top and road below high above Tyne. Six bowstring arches of cast iron each spanning 125ft held in at bottom by wrought iron members with vertical rods of wrought iron. First application of bowstring arch. Nasmyth's Titanic Steam Hammer used for first time here in piling. (Between Tyne Bridge and High Level Bridge is a pivoting road bridge of iron of 1876).

Tyne Bridge, Newcastle. 1928.
Bowstring girder having widest steel arch span in Britain at 531ft. Heavy architectural towers. Useful type for heavy industrial traffic. MOTT, HAY AND ANDERSON (87–8, 115).

Kingsgate Footbridge, Durham. 1965.
Links two groups of college buildings across Wear. Strange, interesting design of reinforced concrete by OVE ARUP AND PARTNERS. Thin white band built on bank sides and then swivelled into place in two halves on two tall tapered fingers. 350ft long (94).

New Scotswood Bridge, Newcastle. 1968.
Steel tied arch of bowstring girder spanning 140ft.

115 Tyne Bridge, Newcastle, Durham.

116 Bourton-on-the-Water, Gloucestershire

GLOUCESTERSHIRE

Eastleach Martin Bridge.
Unknown date. Clapper bridge of five spans.

Bourton-on-the-Water, Cotswolds.
Late 18th century. Delightful collection of small footbridges of wrought stone (116).

Mythe Bridge, Tewkesbury. 1826.
Cast-iron bridge of single low segmental arch spanning Severn in a leap of 170ft. Six main ribs between stone abutments. TELFORD.

Cumberland Basin Swing Bridge, Bristol. 1960s.
Essential part of a major redevelopment for heavy local traffic, through traffic and shipping into City Docks. Long balanced cantilever of twin box girder construction on centre bearing, operated by hydro-electric power.

Almondsbury Interchange. 1960s.
Dramatic four-level steel and concrete structure connecting M4 with M5 motorway.

Winterbourne Railway Bridge. 1960s.
Crosses M4 motorway. Interesting as a fairly rare example of welded, portal frame uncovered steelwork. Main girders, each 254ft long, and piers make two parallel, three-span rigid frames with sloping legs.

Severn Suspension Bridge. 1966.
Magnificent ethereal structure with central span of 3240ft and side spans of 1000ft. Pull of catenary held by massive concrete anchorages. Towers 445ft high of steel portal frames. 18,000 miles of high-tensile steel wire used in cables, deck being shallow box of welded steel plates rigid enough to deal with aerodynamic problem. As an aid to this suspenders of steel wire rope from catenary to deck are not hung vertically but form narrow triangles. Carries M4 motorway (London to South Wales) over Severn between Aust and Beechley. MOTT, HAY AND ANDERSON with FREEMAN, FOX AND PARTNERS (85, 90, 108).

HAMPSHIRE

Northam Bridge, Southampton. 1960s.
Five spans, three of 105ft and two of 85ft. Important as first major prestressed concrete bridge in Britain. Takes coastal traffic between Southampton and Portsmouth.

HEREFORDSHIRE

Wye Bridge, Hereford. c.1490.
Of sandstone rubble faced with ashlar. Six round arches with cutwaters rising to refuges. Widened early 19th century. Main traffic now carried by new neighbour of 1966.

Wilton Bridge, Ross-on-Wye. 1597.
Red sandstone of six spans, five of round, ribbed arches. Strong character with large triangular cutwaters splayed at tops to form half-hexagonal refuges (117).

Bridstoe Bridge. 1960.
Prestressed concrete beams with anchor cantilever and suspended spans. Beautiful bridge with long, low main span of 203ft, whole integrating well with lovely landscape around. Carries Ross-on-Wye bypass over Wye about a mile from Ross.

117 Wilton Bridge, Herefordshire.
(Photograph: Reece Winstone)

HUNTINGDONSHIRE

Huntingdon Bridge. c.1370.

Of stone with decorative moulding in form of a trefoil corbel carrying upstream parapet over two of the six wide, pointed arches. Formerly possessed a chapel dedicated to St Thomas of Canterbury. Oliver Cromwell was born at Huntingdon and must have used the bridge often in his youth and may have returned there in 1645, the first year of the Civil War, when the third arch was temporarily replaced by a draw-bridge.

St Ives Bridge. 1426.

One of few mediaeval bridges still retaining a chapel. Six pointed arches, some ribbed, with debased chapel at centre, now a museum. Crosses the Ouse (26).

KENT

East Farleigh Bridge.

14th or 15th century. Finest mediaeval bridge in south. Kentish ragstone of four pointed arches and a small pointed arch over towpath. Four arches have narrow chamfered ribs. Massive cutwaters on both sides but no parapet refuges. Crosses Medway between East Farleigh and Barming, near Maidstone.

Eynsford Bridge.

Probably 17th century. Packhorse bridge in Kentish ragstone with brick and rubble parapets. Two semi-circular arches of 10ft spans.

Kingsferry Lifting Bridge. 1960.

Important modern lifting bridge carrying road and rail over River Swale between Kent and the Isle of Sheppey. Lifting span rising vertically between reinforced concrete towers has 90ft wide and 95ft high navigational clearance. No beauty but useful. MOTT, HAY AND ANDERSON.

Medway Bridge, Maidstone. 1963.

Two almost equal spans of 145ft and 125ft of post-tensioned beams and cantilevers with piers and foundations of reinforced concrete. Carries Maidstone bypass over Medway two miles downstream from Maidstone.

Medway Bridge and Viaducts. 1963.

Grand, elegant work carrying M2 across Medway near Rochester. Prestressed concrete canti-levered central span of 500ft is longest of its kind in world. Total length with approach viaducts 3340ft. FREEMAN, FOX AND PARTNERS.

Swanscombe Cutting Footbridge. 1960s.

Beautiful post-tensioned concrete span of a three-hinged arch with cantilevered spans. Crosses the A2. J. S. BERGG (21).

LANCASHIRE

Wycoller Village.

Seven small bridges and a ford with stepping stones. Clam bridge of single span and a clapper bridge of three spans. Village formerly a centre of communication on which moorland tracks converged; became busy place of hand-weaving before power-driven looms. Near Yorkshire border and associated with Brontës, Wycoller Hall being the Ferndean Manor of *Jane Eyre*.

Lune Aqueduct, Lancaster. 1796.

Solid classical work of stone having five semi-circular arches each of 75ft span. Carries Rennie's Lancaster Canal across River Lune.

Barton Swing Aqueduct. 1894.

Carries Bridgewater Canal across Manchester Ship Canal. Replaced Brindley's 'Castle in the Air' aqueduct of stone across River Irwell. Steel lattice with pivoting trough which can be swung open full of water, the whole weighing 1500 tons. Ends of trough closed with gates held by tapering wedges weighing twelve tons each and worked by hydraulic rams (62).

Samlesbury Bridge. 1958.

Three spans of 120, 180, 120ft of continuous welded steel box girder construction with concrete piers and abutments faced with Yorkshire stone. Carries M6 over Ribble and the A59.

Lune Bridge. 1959.

Reinforced concrete open spandrel fixed arch of 230ft span, composed of two parallel arches of cellular construction. Light and simple. Carries M6 over Lune about two miles from Lancaster.

Thelwall Bridge. c.1960.

Riveted and welded steel with main span over Manchester Ship canal of 336ft. Deck slab of reinforced concrete. About three miles east of Warrington.

Gleaves Hill Bridge. c.1960.

Three-span continuous prestressed concrete of portal type having inclined legs and side span, deck soffit being curved. Centre span 143ft. Carries Preston–Lancaster motorway over M6 about six miles south of Lancaster.

Gathurst Viaduct. 1962.

Four spans of 150ft and two end spans of 100ft. Deck of welded girders 10ft deep supporting a reinforced concrete deck. Concrete piers. Carries M6 over River Douglas, Leeds–Liverpool Canal and a railway line.

LINCOLNSHIRE

High Bridge, Lincoln.

Mediaeval with later additions. There were shops on the bridge in 1391 but existing buildings on it were not built until 1540 when bridge was widened. A single arch of 23ft 6in at one end and 15ft 6in at other.

West Rasen Packhorse Bridge.
Date unknown. Of stone across River Rase with three ribbed arches. 4ft 6in wide.

Crowland Bridge.
Probably late 14th century. A stone curiosity also called Trinity Bridge or Three-Ways-to-Nowhere. Of rough limestone, it has three branches rising steeply to meet at middle and three arches between the branches forming Gothic points at the crowns. Originally spanning the confluence of three streams which are now dry, it stands as a purely decorative National Monument in the centre of a small fenland town. Each arch has three stone ribs with rough mouldings unusual in mediaeval bridges. Possibly the monks of Crowland Abbey built it as a symbol of the Holy Trinity and it may have formed the base of a large canopied cross rising above the marshes. A rough statue with flowing robes stands against one parapet which may have come from Crowland Abbey church (31).

LONDON'S THAMES

Tower Bridge. 1894.
Last Thames bridge before the sea. Bascule with two rising decks of steel and two bold towers of steel framework faced with granite and Portland stone in kind of Flemish Renaissance style. Bascules formerly raised for shipping by hydraulic power but now by electricity. Two footway beams span the 200ft high up between the towers. SIR HORACE JONES, City Architect, and SIR JOHN WOLFE BARRY (15).

London Bridge. 1973.
Last of a long series on same spot since Romans first erected a wooden bridge here. Replaced Rennie's granite structure of 1831, now rebuilt in Arizona. A practical job without visual thrills. Three spans, central one being 340ft wide. Four prestressed concrete box beams in precast segments strung together with cables like beads form flat 'arches', which are in fact cantilevers with a central suspended span. Piers faced with axed granite; parapets of polished granite. HAROLD KING, City Engineer (99).

Blackfriars Bridge. 1869.
Replaced Robert Mylne's splendid stone structure of 1769. Five low iron arches. Piers embellished with fat columns of red granite supporting pedestrian refuges. JOSEPH CUBITT.

Waterloo Bridge. 1942.
Reinforced concrete of five main spans, widest being 250ft. London's most elegant and beautifully simple bridge (at least in look) in spite of 'architectural' confusions imposed on engineers who nobly solved the problem with use of vast quantities of steel reinforcement. Appearance suggests segmental arch construction; in fact, spans are made up of four main beams, each continuous over two spans with cantilevers projecting to support suspended beam at centre. Spandrels faced with Portland stone. RENDELL, PALMER AND TRITTON (98).

Westminster Bridge. 1862.
Replaced Labelye's fine masonry structure of 1750 when it gave way in 1846 under growing scour. Seven low arches of cast and wrought iron with granite-faced brick piers. Centre span of 120ft. THOMAS PAGE.

Lambeth Bridge. 1930s.
Replaced P. W. Barlow's old suspension of 1862. Four low steel arches between concrete piers and abutments faced with granite. SIR GEORGE HUMPHREYS, Chief Engineer to LCC.

Vauxhall Bridge. 1906.
Replaced London's first iron bridge completed in 1816. Five steel arches with concrete piers and abutments faced with granite, central span being 150ft. Bronze statues above the piers. First London bridge to carry tramway lines. SIR ALEXANDER BINNIE and SIR MAURICE FITZMAURICE, both Chief Engineers to LCC.

Chelsea Suspension Bridge. 1934.
Concise steel bridge which replaced Page's ornamental old iron suspension of 1858. G. TOPHAM FORREST and E. P. WHEELER.

Albert Bridge, Chelsea. 1875.
Endearing eccentric in iron; half suspension, half cantilever, and early case of stayed type. R. M. ORDISH (55).

Battersea Bridge. 1890.
Replaced the 18th-century wooden bridge depicted in Whistler's famous 'Nocturne' in the Tate Gallery. Dull but useful. BAZALGETTE.

Wandsworth Bridge. 1938.
Three arches. Replaced structure of 1873.

Putney Bridge. 1886.
Of granite, replaced old wooden structure of 1729. Widened 1933. BAZALGETTE.

Hammersmith Suspension Bridge. 1887.
Replaced Tierney Clark's elegant suspension of 1827, London's first of this type. Bold ornamented towers and anchorages of painted iron. SIR JOSEPH BAZALGETTE, of the Metropolitan Board of Works (precursor of LCC).

Chiswick and Twickenham Bridges. 1933.
Two reinforced concrete bridges, Chiswick having three arches and Twickenham two extra land arches. ALFRED DRYLAND, County Engineer of Middlesex.

London, general
Serpentine Bridge, Hyde Park. 1826.
Delightful small masonry bridge of five segmental arches with classical balustrade. GEORGE RENNIE, son of John.

Wharncliffe Viaduct, Hanwell. 1837.
One of BRUNEL's fine arched viaducts for his Great Western Railway.

Holborn Viaduct. 1869.

Carries main road to the City over the valley, now underground, of the Fleet River, above which Farringdon Street runs. Part of a local replanning scheme opened by Queen Victoria on same day she opened Blackfriars Bridge at end of street. Splendid Victorian piece of decorated ironwork embellished on top with statuary.

St James's Park Footbridge. 1958.

Replaced Rendel and Wyatt's much mourned small iron suspension of 1857, but a functional, graceful little design of reinforced concrete with main span of 70ft. MINISTRY OF WORKS.

UPPER THAMES

Richmond Bridge. 1777.

Masonry faced with Portland stone, five segmental arches. One of several of its dignified kind across the river. PAINE AND COUSE.

Staines Bridge. 1831.

Fine granite bridge of three segmental arches, central one spanning 74ft and two side arches 66ft. Cutwaters of unusual design. GEORGE RENNIE, son of John.

18 Marlow Suspension Bridge, upper Thames.

Runnymede Bridge. 1961.

Low single arch of 173ft 6in with small arches in abutments. Eighteen encased steel arch ribs and reinforced concrete deck. Facing of Portland stone trim and red handmade bricks. Simple and elegant. Carries Staines bypass over Thames at Bell Weir. C. W. GLOVER AND PARTNERS.

Windsor Bridge. 1824.

Cast iron arches on granite piers. Iron now cracked and bridge limited to foot passengers and bikes, thus happily saving locality from ravages of the motor moloch.

Thames Bridge, Maidenhead. 1960s.

Elegant single arch spanning 270ft in welded steel with small side spans of 38ft, the whole faced with brick. Carries M4 motorway a mile south of Maidenhead. FREEMAN, FOX AND PARTNERS.

Maidenhead Railway Viaduct. 1830s.

One of BRUNEL's three viaducts of red engineering brick carrying the Great Western Railway over the Thames, the two others being at Basildon and Moulsford. Noble structure of two semi-elliptical arches each of 128ft span, one providing a fascinating towpath echo (13).

Maidenhead Bridge. 1772.

Classical masonry of seven wet and eight dry arches having Portland stone facing. SIR ROBERT TAYLOR, architect.

Marlow Suspension Bridge. 1832.

Stone towers with arches, and iron suspension of 218ft span. Makes delightful river picture with neighbouring church spire, long weir and general boskage. TIERNEY CLARK (118).

Henley Bridge. 1786.

Of Portland stone with five arches, very graceful with two keystone heads of Isis and Tamesis carved by Hon. Mrs Damer, cousin of Horace Walpole. HAYWARD.

Sonning Bridge.

18th century. Lovely rich red weathered brickwork of eleven irregular arches rising to centre.

Shillingford Bridge. 1827.

Good classical masonry design with three main arches and ten small flood arches.

Abingdon Bridge. 1416 and later.

Two sections, one over navigable river, other over millstream. Originally had pointed arches but widened upstream with round arches in 1790 and later was given a main wide arch. Main bridge reconstructed 1926 but ancient irregular character largely retained by reinforced concrete faced with local stone preserved from old structure. Main bridge now has one wide arch and four small ones, while millstream section has seven pointed arches.

Donnington Bridge, Oxford. 1962.

Ten portal frames comprising horizontal prestressed concrete beams supported at each end of pair of triangulated inclined legs. Single span of 170ft crossing river on skew and forming part of inner relief road.

Folly Bridge, Oxford. 1827.
Four spans of stone. On site of mediaeval bridge which had a watchtower let in 17th century to one Welcome, thus providing name Welcome's Folly.

Thames Bridge, Oxford. 1961.
Twelve two-pinned prestressed concrete portal frames cast *in situ* of 140ft span. Carries Oxford Southern and Western bypass.

Swinford (Eynsham) Bridge. 1777.
Pleasing classical design of ashlar masonry with nine round arches by the EARL OF ABINGDON. Toll house at one end. Carries the A40.

New Bridge, Kingston Bagpuize. c.1250.
Six pointed arches of rough stone with cutwaters carried up as refuges. Originally ribbed but ribs removed in 1793 to aid navigation. Largely reconstructed in 15th century and again in 1801. Said to be oldest bridge over Thames, but Radcot, higher upstream, may be older; hence name New.

Radcot Bridge.
Probably early 13th century, and so oldest bridge across Thames. Local stone with three arches, two being pointed. From a wharf by the bridge, Upton stone for building St Paul's Cathedral was loaded on to rafts to be floated down to London. Carries A4095 between Bampton and Faringdon (32).

Lechlade Bridge. 1792.
Attractive stone bridge with single segmental arch and two small towpath arches. Sometimes called Halfpenny Bridge on account of toll formerly charged.

NOTTINGHAMSHIRE

West Bridge, Clumber. 1798.
Classical style built for Duke of Newcastle on his estate. Three raised segmental arches 13ft 6in wide of brick and stone. Widened 1931. Carries A614 between Nottingham and Doncaster across River Poulter.

Winthorpe Bridge. 1960s.
Three-span continuous prestressed concrete with centre span of 260ft. Low and elegant. Carries Newark bypass over Trent.

Clifton Bridge, Nottingham. 1960s.
Prestressed concrete with main span of 275ft consisting of two cantilevers and a 100ft suspended span. Fine example of its decade.

NORTHAMPTONSHIRE

Irthlingborough Bridge.
Probably 14th century. Mostly stone of nineteen arches. Triangular refuges remain on downstream side. Restored 1925. Carries A6 between Irthlingborough and Higham Ferrers.

Wansford Old Bridge.
13th, 16th, and 18th centuries. Eleven arches of varying spans, largest being 50ft. Carries A6118 between Huntingdon and Stamford.

NORTHUMBERLAND

Twizel Bridge.
Date unknown but mediaeval character. Graceful single stone arch of 90ft span across Twill between Berwick-on-Tweed and Cornhill. Economical ribbed vaulting (24).

Warkworth Bridge.
14th century. Two wide segmental arches of 60ft span each across River Coquet; of local sandstone. Defensive gateway at one end. Fine broad cutwater with recess at top.

Old Bridge, Berwick-on-Tweed. 1624.
Dressed sandstone of fifteen low segmental arches.

Corbridge. 1674.
Seven segmental arches of stone with heavy piers, carrying A69 between Newcastle and Hexham across Tyne.

Lion Bridge, Alnwick. 1773.
Of dressed local sandstone beside Alnwick Castle with three arched spans, centre 50ft wide crossing River Aln between Newcastle and Berwick. Guarded on parapet by the Northumberland lion with poker tail outstretched.

Cupola Bridge. 1779.
Fine simple job of three segmental arches of dressed sandstone carrying A686 between Hexham and Alstone across West Allen River.

OXFORDSHIRE

Grand Bridge, Blenheim Park. 1711.
Vanbrugh's theatrical baroque gesture in stone crossing a lake in the Duke of Marlborough's park. Never completed owing to the Duchess's contempt for its extravagance (40–1).

Magdalen Bridge, Oxford. 1779.
Fine classical stone bridge with six round arches, carved keystones, balustrade, and rusticated columns at piers. Widened 1882, but original design preserved. Crosses the Cherwell tributary of the Thames. JOHN GWYNN (3, 33).

tions held together with iron keys and screws. Built across Severn by ironmaster ABRAHAM DARBY (58–9).

Welsh Bridge, Shrewsbury. 1795.
Five segmental stone arches. Simple, with pleasing proportions. TILLY AND CARLINE.

Dinham Bridge, Ludlow.
18th century. Simple stone of three segmental arches across Teme.

Coalport Bridge, Coalbrookdale. 1818.
Somewhat like Iron Bridge, showing little development in technique. About one mile downstream from Iron Bridge (119).

Stokesay Bridge. 1823.
Cast iron ribs on masonry abutments with single span of 54ft 9in. Carries A49 across River Onny between Shrewsbury and Ludlow. TELFORD.

Severn Bridge, Shrewsbury. 1964.
Low elegant arches of reinforced concrete. Deck prestressed longitudinally. Carries Ditherington-Monkmoor road over Severn.

119 Detail, Coalport Bridge, Shropshire.

SHROPSHIRE

Ludford Bridge, Ludlow.
Bulky piers suggest Norman period. Stone of three semi-circular ribbed arches each 30ft span across Teme. Once graced with a chapel (25).

English Bridge, Shrewsbury. 1774.
Seven stone arches crowned with balustrade and decorated with carved dolphins on the cutwaters. Central arch 50ft wide. Reconstructed 1927 to increase width and reduce hump-back. JOHN GWYNN, who also designed Magdalen Bridge, Oxford, Atcham near Shrewsbury, and Worcester (4).

Atcham Bridge, near Shrewsbury. 1776.
Seven spans in Grinshill stone rising in size towards centre. GWYNN's most beautiful design with good detailing. Carries London–Holyhead road across Severn. (New concrete bridge nearby of clumsy design built in 1920s) (50).

Tern Bridge, Atcham. 1778.
Elegant structure in Grinshill stone with balustrades, carved keystones and niches at abutments of single segmental arch of 90ft span. Carries London–Holyhead road. WILLIAM HAYWARD.

Iron Bridge, Coalbrookdale. 1779.
First bridge in the world made wholly of iron. Five semi-circular ribs forming single arch of 100ft 6in span. Spandrels filled with iron circles and ogee Gothic arches and deck of cast-iron plates covered with slag and clay. Each of arch ribs cast in two parts. Precast parts floated down river and whole completed in three months. Designer thinking in terms of masonry and carpentry. Joints dovetailed and rectangular sec-

SOMERSET

Tarr Steps, Winsford, Exmoor.
Unknown date, possibly 3000 years old. Low clapper bridge with 17 spans, total length being 180ft. Clapper stones weigh four or five tons each. Crosses the River Barle on the track to Hawkridge. Referred to in *Lorna Doone* as a Devil's bridge. Very picturesque in deep wooded valley.

Horner Water, West Luccombe, Allerford, and Dunster, Exmoor.
Each village has its packhorse bridge: the one at Dunster, called Gallox Bridge, has two arches with slightly pointed tops and double arch rings.

Petherton Bridge.
Possibly 15th century. Rough stone structure crossing River Parrett and carrying the Fosse Way. Pair of quaint, worn stone figures built into the end of a parapet. Thomas Gerard (1633): 'A faire stone bridge, at the end of which I have seen graven on a stone the effigies of the founder and his wife, now much defaced by lewd people, and the memory of them for want of an inscription lost'.

Clifton Suspension Bridge. 1836–1864.
BRUNEL's most famous structure swung high over the Avon Gorge of iron suspension between two stone towers. Original design, considerably altered in the event, won in competition to which Telford also contributed a design. Bridge not completed until after Brunel's death. The chains from the old Hungerford Bridge, London, also by Brunel, were used when that was demolished to make way for the existing railway bridge. Span of 702ft, the Somerset end being three feet lower than the Gloucester end, a

deliberate subtlety instigated by Brunel to counter the effect produced by the land configuration (69).

Bath

Prior Park Palladian Bridge. 1756.
Built for Ralph Allen as an almost exact copy of the Palladian Bridge, Wilton Park, designed by LORD PEMBROKE, the Architect Earl, helped by Robert Morris. Sophisticated classical structure with a colonnade and roof.

Pulteney Bridge. 1769.
The only housed bridge, excepting High Bridge, Lincoln, left in Britain, in a tradition going back to the lakeland village. Designed by ROBERT ADAM in his refined classical style, it was built under patronage of Sir William Pulteney after the Avon had been made navigable up to Bath and when Pulteney had decided to link his Bathwick estate with the city. Of Bath stone on three arches bearing two-storeyed shops and houses. The weir below the bridge was admirably re-designed in 1972 as part of a flood protection scheme by Neville Conder and F. Greenhalgh, a scheme which received a Civic Trust Award (47).

Cleveland Bridge. 1833.
Originally an arched cast iron bridge designed by HAZZLEDINE. Reconstructed 1930 with help of reinforced concrete so that bridge retains its pristine look. Carries A3080 across Wiltshire Avon.

North Parade Bridge. 1836.
Handsome cast iron arch rib bridge with single span of 111ft. Probably also by HAZZLEDINE. Crosses Avon within the city.

STAFFORDSHIRE

Shugborough, or Essex, Bridge.
16th century or earlier. Stone of 14 arches and triangular cutwaters with refuges, whole being low and 312ft long with width between parapets of only 4ft. A bridle or packhorse bridge crossing Trent in Shugborough Park near Great Haywood.

Viator's Bridge, Milldale.
Unknown date. Pack-horse bridge across River Dove at northern end of Dove Dale. Rough stone of two segmental arches. Izaak Walton: 'Why, a mouse can hardly go over it'.

SUSSEX

Stopham Bridge.
Possibly 16th century. Picturesque in Sussex sandstone with seven main arches with semi-circular heads and one larger, taller central arch which is segmental and turned in brick, perhaps of later date than other arches built high to aid navigation. Nine recesses for pedestrians. Crosses River Arun on A283 between Pulborough and Petworth (35).

Balcombe Viaduct.
Mid-19th century. Magnificent example of railway engineering with its long rhythm of brick arches. A remarkable perspective below bridge with its row of voids arched above and below. Takes the old London, Brighton and South Coast Railway across the Ouse Valley (80).

WARWICKSHIRE

Old Stare Bridge.
Late 13th century. Built by Cistercian monks of Stonleigh Abbey. Sandstone ashlar with nine pointed arches of about 12ft span. Enormous cutwaters with refuges above as wide as the arches.

Clopton Bridge, Stratford-upon-Avon. 1480.
At one time even longer than Bideford Bridge, Devon, at 1100ft. Now only 500ft. Shakespeare must have crossed it many times. Of ashlar masonry of fourteen spans each about 19ft wide, all arches being pointed. Widened 1811. Financed by Sir Hugh of Clopton, Mayor of London, who bought New Place, Stratford from Shakespeare (120).

Warwick Castle Bridge. 1793.
Grey sandstone with single arch unusually wide for period at 105ft. Carries A41 between Warwick and Banbury across Avon.

Tramway Bridge, Stratford-upon-Avon. 1823.
Simple bridge of red brick with seven semi-elliptical arches originally built to carry a horse tramway.

WESTMORLAND

Crook-of-Lune Bridge.
Probably 17th century. Two segmental arches of rough masonry crossing Lune between Grayrigg and Sedbergh.

Bridge House, Ambleside, Lake District.
Date unknown. A curiosity with rubble-stone cottage supported on an arch across a stream said to have been built thus by owner to avoid taxes. Now office of National Trust.

WILTSHIRE

Bradford-on-Avon Bridge.
14th century. Nine arches of stone and a charming small oratory (only one of its kind), having a dome added in the seventeenth century when bridge was widened. Oratory became a lock-up in 18th century and John Wesley was interned there for a night in 1757.

Lacock Bridge.
Date unknown, probably mediaeval. Four pointed arches of stone. Attractive small bridge Carries road between Lacock and Bowden Hill

Combe Bissett Bridge.
Mediaeval packhorse bridge of stone across
Avon. Three pointed arches and no parapets (to
avoid scraping of projecting packs); now has
wooden railings. 6ft wide. One side refaced with
brick. (Close by is a modest eighteenth-century
road bridge of three arches).

Wilton Park Palladian Bridge. 1737.
Elaborate, classical, roofed bridge of decorative
kind with Ionic portico, balustrades, carved keystones and rusticated pediment. Outstanding
product of Age of Taste and landed aristocracy.
Built by ninth EARL OF PEMBROKE, the Architect
Earl, one of the first landscape gardeners who
superintended the construction of Labelye's
Westminster Bridge, London. Probably designed
the bridge himself with the aid of Robert Morris,
Copies stand at Stowe and Prior Park, Bath
(44).

WORCESTERSHIRE

Pershore Old Bridge.
Mediaeval. Stone with brick parapets. Six round
arches, centre spanning 27ft 6in.

Worcester Bridge. 1781.
Stone of five arches each 40ft span. Widened and
reconstructed 1932 in concrete faced with stone.
JOHN GWYNN.

Bewdley Bridge. 1799.
Sandstone of seven spans across Severn, longest
being 59ft 6in. Strengthened 1926. TELFORD.

Holt Fleet Bridge, Ombersley. 1828.
Single low arch spanning 150ft of cast iron with
open spandrels and sandstone abutments.
Crosses Severn. Strengthened 1928. TELFORD.

Knightsford Bridge. 1959.
Three-span, cantilever type with centre span of
90ft. Superstructure of reinforced concrete cellular construction. Piers, abutments and training
walls of mass concrete faced with brickwork.
Civic Trust Award 1959. Carries Worcester–
Bromyard road (A44) over Teme at Knightwick,
nine miles west of Worcester.

Queenhill Bridge. 1960s.
Mostly concrete with three central spans of steel.
2466ft long in 27 spans on a curve. Carries Ross
Spur motorway (M50) over Severn, about three
miles north of Tewkesbury.

YORKSHIRE

Wakefield Chantry Bridge.
Mid-14th century. Stately stone bridge of twelve
pointed arches. West elevation of chapel restored by Scott, 1847 (27).

Rotherham Chantry Bridge. 1483.
Formerly across River Don but now no water
flows below its four pointed arches (28).

Knaresborough High Bridge.
Mediaeval of two arches, older one being ribbed.
Crosses Nidd on Harrogate–Knaresborough
road. Widened 1826.

Barden Bridge.
Mid-17th century. Pleasing masonry of three
segmental arches across River Wharfe on
Barden-Appletreewick road.

Ferry Bridge, Knottingley. 1797.
Dignified design of rusticated masonry with three
segmental wet arches and a number of dry ones.
Takes A1 across Aire between Doncaster and

129

121 Middlesbrough Transporter Bridge, Yorkshire.

Wetherby. JOHN CARR, architect, of York, who designed Harewood House and mansion at Basildon Park.

Nidderdale, West Riding.
Two packhorse bridges, one at Thronthwaite, other at Haxby across Nidd between Burnt Yates and Birstwith. Latter a beautiful, humpbacked, single span of 63ft.

Middlesbrough Transporter Bridge. 1911.
Spans 470ft between steel towers 225ft above Tees high water. Cantilevers of steel taking travelling car (121).

Wharfe Bridge, West Riding. 1959.
Reinforced concrete of cantilever and suspended span with central span of 160ft. Suspended span of 70ft of precast post-tensioned I-beams. Elegant. Carries A1 over Wharfe on Wetherby bypass.

Wentbridge Viaduct. 1961.
Reinforced concrete, 470ft between outside bearings with pair of inclined, tapering legs between prestressed deck of cellular construction. Centre span of 190ft. Grand, simple design. 90 miles of steel tubing used for scaffolding during construction. Carries A1 over Went Valley (97).

Tinsley Viaduct, Sheffield. 1967.
Composite of steel and concrete. Spans Don Valley with two decks carrying M1 motorway on upper level and all-purpose road below.

Scotland

ABERDEENSHIRE

Balgownie Bridge, near Aberdeen. c.1320.
Built, according to legend, by order of Robert the Bruce (122).

Dee Bridge. 1527.
Seven ribbed arches. Widened 1841.

Brig o' Dye, near Aberdeen.
Possibly late 17th century, but mediaeval character. Single arch of 43ft span.

ARGYLL, INVERARAY

Aray Bridge.
18th century. Stone with pierced central spandrel. Attributed to ROBERT ADAM (46).

AYRSHIRE

Brig of Ayr.
13th century. Restored 1910 in memory of Robert Burns and his poem 'The Brigs of Ayr'.

Brig o'Doon, near Ayr.
15th century. Five single round-arch span of 70ft. Monument nearby to Robert Burns whose ballad 'Tam O'Shanter' describes an incident on the bridge when Tam is pursued by warlocks in the mirk.

Howford Bridge, Ayr. 1962.
Reinforced concrete of single span of 300ft with open spandrels. In spectacular Ballochmyle gorge on Kilmarnock–Dumfries road.

BERWICKSHIRE

Berwick Old Bridge. 1624.
Fifteen spans.

Coldstream Bridge. 1766.
Crosses Tweed on Northumberland border. Five arches with tunnelled spandrels. JAMES SMEATON (38).

Kelso Bridge. 1803.
Five arches of 72ft span each. One of first in Britain to carry level roadway and to contain elliptical arches. Forerunner of London's Waterloo. JOHN RENNIE.

Union Bridge. 1820.
449ft span across Tweed. First suspension to take carriages. SIR SAMUEL BROWN (123).

Royal Border Bridge. 1850.
28 semi-circular stone arches of 60ft span rising 126ft above Tweed Valley. ROBERT STEPHENSON.

EDINBURGH

Dean Bridge. c.1800.
One of TELFORD's best masonry bridges with four tall arches rising 100ft above the Water of Leith (124).

Forth Railway Bridge, near Edinburgh. 1890.
Cantilever and beam of steel. BAKER AND FOWLER (9, 83–4).

Forth Road Bridge, near Edinburgh. 1964.
Steel suspension with span of 3300ft. FREEMAN, FOX AND PARTNERS with MOTT, HAY AND ANDERSON (93).

122 Below, *Balgownie Bridge, near Aberdeen.* *123* Right, *Union Bridge, Berwickshire.* (Photograph: Adam J. Scott)

*124 Dean Bridge,
Edinburgh.*

FIFESHIRE

Guard Bridge. 1450.
Well built of six irregular arches in stone.

Tay Road Bridge. 1960.
Connects Fifeshire with Dundee. Steel and concrete 7365ft long with 42 spans. W. A. FAIRHURST.

GLASGOW

Clyde Street Footbridge.
Early 19th century. Iron suspension between classic stone towers decorated with Ionic columns.

Erskine Bridge. 1972.
Nine miles west of Glasgow across Clyde. Fine steel and concrete structure with approach viaducts. Centre span supported by two stayed girders of steel.

INVERNESS-SHIRE

Craigellachie Bridge. c.1800.
Trussed iron arch of 152ft span with castellated stone abutments. First truly modern bridge of iron. TELFORD.

Ness Bridge, Inverness. 1961.
Three-span prestressed concrete with centre span of 120ft.

KIRKCUDBRIGHT

Tongueland Bridge. 1805.
Single masonry span of 112ft across Dee with hollow spandrels. TELFORD.

LANARKSHIRE

Mouse Water Bridge, Cartland Craigs.
Immensely tall stone arches across wooded gorge. TELFORD.

PERTHSHIRE

Millhaugh Old Bridge, Glenalmond. 1619.
Single, graceful arch of 63ft span, with cutwaters and refuges each end. Pierced spandrels.

Aberfeldy Bridge. 1733.
One of General Wade's military bridges in scheme for opening up Highlands. One of very few with baroque character (37).

STIRLING

Stirling Bridge. c.1400.
A war bridge of strategic importance as it is the lowest crossing of the Forth. Until the late eighteenth century almost only access to north of Scotland (30).

Wales

BRECKNOCKSHIRE

Taf Fechan Bridge. 1960s.
Between Hirwaun and Abergavenny. One of three reinforced concrete, open-spandrel fixed arch bridges in the Heads of the Valleys. Curved on plan with span of 227ft. Built by cantilever construction with cables instead of staging (95).

Taf Fawr Bridge. 1960s.
Crosses tributary of River Taff 110ft above valley. Also balanced cantilever construction. Three box girder spans, centre of 216ft. Elegant.

Nant Hir Bridge. 1960s.
On Heads of the Valleys road. Similar to Taf Fechan, with concrete arch of 184ft.

CAERNARVONSHIRE

Waterloo Bridge, Bettws-y-Coed. 1815.
An iron curiosity by TELFORD taking Holyhead road across Conway River. 105ft arch span with brilliant casting which reads 'This Bridge was constructed in the same year the Battle of Waterloo was fought'. In each spandrel the rose, thistle, shamrock, and leek are brightly painted. Strengthened recently by having interior ribs unobtrusively encased in concrete (74).

Conway Suspension Bridge. 1826.
TELFORD's iron suspension between castellated towers below Conway Castle. Next to it Conway Tubular and modern steel arch road bridge of 1958 (70).

Menai Bridge. 1826.
TELFORD's suspension masterpiece crossing Menai Straits and linking Anglesey to mainland on Holyhead road. Central span between masonry towers 579ft. Refurbished 1940 by Sir Alexander Gibb whose great-grandfather had been Telford's resident engineer on building of Aberdeen Harbour (67–8, 125).

Conway Tubular Bridge. 1848.
GEORGE STEPHENSON's railway structure similar to Britannia in principle but lower and smaller, single span of two tubes, each 412ft long (77).

Britannia Railway Bridge. 1850.
GEORGE STEPHENSON's famous structure of iron tubes of four spans between stone towers, two main ones 460 ft, across Menai Straits near Menai Bridge. Damaged by fire caused by children in 1970, pristine form now marred by supporting arch (8, 76, 78).

CARMARTHENSHIRE

Dolau-Hirion Bridge. 1773.
Single segmental arch of 84ft span, with pierced haunches across the Towy near Llandovery. WILLIAM EDWARDS of Pont-y-Pridd fame.

Llandeilo Bridge. 1848.
Widest and highest single span of its masonry type in Wales.

DENBIGHSHIRE

Llangollen Bridge.
Part 1131 but largely rebuilt mid-14th century and again about 1500. Irregular of four arches.

Holt Bridge. 1545.
Low red sandstone of eight arches and pleasing proportions. Originally strategic with draw-bridge, tower and gateway.

Bangor Isycoed Bridge.
17th century. Fine design of red sandstone crossing Dee with five segmental arches and shallow refuges. Attributed to INIGO JONES.

Llanrwst Bridge. 1636.
Also called Pont Fawr, or the Great Bridge. Masonry with centre span of 60ft and side spans of 45ft with segmental arches. Elegant design in spite of undressed ashlar. Known as Shaking Bridge since it vibrates if parapet above centre arch is struck. Also attributed to INIGO JONES.

Chirk Aqueduct. 1801.
Ten round-headed stone arches of 40ft span each carrying iron trough to reduce weight which puddled clay would impose. Carries Welsh Section of Shropshire Union Canal over Ceiriog. TELFORD.

125 Menai Straits Bridge, Caernarvonshire.

126 Thomas Telford.

Chepstow Bridge. 1816.
Open ironwork of five spans across Wye (73, 127).

Pant-y-Goytre Bridge. c.1821.
Fine stone bridge across Usk with tunnels in spandrels. JOHN UPTON of Gloucester (39).

Newport Transporter Bridge. 1906.
Elegant steelwork with beam 177ft above water carrying hanging carriage across 145ft span. R. H. HAYNES and Frenchman F. ARNODIN (designer of Pont Transbordeur, Marseilles, destroyed in Second World War) (17).

George Street Bridge, Newport. 1960s.
Cable cantilever design with main span of 500ft across Usk. Ropes of steel wire, deck of cellular steel boxes, towers of hollow concrete (92).

Wye Viaduct. 1960s.
Ten steel spans and a stayed girder across Beachley Peninsula west of Severn bridge carrying M4 motorway (91).

Coldra to Crick.
On London–South Wales motorway. 1960s. Eleven underbridges, six overbridges and two viaducts, all of interest.

Pont Cysylltau Aqueduct. 1805.
Four miles from Chirk taking the Welsh Section of the Shropshire Union Canal across River Dee. Exposed iron trough on iron arches carried on 18 slender masonry piers at 127ft above river. 1000ft long. Walter Scott: 'The most impressive work of art I have ever seen'. Next to Menai Bridge, TELFORD's masterwork (61).

FLINTSHIRE

Queensferry Bridge. 1960s.
On Queensferry bypass, built to be converted later into a vertical lifting bridge. Three spans of welded plate girders.

GLAMORGANSHIRE

Pont-y-Pridd. 1750.
Most beautiful single-span bridge in Britain and landmark in bridge construction on account of its high arch of 140ft span across River Taff. Haunches pierced with tunnels. WILLIAM EDWARDS, farmer and mason (1).

Neath Bridge. 1955.
Carries bypass over River Neath between Briton Ferry and Earlswood. Reinforced concrete, three-quarters of a mile long.

MONMOUTHSHIRE

Monnow Bridge, Monmouth.
1272 but widened later. Best preserved war bridge in Britain with tower. Ribbed arches (29).

Usk Bridge. 1563.
Sturdy with seven segmental arches. Widened 1794.

*127 Chepstow Bridge,
Monmouthshire.*

128 Next page,
*Spettisbury Bridge,
Dorset.* (Photograph:
B. C. Clayton)

DORSET
ANY PERSON WILFULLY INJURING
ANY PART OF THIS COUNTY BRIDGE
WILL BE GUILTY OF FELONY AND
UPON CONVICTION LIABLE TO BE
TRANSPORTED FOR LIFE
BY THE COURT
7&8 GEO 4 C30 S13   T FOOKS